"This book consists of personal reflections, insights, metaphors, observations, judgments on readings and events. The material is taken from notebooks which I have kept since 1956. Though they are personal and conversational and represent my own version of the world, these entries are not of the intimate and introspective kind that go to make up a spiritual journal. There is certainly nothing private or confidential here.

"As I said, these notes add up to a personal version of the world in the 1960s. In elaborating such a version one un-avoidably tells something of himself, for what a man truly is can be discovered only through his self-awareness in a living and actual world. But these pages are not a venture in self-revelation or self-discovery. Nor are they a pure soliloquy. They are an implicit dialogue with other minds, a dialogue in which questions are raised. But do not expect to find "my answers." I do not have clear answers to current questions. I do have questions, and, as a matter of fact, I think a man is known better by his questions than by his answers. To make known one's questions is, no doubt, to come out in the open oneself. I am not in the market for the ready-made and wholesale answers so easily volunteered by the public and I question nothing so much as the viability of public and popular answers, including some of those which claim to be most progressive.

"Maybe the best way to characterize this book is to say that it consists of a series of sketches and meditations, some poetic, and literary, others historical and even theological, fitted together in a spontaneous, informal philosophic scheme in such a way that they react upon each other. The total result is a personal and monastic meditation, a testimony of Christian reflection in the mid-twentieth century, a confrontation of twentieth-century questions in the light of a monastic commitment, which inevitably makes one something of a 'bystander.'"

*Thomas Merton*

# BOOKS BY THOMAS MERTON

*The Ascent to Truth*
*The Behavior of Titans*
*Bread in the Wilderness*
*Conjectures of a Guilty Bystander*
*Disputed Questions*
\* *Life and Holiness*
*The Living Bread*
*The New Man*
\* *No Man Is an Island*
*Raids on the Unspeakable*
*Seasons of Celebration*
*Seeds of Contemplation*
*Seeds of Destruction*
*The Seven Storey Mountain*
\* *The Sign of Jonas*
*The Silent Life*
*The Secular Journal of Thomas Merton*
*The Thomas Merton Reader*
*Thoughts in Solitude*
\* *The Waters of Siloe*
*The Way of Chuang Tzu*

POETRY

*Emblems of a Season of Fury*
*A Man in the Divided Sea*
*The Strange Islands*
*Selected Poems*
*The Tears of the Blind Lions*
*The Tower of Babel*
*Figures for an Apocalypse*
*Thirty Poems*

TRANSLATIONS

*Clement of Alexandria* (Selections)
*The Wisdom of the Desert*

\* Available in Image Books editions

# THOMAS MERTON

# CONJECTURES OF A GUILTY BYSTANDER

*Remember that you were a slave in the land of Egypt,*
*and the Lord your God brought you out of there.*
Deuteronomy 5:15

*My life is like the crane who cries a few times*
*under the pine tree*
*And like the silent light from the lamp*
*in the bamboo grove.*
Po Chu-i

## IMAGE BOOKS

A Division of Doubleday & Company, Inc.

Garden City, New York

Image Books edition 1968
by special arrangement with Doubleday & Company, Inc.

Image Books edition published February 1968

*Ex parte ordinis*

*Nihil obstat:*           Fr. Charles English, O.C.S.O.
                               Fr. Benjamin Clark, O.C.S.O.

*Imprimi potest:*        Fr. Ignace Gillet, O.C.S.O.
                               Abbot General
                               February 14, 1966. Rome

*Nihil obstat:*           John A. Goodwine, J.C.D.
                               *Censor Librorum*

*Imprimatur:*        ✠ Terence J. Cooke, D.D., V.G.
                               Archdiocese of New York
                               June 29, 1966

The nihil obstat and imprimatur are official declarations that a book
or pamphlet is free of doctrinal or moral error. No implication is
contained therein that those who have granted the nihil obstat
and imprimatur agree with the contents, opinions or statements
expressed.

Grateful acknowledgment is made to the following for permission to
reprint copyrighted material:
The Macmillan Company and the Student Christian Movement
Press Ltd., for excerpts from *Ethics* by Dietrich Bonhoeffer, copy-
right 1955 by The Macmillan Company; and from *Letters and
Papers from Prison* by Dietrich Bonhoeffer, copyright 1953 by The
Macmillan Company. Reprinted by permission.
New Directions Publishing Corporation and San Francisco Review
for lines from "Sara in her Father's Arms" from *The Materials* by
George Oppen, copyright © 1960, 1961, 1962 by George Oppen;
and from "A Language of New York" and "A Narrative" from
*This in Which* by George Oppen, copyright © 1962, 1963, 1964,
1965 by George Oppen. Reprinted by permission.
Oxford University Press, Inc. and Chatto & Windus Ltd., for lines
from "Analogy of Unity in Multeity" from *Collected Poems 1930–
1960* by Richard Eberhart, copyright © 1960 by Richard Eberhart.
Reprinted by permission.
Random House, Inc. and Faber and Faber Ltd., for lines from "For
the Time Being," copyright 1944 by W. H. Auden, and from "Mon-
taigne," copyright 1945 by W. H. Auden, from *The Collected
Poetry of W. H. Auden*. Reprinted by permission.

# PREFACE

This is not a sequel to *The Sign of Jonas*, a spiritual journal which appeared in 1953. True, the reader will find here some of the brief notes on nature and life, the occasional meditations and some of the comment which recall the earlier work. The book does, indeed, consist of personal reflections, insights, metaphors, observations, judgments on readings and events. The material is taken from notebooks which I have kept since 1956. Though they are personal and conversational and represent my own version of the world, these entries are not of the intimate and introspective kind that go to make up a spiritual journal. There is certainly nothing private or confidential here.

As I said, these notes add up to a personal version of the world in the 1960s. In elaborating such a version one unavoidably tells something of himself, for what a man truly is can be discovered only through his self-awareness in a living and actual world. But these pages are not a venture in self-revelation or self-discovery. Nor are they a pure soliloquy. They are an implicit dialogue with other minds, a dialogue in which questions are raised. But do not expect to find "my answers." I do not have clear answers to current questions. I do have questions, and, as a matter of fact, I think a man is known better by his questions than by his answers. To make known one's questions is, no doubt, to come out in the open oneself. I am not in the market for the ready-made and wholesale answers so easily volunteered by the public and I question nothing so much as the viability of public and popular answers, including some of those which claim to be most progressive.

Maybe the best way to characterize this book is to say that it consists of a series of sketches and meditations, some poetic,

and literary, others historical and even theological, fitted together in a spontaneous, informal philosophic scheme in such
a way that they react upon each other. The total result is a
personal and monastic meditation, a testimony of Christian
reflection in the mid-twentieth century, a confrontation of
twentieth-century questions in the light of a monastic commitment, which inevitably makes one something of a "bystander."

At no point in this book are any questions treated systematically. Aspects of them are briefly noted, when they come
to mind or when they fit in with the organic pattern of the
book. Such a procedure is obviously unsatisfactory from the
viewpoint of professional theology, but perhaps it may keep
the book from being dry and doctrinaire.

Though there are frequent references to Barth and Bonhoeffer, among others, this is not a book of professional ecumenism. There is no systematic examination of the differences
between the theologies of various Churches, or between Eastern and Western philosophy and mysticism. There is no attempt to map out areas of agreement and of difference,
proposing means of improving mutual understanding. On the
contrary, the approach is completely personal, informal, and
tentative. I simply record ways in which theologians like Barth
have entered quite naturally and easily into my personal and
monastic reflections, indeed, into my own Christian world-
view. To put it plainly, the book attempts to show how in
actual fact a Catholic monk is able to read Barth and identify
with him in much the same way as he would read a Catholic
author like Maritain—or indeed a Father of the Church. This
is not a critical—if sympathetic—analysis of Protestant thought
by a Catholic, but a Catholic sharing the Protestant experience—and other religious experiences as well. This is not to
say that I am in perfect agreement with everything in Barth
and Bonhoeffer, still less in J. A. T. Robinson. That would be
impossible, since, in the first place, these writers are not in
agreement with each other, and all of them make statements
which a Catholic would not readily accept as they stand.
Nevertheless, some of their books have proved relevant and
stimulating to me in a cloistered and contemplative monas-

tery. In the climate of the Second Vatican Council, this no longer requires apology or justification.

Yet the ecumenical view is not what is most important in this book. There are many other concerns appropriate to an age of transition and crisis, of war and racial conflict, of technology and expansion. Above all, there are the day-to-day impressions, the simple conjectures, of a man in his own world with its own challenges. It is a monastic world, and doubtless strange to those who have no experiences of any such thing. Yet it is, I think, open to the life and experience of the greater, more troubled, and more vocal world beyond the cloister. Though I often differ strongly from that "world," I think I can be said to respond to it. I do not delude myself that I am not still part of it.

The contemplative life is unfortunately too often thought of in terms purely of "enclosure," and monks are conceived of as hothouse plants, nursed along in a carefully protected and spiritually overheated life of prayer. But let us remember that the contemplative life is first of all *life*, and life implies openness, growth, development. To restrict the contemplative monk to one set of narrow horizons and esoteric concerns would be in fact to condemn him to spiritual and intellectual sterility.

If the Catholic Church is turning to the modern world and to the other Christian Churches, and if she is perhaps for the first time seriously taking note of the non-Christian religions in their own terms, then it becomes necessary for at least a few contemplative and monastic theologians to contribute something of their own to the discussion. That is one of the things this book attempts to do. It gives a monastic and personal view of these contemporary questions. The singular, existential, poetic approach is proper to this monastic view.

*Abbey of Gethsemani*
*November 1965*

NOTE: The notes in the book are not in strictly chronological order, and in preparing the book for publication in 1965, I added many new ideas throughout.

# PART ONE

## Barth's Dream

THE *servant Kabir sings: "O Sadhu!*
  *finish your buying and selling, have done*
  *with your good and your bad—for there*
  *are no markets and shops in the land*
  *to which you go!"*                    —Kabir

BUT *little did the infant dream*
  *That all the treasures of the world were by*
*And that himself was so the cream*
  *And crown of all that round about did lie.*
                    —Thomas Traherne

Karl Barth had a dream about Mozart.

Barth had always been piqued by the Catholicism of Mozart, and by Mozart's rejection of Protestantism. For Mozart said that "Protestantism was all in the head" and that "Protestants did not know the meaning of the *Agnus Dei qui tollis peccata mundi.*"

Barth, in his dream, was appointed to examine Mozart in theology. He wanted to make the examination as favorable as possible, and in his questions he alluded pointedly to Mozart's masses.

But Mozart did not answer a word.

I was deeply moved by Barth's account of this dream and almost wanted to write him a letter about it. The dream concerns his salvation, and Barth perhaps is striving to admit that he will be saved more by the Mozart in himself than by his theology.

Each day, for years, Barth played Mozart every morning before going to work on his dogma: unconsciously seeking to awaken, perhaps, the hidden sophianic Mozart in himself, the central wisdom that comes in tune with the divine and cosmic music and is saved by love, yes, even by *eros*. While the other, theological self, seemingly more concerned with love, grasps at a more stern, more cerebral *agape*: a love that, after all, is not in our own heart but *only in God* and revealed only to our head.

Barth says, also significantly, that "it is a child, even a 'divine' child, who speaks in Mozart's music to us." Some, he says, considered Mozart always a child in practical affairs (but Burckhardt "earnestly took exception" to this view). At the same time, Mozart, the child prodigy, "was never allowed to be a child in the literal meaning of that word." He gave his first concert at the age of six.

Yet he was always a child "in the higher meaning of that word."

Fear not, Karl Barth! Trust in the divine mercy. Though you have grown up to become a theologian, Christ remains a child in you. Your books (and mine) matter less than we might think! There is in us a Mozart who will be our salvation.

⁌ ⁌ ⁌

I never tire of reading the *Crusoe* of St. John Perse. It never ceases to move me. Such joy in reading it, and such agreement!

The wonderful legend has to be dissipated, in all its elements, by the sordid confusion of the city. That does not mean the legend was not real. On the contrary, this treatment is the final rejection of all sentimentality about "the island." It is the affirmation that *only the island was real.* That the city, the squalor, the exhausting mess of life remade to our diminished measure is utterly false. The *Crusoe* of Defoe was still perhaps legendary. The *Crusoe* of St. John Perse affirms, ten times over, the reality of his island, and of its own adventure.

I write this in the woodshed, surrounded by the charred, sweet-smelling wood of smashed-up whiskey barrels: not ours, naturally. Kegs given to the monks to break up for firewood.

⁌ ⁌ ⁌

Mark Van Doren, who is a friend of St. John Perse, says that St. John Perse had always thought of Cape Hatteras as a legendary, dreadful place, with perpetual hurricanes, like Cape Horn, and that it was the first thing he wanted to see when he was appointed to the French Embassy in Washington. So he went there at once. Sure enough there was a wild storm that very day. Ships were broken to pieces. You see! Things are often exactly what we want them to be!

✓ ✓ ✓

Another story of Mark Van Doren's. A doctor was called in the night and came home exhausted after working with the patient all night long. When asked what had happened, he groaned: "I have had a terrible time with the delivery of a child called Victor Hugo."

✓ ✓ ✓

The Brazilian poets: a whole new world. To begin with, Portuguese is a wonderful language for poetry, a language of admiration, of innocence, of joy, full of human warmth and therefore of humor: the humor that is inseparable from love, that laughs at the uniqueness of each individual being not because it is comical or contemptible but because it is unique. Uniqueness, the innocent self, is always surprising, and surprise is humorous as well as wonderful, on this human level.

I find the Brazilian poets different from the other Latin Americans. Their mild temper, their Franciscan love of life, their respect for all living things is fully reproduced as far as I know only in Carrera Andrade of Ecuador and Ernesto Cardenal of Nicaragua. There is in the Brazilians none of the hardness, none of the sour, artificial, doctrinaire attitudes which you find in so many of the Spanish-American poets, wonderful as they are. What a difference between Manual Bandeira, or Jorge de Lima, whose love is for *men*, and some of the Marxist poets writing in Spanish whose love is for a *cause*.

How quickly one discovers, below the surface of this devotion to causes, the deep current of hatred for men announced by the fallacious exaltation with which each string of curses and imprecations ends with an accolade among the select partisans: "BUT WE, brothers, will lift our heads and march into the future." A mechanical gag, a final pirouette after many crudely engineered moments of truth in which the bull is hacked to bits with a blunt axe.

Yet this bitterness must be; it is inevitable. I am moved by Alfonso Reyes, and Neruda, both of whom are deeply human, and Neruda remains so in spite of the unutterable banality and pompousness of his party-line exercise books—the later poems.

Returning to the Brazilians: I find Jorge de Lima above all a profoundly exciting poet, a mystic of cosmic as well as Christian vision. I wrote to Lax about him right away, when I discovered his great, incomparable circus. The same paradisaical humor, viewing the universe as "play"

—see the eighth chapter of *Proverbs*.

✓ ✓ ✓

One has either got to be a Jew or stop reading the Bible. The Bible cannot make sense to anyone who is not "spiritually a Semite." The spiritual sense of the Old Testament is not and cannot be a simple emptying out of its Israelite content. Quite the contrary! The New Testament is the fulfillment of that spiritual content, the fulfillment of the promise made to Abraham, the promise that Abraham believed in. It is never therefore a denial of Judaism, but its affirmation. Those who consider it a denial have not understood it.

✓ ✓ ✓

There is nothing whatever of the Ghetto spirit in St. Benedict. That is the wonderful thing both about the Rule and about the Saint: the freshness, the liberty of spirit, the sanity, the broadness, the healthiness of early Benedictine life.

You find the same sanity and breath in the early commentaries on the Rule: Smaragdus, Hildemar (and therefore Warnefrid).

But when the monastery turns in on itself, interpreting interpretations of interpretations, it becomes a Ghetto. Reforms that concentrate too exclusively on a "return to the letter" get involved in a web of interpretations, and fail to break the spell. They tend to let in some fresh air in one way, and in others they increase the danger of suffocation by locking all the windows that look outward to the world, or toward the sky.

Yet the air of the outside world is not fresh air. Just to break out and walk down the boulevards is no solution. The fresh air we need is the clean breath of the Holy Spirit, coming like the wind, blowing as He pleases. Hence the window must open, or be able to open, in any direction. The error is to lock the windows and doors in order to keep the Holy Spirit in the monastery. The very action of locking the doors and windows, in that sense, may be fatal.

St. Benedict never said the monk must *never* go out, *never* receive a letter, *never* have a visitor, *never* talk to anyone, *never* hear any news. He meant that the monk should distinguish what is useless or harmful from what is useful and salutary, and *in all things* glorify God.

Rejection of the world? The monk must *see Christ* in the pilgrim and stranger who come from the world, especially if they are poor. Such is the spirit and letter of the Rule.

✓  ✓  ✓

This sentence from a book now being read in the refectory, about the wonders of nature, leaves me lost in thought:

"After his two-legged master, the pig is the most abundant large mammal on the face of the earth."

Perhaps the time has come for a formal and conciliatory speech addressed to men and swine together, beginning something like this:

"There is a tide in the affairs of abundant large mammals . . ."

✓  ✓  ✓

This morning, before Prime, in the early morning sky, three antiquated monoplanes flew over the monastery with much noise, followed by a great heron.

✓  ✓  ✓

In a dream I saw people dancing new dances, with great gestures: a ballet. One of the dancers, in tight-fitting velvet of olive green, was a dark-haired woman, her hair cut close and shapeless like a boy's. In the middle of the dance she turned over sideways or backwards and touched the floor with her hands, very easily, but with a curious impossible gesture. I observed that all the dancers were serious, elegant, and bored. Their expressions of boredom were, however, slightly different from what they once were when I was in the world.

Then men came into the room with straw caps. Kentucky politicians.

✓ ✓ ✓

Governor Chandler of Kentucky, "Happy" Chandler: he came to the monastery with a party of friends and stood in the bright sun on the steps of the old guest house. He made a speech appropriate to the occasion, in which he mentioned "my young friend Thomas Merton," as if that were capable of getting him a vote—even mine.

Poor syntax, in one of his statements, resulted in a curious paradox: "You monks," he said, "know you cannot be happy because you have material possessions." I spoke of this later to the novices, pointing out the exact meaning of these words —that we were in despair because of our great possessions. One novice protested at once: "That was not what he *meant*." Naturally. What he meant was that we monks knew that poverty and not possessions would make men happy. How true it is that everyone instinctively pays attention not to what a politician actually says, but to what he seems to want to say.

✓ ✓ ✓

As I was coming back from Dom Frederic's lake, a green heron started up from the water in the culvert under the roadway where all the blackberry bushes are, and flew up into the willows. I could see his beautiful mahogany neck, and his crest was up as he looked back at me. His legs were bright yellow. This was perhaps the same heron I saw the other day at a distance over the night pasture, hardly bigger than a crow.

✓ ✓ ✓

I read a depressingly inane magazine article by a Logical Positivist—someone wanted my comment on it.

What can I say? The burden of his teaching seems to be this: "Since we cannot really say anything about anything, let us be content to talk about the way in which we say nothing." That is an excellent way to organize futility.

After all, even nothingness has its dignity: but here not even the dignity of nothingness is respected. There must be the mechanical clicking of the thought machine manufacturing nothing about nothing, as if even nothing had at all costs to be organized, and presented as if it were something. As if it had to be talked about.

The atheist existentialist has my respect: he accepts his honest despair with stoic dignity. And despair gives his thought a genuine content, because it expresses an experience —his confrontation with emptiness. But these others confront only the mechanical output of their own thinking machine. They don't have the imagination or the good sense to stand in awe at real emptiness. In fact, their rationalizations seem to be a complacent evasion: as if logical formulas somehow could give them something to stand on in the abyss.

And now: just wait until they start philosophizing with computers!

✴ ✴ ✴

Karl Barth asked (in a Christmas sermon preached in 1931): "Is perhaps an unconditional faith in all sorts of principles not the typically German form of unbelief?" A cogent question, with which I have no quarrel except that it restricts itself to Germany. Why not everybody else?

Barth says remarkable things in this sermon. Man must assuredly be able to live without principles as well as with them, for the "Light which entered the world at Bethlehem is, if its testimony is to be trusted, certainly *the most unprincipled reality* one can imagine."

The Incarnation is not something that can be fitted into a system, and though I know Barth draws from this many conclusions with which I would not agree, yet I think what he says must be remembered, and in this I would lean toward Barth much more readily than toward Teilhard de Chardin, for example. "Divine revelation," Barth continues, "cannot be discovered in the same way as the beauty of a work of art or the genius of a man is discovered. . . . It is the opening of a door that can only be unlocked from the inside."

✓ ✓ ✓

There are seven fascinating lines in the book of Wisdom about ships (14:1–7): how the wood of ships carries men across the sea, even though "a man went to sea without art." It is a lovely and basically humorous passage, with all the bustle and business of building the ship and planning the voyage, and trusting life and fortune to a piece of wood, and going off to sea without knowing what it is really all about, and praying to a piece of wood even more frail than the wood that carries the voyager: and all the while God draws the madman over a safe path among the waves and saves him in spite of his nonsense and his idol: "For blessed is the wood by which justice cometh." If the author of Wisdom has nothing but approval for ships and shipbuilders, he has no patience with idols and their makers.

✓ ✓ ✓

"*Parmi ses signes il y a les vaisseaux qui, sur la mer, sont comme dans le desert.*" This is a line which sounds a bit like St. John Perse. Actually it is from a French translation of the Koran (xlii–31). It moves me deeply, with its spirit of loneliness, independence of men, dependence on God, emptiness, trust . . . the spirit of the desert which, for Muslims, is not the prerogative of a few. It is for everyone.

✓ ✓ ✓

The lapidary sentences of Isaac of Stella: splendid austere light, fire struck from stone. In his Easter sermon, he sees faith as a resurrection because it is an act of obedience to God, who is Supreme Life. To believe: to obey Him Who is Life, and consequently to live. To live by submission to the Supreme Authority of Life—self-commitment and submission to God's Truth precisely in its power to give life, *to command to live.*

Hence faith is by no means a mere act of choice, an option for a special solution to the problems of existence. It is birth to a higher life by obedience to the Source of Life: to believe is thus to consent to hear and to obey a creative command that raises us from the dead. And what can be a deeper motive for belief?

We believe, not because we want to *know,* but because we want to *be.* And supernatural faith responds to the mystery of that natural faith which is the core and center of our personal being, the will to be ourselves that is the heart of our natural identity. The higher faith is the will not only to be ourselves, but to find ourselves truly in Christ by obedience to His Father.

✓ ✓ ✓

To be a solitary but not an individualist: concerned not with merely perfecting one's own life (this, as Marx saw it, is an indecent luxury and full of illusion). One's solitude belongs to the world and to God. Are these just words?

Solitude has its own special work: a deepening of awareness that the world needs. A struggle against alienation. True solitude is deeply aware of the world's needs. It does not hold the world at arm's length.

✓ ✓ ✓

If as Christians we thought that Church and Synagogue no longer affected one another, everything would be lost. And where this separation between the community and the Jewish nation has been made complete, it is the Christian community which has suffered. The whole reality of the revelation of God is then secretly denied and as an inevitable result philosophy and theology take the upper hand, and Christianity of a Greek or German or some other freely chosen kind is invented.                                                    —Karl Barth

In consequence of this, Barth sees clearly that Nazi anti-Semitism was also an attack *on Christ.*

✓ ✓ ✓

The reader in the refectory this week, particularly serious, announces at each meal the title of the book: *A Right to be Merry*. He drops his voice ever so slightly on the word "merry" as if he hesitated to utter it, almost as if he would question the title altogether. "God forbid, not a right to be *merry!*" If anything in the book concerns eating and drinking, he dims his voice ever so slightly with the same type of concern, as if withdrawing his will out from under the word "eat" and letting it float on its own, irresponsibly, before the face of a divine reproof.

But when he reads words like "death" and "dead" he lays them down squarely in the middle of the refectory, with satisfaction and with utter finality.

I have noticed that another very austere member of the community, who is severe with everything that concerns nature and is sparing at table, eats very slowly, after mashing all his food up like the food of a baby. I am glad that he gets a very evident satisfaction out of this private ritual.

✓ ✓ ✓

Refrain for a pensive song:

> *Le beau phénix est mort*
> *Il s'était trop brûlé.*

✓ ✓ ✓

We have to remember the principle that certain desires and certain pleasures are willed for us by God. We cannot live in the truth if we automatically suspect all desires and all pleasures. It is humility to accept our humanity, pride to reject it.

Von Hügel, in one of his letters, writes of W. G. Ward ("Ideal Ward") as an "eager, one-sided, great, unintentionally unjust soul" who on his deathbed saw the mischief of his life—he had consistently demanded that all others be like himself!

This is the root of inhumanity!

It is often more perfect to do what is simply normal and human than to try to act like an angel when God does not will it. That is, when there is no need for it, except in the stubborn passion of our own impatience with ourselves.

It is not practical, it is not honest, it is not Christian to fly from "every desire" and "every pleasure" that is not explicitly pious.

For others who are human enough to be ascetics without losing any of their humanity, it is all right to risk things that seem inhuman. For one as deficient and self-conscious as I am, the ordinary ways are safer. They are not just an evasion to be tolerated; they are a more perfect way.

✓ ✓ ✓

If I can unite *in myself* the thought and the devotion of Eastern and Western Christendom, the Greek and the Latin Fathers, the Russians with the Spanish mystics, I can prepare in myself the reunion of divided Christians. From that secret and unspoken unity in myself can eventually come a visible and manifest unity of all Christians. If we want to bring together what is divided, we can not do so by imposing one division upon the other or absorbing one division into the other. But if we do this, the union is not Christian. It is political, and doomed to further conflict. We must contain all divided worlds in ourselves and transcend them in Christ.

✓ ✓ ✓

Karl Marx would not work for his living, or even write for money. Yet he got Engels to write articles for him, which he sold to the New York *Tribune*.

Engels practically supported Marx in England: Engels, who was one of the bosses in his father's capitalist firm in Manchester. Out of these contradictions springs the genial theory of alienation, and the humanism of labor.

Marx the humanist was also a misanthrope, with piles, who liked scatological humor, understood the fetish-character of money and the propensity to adore golden calves.

A cynic, he relentlessly purified the labor movement of all semblance of sentiment, all aspirations to brotherly love. Yet he was also a kind father.

He was totally ignorant of machinery.

Like many scholars, he kept his room in a frightful mess, and wore a trail in the carpet, walking up and down in resentful meditation. Because he was thoroughly convinced of his own rightness, he would alter historical facts to suit his theories (says Edmund Wilson).

Shall we on this account disbelieve everything he said? No, for he was a great diagnostician. He saw the disease of modern man, who has come to be ruled by things and by money, and by machines. Marx thought he had a remedy. Whether or not those who followed him understood his remedy, whether or not they have applied it, it does not seem to have worked. Some still think it has not yet been tried.

In any case, there is no point in judging the inner contradictions of Marx's character and life with an exaggerated severity. All men, especially all who have talent, tend to be inconsistent. Their very struggle with their inconsistency seeks an outlet and a solution in creative works. But what is significant in Marx is that his analysis of society is a keenly intuitive analysis of inconsistency. He is quick to see the hidden contradictions in every ideology, every social structure. He believes that religion exists for the express purpose of assuaging the guilt created by these inconsistencies; to do this, it imagines an ideal and supraterrestrial condition in which the inconsistencies are all resolved.

Marx himself sought to bring about a condition, no less ideal, almost celestial, a paradise on earth in which the inner contradictions of man—particularly the inner contradictions of Karl Marx—would be resolved. Hence his philosophy lent itself very readily to pseudoreligious manifestation. Russian Communism is, in fact, an ersatz for religion.

The fact remains that, when Marx makes observations about inconsistencies and inner contradictions in society, his intuitions are sometimes very keen. It is a pity that his followers, raising his thought to the level of dogma, have enabled themselves to write theological glosses on it without perceiving its real relevance and its condemnation of their own inconsistency.

Marx said: "All our inventions and progress seem to result in endowing material things with intellectual life and stultifying human life into a material force."

And who has done more than the Marxists, at least the Stalinist variety, to bring this about?

✢ ✢ ✢

A woodpecker with a cry as sharp as a dagger terrifies the lesser birds, while he is himself benevolent and harmless. The beautiful kingfisher in dazzling flight rattles like a bird of ill omen. So we fear beauty!

✢ ✢ ✢

Those of whom God demands the most perfect hope must look closely at their sins. This is to say that they must let God shine His lamp suddenly upon the darkest corners of their souls—not that they themselves must search out what they do not understand. Too much searching conceals the thing we really ought to find. Nor is it certain that we have any urgent obligation to *find* sin in ourselves. How much sin is kept hidden from us by God Himself, in His mercy? After which He hides it from Himself!

✢ ✢ ✢

Our glory and our hope: we are the Body of Christ. Christ loves and espouses us in His own flesh. Isn't that enough for us? But we do not really believe it. No! Be content, be content. We are the Body of Christ! We have found Him because He has sought us. God has come to take up His abode in us, in sinners. There is nothing further to look for except to turn to Him completely, where He is already present. Be quiet and see that He is God.

✢ ✢ ✢

The Church militant: the Church "that fights." The Church that fights what? Why, Communism of course. What else?

The Church that fights *only* Communism, or some other political system that is hostile to it, has ceased to be militant.

✓  ✓  ✓

Yesterday I killed a big, shiny, black widow spider in her nest in a rotten tree stump. A beautiful spider, more beautiful than most other kinds. But I thought I had better kill her, for I myself had sat down right next to the stump before I saw her there. Someone else might do the same and get bitten.

It is strange to be so very close to something that can kill you, and not be defended by some kind of an invention. As if, wherever there was a problem in life, some machine would have to get there before you to negotiate it. As if we could not deal with the serious things of life except through the intermediary of these angels, our inventions. As if life were nothing, death were nothing. As if the whole of reality were in the inventions that stand between us and the world: the inventions which have become our world.

✓  ✓  ✓

Two great men impress themselves more and more upon my heart. I revere them deeply, though formerly I ignored and misunderstood them. They are Newman and Fénelon.

What moves me is their greatness, the polish of "finished" men, masterpieces, who because they are perfect beyond the ordinary seem to have reached a stasis, a condition that is not of time. They are not of their time, or ahead of it, or behind it. They are outside of it. Indeed, they reach this condition by suffering a kind of rejection which liberates them into a realm of a final perfection, a uniqueness, a humility, a wisdom, a silence that is definitive and contains all that they have ever said. So that, even when they quietly continue to speak and to write, perhaps for a few people only or for no one at all, they are saying things for everyone of all time who can grow to understand this peculiar type of greatness. They seem "old," and belong to the past, yet they survive indefinitely. Newman is always young: and yet his contempo-

rary and *bête noire*, Faber . . . compared with the fine-
grained Newman . . . the popular and effective Faber is
coarse and shallow.

Fénelon and Newman look alike, in their portraits. They
often speak alike. They must have had the same gestures, the
same way of looking at you, of listening to you, with a respect
you could not imagine you had suddenly deserved. Both
had, above all, style. And this, a fact which contradicts identification of banality with modesty, is necessary for perfection.

↑   ↑   ↑

"Whatever is done naturally may be either sacred or profane, according to our own degree of awareness; but whatever is done unnaturally is essentially and irrevocably profane."
                                        —A. K. Coomaraswamy

Technology is not in itself opposed to spirituality and to
religion. But it presents a great temptation. For instance,
where many machines are used in monastic work (and it is
right that they should be used), there can be a deadening of
spirit and of sensibility, a blunting of perception, a loss of
awareness, a lowering of tone, a general fatigue and lassi-
tude, a proneness to unrest and guilt which we might be less
likely to suffer if we simply went out and worked with our
hands in the woods or in the fields. The acceptance of lassi-
tude and enervation is then proposed as a sacrifice, and, of
course, it can be a sacrifice. It is the lot of the poor, and we
are supposed to share that lot. But the mere fact that these
new routines weary and exhaust nature, deaden our percep-
tions, and diminish our spiritual vitality is wrongly treated as
per se "supernatural." To do this is to equate the supernatural with the unnatural, sacrifice with frustration, and this
leads logically to the absurd proposition that, in practice, we
must sacrifice the spiritual life itself.

We must be detached from the spiritual life, but we must
still live it. And the purpose of the detachment is only to enable us to live it on a higher level. To resign ourselves to the
degradation and ruin of our spiritual life is not a sacrifice
that we can offer up as pleasing to God.

Hence a certain prudence is needed in the use of machines, and we cannot shrug off both bad ends and bad means by invoking the concept of the "supernatural."

The axiom that grace builds on nature has often been misused. But the fact remains that, if nothing is left of nature, there is nothing for grace to build on, there is nothing left to be sanctified and consecrated to God. This is not consecration, but desecration of the temple of our being.

✗ ✗ ✗

It would be easy and consoling to be able to say, at any moment: this thing I am now doing is regarded by every believer as a perfect act, as something having genuine and unquestionable value in the eyes of God. But would the peace and consolation I felt necessarily have anything to do with God? Might it not, after all, turn out to be another illusion, all the more illusory because it seemed so safe? A surrender to the authority of common opinion: "they say." But what do *they* know about it? How weak our consciences are. We give in and shut our eyes. We have conformed to "them." We are at peace, because we are what "they say" we should be. When Christ was nailed to the Cross, "they" were all certain that He was a blasphemer and a rebel, and the Apostles themselves did not dare to oppose "them."

✗ ✗ ✗

I want as many of the novices as possible to learn how to weave baskets. Brother Gerard is an aged monk who has made baskets for a long time, and he is now seventy-four. I want some novices to learn from him how to make baskets before he dies, or before he grows too old for anything of the sort. For when a brother is very old he sits only in the infirmary chapel, close to the window, right at the side of the altar, reading from a prayer book or a book of meditations, no longer weaving baskets.

Brother Basil and Brother Isaias will learn first to make baskets. Then others will learn. Brother Gerard cannot teach more than two at a time because there is no room for more than three to work in the potato cellar, where he weaves baskets.

"I moved a lot of the trash over to one side," said Brother Gerard. "It is warm in there. It will be nice in there. It is right in the next cellar to where I was last year." I received permission to speak to him about the baskets. He received permission to speak to the novices, but they did not get permission to speak to him. They make signs. He asked them, however, to tell him their names. "Speak," he said, "just for that only. Your names." That was enough speaking. They went ahead with the baskets. This afternoon the sun is warm. They are out cutting willows.

Brother Gerard said: "You don't remember Brother Stephen." He was condescending about my not knowing Brother Stephen. I have been here only twenty years. Brother Stephen apparently was here long before that, probably died thirty-five or forty years ago. "Brother Stephen was one who made baskets. Of course, he was French. He made all the baskets for everyone. But he died suddenly. We were all left without any more baskets. Anyone who wanted baskets had to get out and make his own. Well, I was in charge of the wardrobe and all the old baskets were falling to pieces. So I would repair them, and get a good look at how they were made, and then I began to make them for myself. That is how I learned how to make them. Of course, I could have learned at home before I entered the monastery. My father and brothers all made baskets. But you can imagine when I was out there I was not thinking about *baskets!*" This evoked a very quiet laugh on his part, as if it were the greatest joke in the world to imagine him thinking about baskets when he was "in the world."

"Then before we had the cheese business," he continued, "Brother Cellarer came to me and said, 'Reverend Father needs money and he needs it bad. Why don't you go and see him about those baskets?' So I went to Reverend Father and he said: 'How many baskets can you make in one day?' 'Oh,' I said, 'the little ones, I can probably make three or four of the little ones.' And he said to me: 'How much are we going to sell them for?' I said I thought about seventy-five cents apiece would probably be all right. But he said he thought five dollars apiece would be more like it. He said that nowadays you have to pay a man a dollar an hour at least, and the labor alone would add up to that. I said to him: 'A dollar an hour for making *baskets?*'" Again, the quiet laugh. What a world! Baskets! Five dollars for a basket. Dollar an hour for working, when you *like* it.

"Captain Kinnarney came around and he said if we put the baskets on sale in the gatehouse he would be the first to buy one. We sold them for three dollars, and he bought the first one. Then that year we sold a lot of baskets. Everyone bought a basket. But the next year I did poorly. The same people came back and they already had baskets, so we didn't sell any. But when we opened up a new guest house, and ladies were admitted to see it, then the brothers had the baskets spread all over the place and the women saw them. The baskets went fast, but the gatekeepers were selling them for fifty cents, sometimes. It depended. You could get a basket for any price you liked."

"You are making big ones again now?" I asked.

"Yes," he said, "I am making some for the foundation in California. The ones they took out with them are all broken up. Brother Procurator was out there and he just came back saying they needed baskets badly. So I said: 'All right, I will make them eight big ones.'" He held up eight fingers, laughed quietly and went away.

✓  ✓  ✓

Winter morning, pale sunshine. White smoke rises up in the valley, against the light, slowly taking on animal forms, against the dark wall of wooded hills behind. Menacing and peaceful forms. Probably this is the smoke of brush fires in the hollow. It might be the smoke of a burning house. Probably not a burning house. Big animal against the blue wall of the hill, a lion of smoke changing into a smoke bear. Cold, quiet morning, the watch ticks on the table, nothing happens. The smoke dragon rises, claws the winter sunlight, and vanishes over the hills.

✓ ✓ ✓

According to Gilson, Duns Scotus says of God that He is free "to set up any moral code He pleases so long as it deals with rules of human conduct whose relations to His own essence are not necessary ones." This is against those who assume that all moral relationships with God are necessary ones, excluding spontaneity; that to serve God is not to be free but finally and irrevocably bound. A moral code does not suppress choice, but educates and forms liberty. But for some, morality is opposed not only to evil choice (sin) but to *any* choice at all, any personal act of the will, any initiative, and obedience is therefore compulsion, not a matter of love. For them God is not love but power, obedience is not freedom but submission and inertia.

✓ ✓ ✓

Meadow larks singing in the snow, along the road from the cow barns. Icy water of the running stream, full of sun, flowing over green watercress between banks of snow. Dark blue water of the lake, edged with melting ice and snow.

✓ ✓ ✓

Evening: cold winter wind along the walls of the chapel. Not howling, not moaning, not dismal. Can there be anything mournful about wind? It is innocent, and without sorrow. It has no regrets. Wind is a strong child enjoying his play, amazed at his own strength, gentle, inexhaustible, and pure. He burnishes the dry snow, throwing clouds of it against the building. The wind has no regrets. The chapel is very cold. Two die-hard novices remain there alone, kneeling both upright, very still, no longer even pretending to enjoy or to understand anything.

✓ ✓ ✓

A dream:

I am invited to a party. The people are dressed in fine new clothes, walking about by the waterfront of a small fishing village of old stone houses. The gay, light dresses of the women contrast with the dark stones of the houses. I am invited to the party with them, and suddenly they are all gone, and the party is much farther away than I thought it would be. I must get there in a boat. I am all alone; the boat is at the quay.

A man of the town says that for five dollars I can get across on a yacht. I have five dollars, more than five dollars, hundreds of dollars, and also francs. He takes me to the yacht, but it is not a yacht. It is a workaday fishing schooner, which I prefer. But it does not move from shore. It is very heavy. We try to push it off, it does not move, we try in many ways to make it move, and it seems to have moved a little. But then I know that I must strike out and swim.

And I am swimming ahead in the beautiful magic water of the bay. From the clear depths of the water comes a wonderful life to which I am not entitled, a life and a power which I both love and fear. I know that by diving down into the water I can find wonders and joys, but that it is not for me to dive down; rather I must go to the other side, and I am indeed swimming to the other side. The other side is there. The end of the swim. The house is on the shore. The wide summer house which I am reaching with the strength that came to me from the water. The water is great and vast beneath me as I come toward the shore. And I have arrived. I am out of the water. I know now all that I must do in the summer house. I know that I must first play with this dog who comes running from one of the halls.

I know the Child will come, and He comes. The Child comes and smiles. It is the smile of a Great One, hidden. He gives to me, in simplicity, two pieces of buttered white bread, the ritual and hieratic meal given to all who come to stay.

✦ ✦ ✦

Among the martyrs of Uganda, all one in the witness of their death and of their blood, were several who were not Roman Catholics. Who is to say these were not canonized along with the others? A great sign is seen in Africa!

✓ ✓ ✓

The Congo: because Albert Schweitzer is there in the jungle, we are firmly convinced that we are all benevolent, all brave, all self-sacrificing: that we have *all* loved Africa. That it is our very nature to love Africa, Asia, "inferior races," etc., etc. And that if they do not recognize this at once, it is proof that they are by nature inferior since they cannot appreciate the superior benevolence and culture of the white race. This perversity, itself a sign of ingrained malice, predisposes them to Communism.

Thus Africa becomes part of our own pathological myth, part of our own sickness. Not only Africa: much nearer home is the American Negro. Same syndrome: We have offered him everything, he has rejected it ungratefully because he does not like our terms! What we give him is a sign of our superiority. . . .

Whole continents and whole races do not take well to imaginary roles, roles assigned to them by minds they find it difficult to understand, and which look quite strange to them. Thus they finally insist, if necessary with violence, on asserting what is least imaginary—and least acceptable to our collective imagination. "Here," they say, setting fire to a building, "see what you can make of *this!*"

We do not make much of it. Or else, perhaps, we decide it is a Communist plot. . . . Thus we dispense ourselves from the need to think, and convince ourselves that there is only one way: to go into action with weapons.

Thus we drive them all into the arms of the Communists, since we have left them nowhere else to go!

✓ ✓ ✓

The core of the race problem as I see it is this: the Negro (also other racial groups of course, but chiefly the Negro) is victimized by the psychological and social conflicts now inherent in a white civilization that fears imminent disruption and has no mature insight into the reality of its crisis. White society is purely and simply incapable of really accepting the

Negro and assimilating him, because white people cannot cope with their own drives, cannot defend themselves against their own emotions, which are supremely unstable in a rapidly changing and overstimulated society.

In order to minimize the sense of hazard and disaster always latent in themselves, the whites *have to* project their fears on to some object outside themselves. The Cold War conflict of course provides ample opportunities—and the more insecure men are on one side or the other, the more they resort to paranoid accusations of "Communism" or "imperialism," as the case may be. The accusations are not without basis, though still pathological.

Caught in this inescapable syndrome is the Negro, who has had the misfortune to make himself, his presence, his wretchedness, his own conflicts, his own disruption clearly visible at the precise moment when white society is least prepared to cope with an extra load of hazard.

What is the result? On one hand a rather pathetic but still comprehensible rush of liberal tenderness to welcome and conciliate this tragic woe. On the other, a viciously pathological hardening of the insecure, a tightening of resistance, a confirmation in fear and hate on the part of those (conservative or otherwise) who are determined to blame someone else for their own inner inadequacies.

The incredible inhumanity of this refusal to listen for a moment to the Negro in any way whatever, and of this determination to keep him down at all costs, is, it seems to me, almost certain to provide a hopelessly chaotic and violent revolutionary situation. More and more the animosity, suspicion, and fear which these whites feel (and it remains in its roots a fear of their own inner misery, which they probably cannot feel as it really is) develop into a self-fulfilling prophesy. The white racist's hate of the Negro (I repeat, hate, for this is only a mild word to represent the reality in the hearts of these disturbed people) is made acceptable to him when he represents it as a Negro hatred of the whites fomented and stimulated by Communism. Cold War and racist fears neatly click together in one unity! Everything is so simple!

The Negro is clearly invited to one response. He has had untold reasons for hating the white man. They are now being solidly compounded and confirmed. Even though he has nothing whatever to gain by violence, he has also nothing to lose. And violence will at least be one decisive way of saying what he thinks of white society!

The result is likely to be very unpleasant, and the blame will rest squarely on the shoulders of white America, with its emotional, cultural, and political immaturity and its pitiable refusal of insight.

*    *    *

Blaming the Negro: this is not just a matter of rationalizing and verbalizing. It has become a strong emotional need for the white man. Blaming the Negro (and by extension the Communist, the outside agitator, etc.) gives the white a stronger sense of identity, or rather it *protects* an identity which is seriously threatened with pathological dissolution. It is by blaming the Negro that the white man tries to hold himself together. The Negro is in the unenviable position of being used for *everything*, even for the white man's psychological security. Unfortunately, a mere outburst of violence will only give the white man the justification he desires. It will convince him that he is for real because he is *right*. The Negro could really wreak havoc in white society by psychological warfare if he knew how to use it. Already the psychological weapon of nonviolence has proved effective as an attack on the white man's trumped-up image of himself as a righteous and Christian being.

*    *    *

When a myth becomes a daydream it is judged, found wanting, and must be discarded. To cling to it when it has lost its creative function is to condemn oneself to mental illness. I do not say we must learn to live without myths (such an idea is dangerous self-deception: it is itself a false myth, or a daydream), but we must at least get along without evasions. A daydream is an evasion.

When a myth becomes an evasion, the society that clings to it gets into serious trouble.

What is the conventionally accepted American myth? Is this myth still alive, or has it expired and become an evasion? Is the present crisis—in race relations, delinquency, etc., a judgment of our public daydream?

*"America is the earthly paradise."*

To say that this was once a valid and creative myth is not to say that there was no basis of truth in it. On the contrary, this belief in the obvious possibilities of an immense new continent, a place fabulously endowed and blessed, had fantastic potency. The discovery of America (and you should read the first descriptions of Hispaniola!) galvanized and inebriated the Western World. It did more than anything else —even Copernicus and Galileo—to overturn the world-view of the Middle Ages. It revolutionized the thought of Western man. He was now convinced that human society was getting off to *an entirely new start.* This was a much more potent and influential myth than that of Holy Russia, for example, which has never had, and now can never have, the same universal effect. Russia, after all, is Russia. It is inexorably rooted in its peculiar history, and no matter what new forms it may assume, no one is fooled: before Khrushchev was Stalin, before Stalin was Ivan the Terrible.

But the New-Found-Land was a world *without history,* therefore without sin, therefore a paradise. To this world came the victims of a Europe grown old in wickedness, with its history of arbitrary authority. To escape from history, that is to say from Europe, to escape from the burden of the past, to return to the source, to begin again a new history, starting from scratch, *without original sin.* This was what America offered to the oppressed, the persecuted, the unsuccessful, the disinherited—or the merely discontented. To be "baptized" by emigration, to leave one's sins and one's past in the Atlantic, to start out for a new life in the wilderness with one's hand in the hand of God . . . !

For four hundred years American horizons kept widening. There were no limits. There was always a frontier beyond which there was still more paradise, even though on this side of the frontier there was now history, there was sin, and paradise had begun to close down. Yet it did not close down altogether, as long as there was a frontier. There was always a new start, over the mountains, over the plains.

Then there was the ocean—a permanent barrier against the "old world" of sin and history. As long as our "history" was self-contained, we could regard it as a series of paradisiacal incidents—or of innocent excesses. It took place in the great unlimited garden where, in some mysterious way it was not judged because it did not have any part in the ancient inscrutable intrigues of the Old World. Europe after all had roots in a past so ancient it could never be remembered: as far back as Egypt and Babylon and Ur. America was cursed with no past that could not be remembered, explained, justified. Everything was *clear*. Everything was well meant. Since there were no hidden meanings, no implications dictated by the past, no reservations in view of agreements that might be violated, everything was considered *sincere*. There was not yet a heritage of official and known duplicity to poison the national memory. Even though there were distressing episodes, we were honest about them, and if they happened on our side of the ocean they were regarded as without sin because *well meant*. At any rate there was always another frontier; one could begin again.

Thus the word "frontier" became the symbol not only of adventure but of clear-eyed innocence—pathetic overtones, in Kennedy's "new frontier," when the frontiers are closed forever! Kennedy is trying to keep the myth alive in spite of everything.*

When there were in reality no more frontiers, America gradually became the prisoner of that curse, the historical memory, the total consciousness of an identity responsible for what had happened to the Indians, for instance. (As long as there was merely the frontier, and one camp of pioneers here, another there, what happened to the Indians was, in a way, happening to the devil. It was at any rate heroic—and

* Johnson's Great Society is another variation, but the overtones of innocence are slightly different. We are innocent not because we are new, but because we are *a success*, and this justifies everything.

*well meant.* The Indian could somehow seem to be the serpent in Paradise, because he was outside the myth. For the greatest of the pioneers, for people like Daniel Boone, the Indian remained *part* of the myth because someone like Boone had a heart and a mind broad enough to embrace both sets of opposites at the same time. He could accept correlatives. Others, however, had no way of conceiving "pioneer" and "Indian" as correlative.)

The South, too, was an earthly paradise. Not of course at all times, for all its inhabitants. There were the slaves. Yet the South, before the War between the States, had this of paradise left to it: it still had the wholeness that embraced white and black in an apparent unity, even though the relationship was out of order. This unified feudal society was nevertheless conceived as a realistic possibility that did not conflict with the living and efficacious paradise myth. For the South, on the contrary, it *was* paradise, in which the benevolent and cultured planters paternally loved and protected the joyous, singing "darkies," etc.

The brutal national trauma of that war destroyed the myth for the South, and in doing so (though no one realized it at the time) destroyed it for everybody.

Since the Civil War, the whole nation has been "in sin," and the sin has been inescapable. The pioneer child, or the plantation child if you prefer, had been cruelly awakened. And he has faced in himself the cruelty that he did not realize was there: the meanness, the injustice, the greed, the hypocrisy, the inhumanity! He knows there is a mark on his forehead, and is afraid to recognize it—it might turn out to be the mark of Cain!

Rather he has consistently refused to accept his expulsion from "Paradise." He has insisted that he is what he has always dreamed he was—gentle, kind, fair, noble, courteous, yet simple, with the clear-eyed simplicity of the frontiersman—or the noble directness of the Confederate gentleman: the frankness of General Lee.

At this point, the myth becomes an evasion. The refusal is culpable. The beautiful story we are telling ourselves is no longer much more than an ordinary lie.

There have been foreign wars, in which America has been persuaded to take part only when convinced that we would ride into battle as cowboys. We took over Cuba from Spain. Why? Because we were roughriders, of course. Clear-eyed, independent, with the honesty that is bred by gazing out over great plains, we jumped on our horses and rode up San Juan Hill, to liberate the poor, defenseless, nonindependent Cubans. They, too, have plains, of course. But looking out over the small plains of Camaguey is somehow different.

We strode into World War I no longer busting broncos as we went: but we still had cowboy hats.

And today? All we do is watch ourselves in the mirror of TV. Yes, that is you and me, pardner. Tight-lipped, straight-shooting, hard-hitting, clean-loving: we are still on the frontier, we are still in paradise. There has really been no history. There is not even a change in the script: same mesquite, same arroyo, same dead man's gulch, same forty-niners, and is the daughter's name Eve or Clementine? And the same serpent: the foreign type, the man with a record (for sin, remember, equals history), the man with roots in Europe or Mexico . . . or perhaps the same Indian. The Indian, too, is serpent, for he is older, he was there before, he had roots in the ground when we arrived. He did not have any history, but at least he had a past (and as time went on we traced him back to Asia, to *China:* what a record *that* turned out to be! He was a criminal before he got here, and he brought it all with him, because he obviously came by gradual stages. There was continuity. Whereas we arrived suddenly, we stepped off the *Mayflower* in perfect innocence, for we had left all our sins in the ocean. Indeed, the fact that we were persecuted meant that we were sinless in the beginning.).

After every war (which we, being the good guys, have always won) we have, with the utmost sincerity, exported just a little bit of our innocence, just a little bit of our paradisaical idealism, to the lands sunken in history and sin. Wilson was still a creature of another world, and they almost believed him for a while. The Marshall Plan: surely a thought born of a simple and magnanimous mind. (The Alliance for Progress—the bare ideal remained for a while.)

Yet more and more the lands of sin, the countries of history, have tended to observe, with ever greater malice and with ever more intolerable arrogance, and with manifest satisfaction, that we, too, have a history, that we are no longer the earthly paradise! They claim now to be able to see this clearly, and they never hesitate to offer what seems to them to be convincing evidence. They proclaim the fact tirelessly from day to day. We know, of course, that they are devoured with jealousy: but ought we, perhaps, to ask ourselves if they have something?

They tell us: Yankee go home. And we would gladly go: but somehow when we get back, we find we don't have a home any more. We have fallen into history like everyone else; we are involved, beyond repair, in the fantastic problems of everybody, and we are part of their accursed history. We go home, and when we get there we find—revolution! Home is not home any more. It is no longer paradise.

There is a great depth of cruelty in that taunt: Yankee go home!

The people who yell that at us exult with hate because they see the flaming sword and the locked gate behind us. We do not look around because we are afraid to see them too. What will we do when we finally have to realize that we are locked out of the lone prairie and thrust forth into the world of history along with all the other people in the world: that *we are just as much a part of history as all the rest of them?*

That is the end of the American myth: we can no longer lean out from a higher and rarified atmosphere, and point down from the firmament to the men on earth to show them the patterns of our ideal republic. *We are in the same mess as all the rest of them.* And what is worse, there are even some people (Pope John, for instance) who seem to think that it is our duty, along with everybody else's, to cooperate in solving common problems, problems of history, problems of sin, problems of crime. . . .

Shall we turn our backs on all that? Shall we open another can of beer and flip the switch, and find our way back to the familiar mesquite, where all problems are easily solved? The good guys are always the straight shooters and they always win. The bad guys are always shifty because they have a history.

What is history?

If you mean a *personal* history, it is perhaps what one would most like to forget.

Back to the rancho! Back to the old mesquite!

But now, even supposing that we *could* stay at home, and mind our own business: even though we have "the deterrent" (our own kind of flaming sword to hold history at bay) what happens? We have Negroes at home, disturbing the peace of paradise, and trying to force us, against our own best judgment, to move, to change, to make history, instead of going back, over and over again, to what can never be a new start any more.

✔ ✔ ✔

There is a divine judgment upon national complacencies: it condemns the complacent to eat their fine words—in detail, in the crudest, most inexorable fashion, and not to realize that they are doing it.

To call it a "judgment" is to suppose, normally, that the one judged has a conscience. In which case, he is all the more severely judged by the flagrant evasions with which he seeks to escape the contradiction between his actions and his formal ideals: for instance, we celebrate in America the Boston Tea Party, the Declaration of Independence, etc. Rightly. But now, let anyone start the equivalent of the Boston Tea Party in Viet Nam, in Peru, in Brazil, in Venezuela, or in Alabama.

Meanwhile, the Declaration of Independence was celebrated this year with more death in automobile accidents than ever before. This, too, says something.

✔ ✔ ✔

There was a theological conference in the Monastic Chapter. Even more disconcerting than usual. The thesis: "That it is impossible to know with certitude of faith that one is saved." So there was much fumbling and bumbling about certitude, moral certitude, this or that certitude, anything but faith. All right. We have not yet paid too much attention to the ecumenical movement, have we? We are intent on proving the Protestants wrong. But someone might conceivably have mentioned *hope*. No one did. Are we, then, in despair?

✓    ✓    ✓

In the refectory, instead of reading (for a day or so), they are playing one of those "liturgical tapes"—a tape-recorded exhortation on the liturgy from some conference or congress on the subject. It is a deafening harangue, blasting everybody's head off. The material in itself is not bad: the standard approach on the theology of the mysteries of Christ in the liturgy—standard since *Mediator Dei* at any rate. Certainly nothing beyond or besides *Mediator Dei*.

But the blast, the emphasis. Everything is pounded out with both fists. I would not believe it possible, but it is true. Constant, impassioned pointing to the "ca-ROSS." (That is how he emphasizes the word "cross." Makes it into two syllables and lands with both feet on the second.)

One of the older monks gets tired of it and walks out of the refectory, banging the door. Not exactly virtuous, but fully understandable.

Pontiffs! Pontiffs! We are all pontiffs haranguing one another, brandishing our croziers at one another, dogmatizing, threatening anathemas!

Recently in the breviary we had a saint who, at the point of death, removed his pontifical vestments *and got out of bed*. He died on the floor, which is only right: but one hardly has time to be edified by it—one is still musing over the fact that he had pontifical vestments on *in bed*.

Let us examine our consciences, brethren: do we wear our mitres even to bed? I am afraid we sometimes do.

Reflections after this booming tape: sympathy for Peguy, Simone Weil, who preferred not to be in the middle of the Catholically approved and well-censored page, but only on the margin. And they remained there as question marks: questioning not Christ, but Christians.

✓ ✓ ✓

A letter arrives stamped with the slogan "The U. S. Army, key to peace." No army is the key to peace, neither the U. S. Army nor the Soviet Army nor any other. No "great" nation has the key to anything but war. Power has nothing to do with peace. The more men build up military power, the more they violate peace and destroy it.

✓ ✓ ✓

All Souls' Day:

Some seem to want to make All Souls' Day a feast of death, with much rattling of bones and many skulls. The cult of cemeteries not as places where bodies sleep in peace awaiting the Resurrection, but where they lie and rot, eaten by worms. In this cult of death more than anywhere else there is danger of the universal vulgarity and stupidity of middle-class culture corrupting the Christian spirit. Money has a lot to do with this. The disposal of dead bodies is a lucrative and scandalous business—scandalous in the way sorrow is exploited and insulted with small, unctuous, frightful, utterly useless, and expensive toys. The paint, the cushions, the things that light up, the things that play music.

But our dead rest in Christ. The cemetery is the symbol of Christ. To rest in Christ is to live (hence cypresses, green even in winter, are not supposed to suggest melancholy thoughts, as the Romantics imagined—just the opposite)! Yet the dead do not all live totally in Him. What Purgatory is we neither fully know nor fully understand. But why treat it as a preternatural reform school?

Walking in the monastic cemetery I am appalled by the dates on the crosses: it is already four years since old Brother Albert died, eleven since Father Odo died, etc. And back in another age, twenty years ago, the first funerals I saw here: old monks who were still medieval, or at least seventeenth-century Trappists, with just a touch of American foolishness in them (Brother Andrew had been a circus clown anyway!) but who for the most part lived and died so seriously. Even their apparent flippancies were rooted in a crude solidity.

Even their jokes, silly as they were, had a kind of seriousness behind them. (Perhaps even at times a kind of desperation!)

The dim past! The postulant who left yesterday was not yet born when Frater Alfred, a fellow student in my theology class, a strange one, dropped in at the cloister after Compline and was dead before morning, no one ever knew what of. One could hardly be more completely forgotten than he is now, except by a few of us who used to see him every day.

✓ ✓ ✓

When the Dalai Lama was young, still a boy, he was lonely in his palace, the Potala, and would walk on the roof looking through field glasses down upon the houses of his subjects to see if they were having parties, and in order to watch them enjoying themselves. They, in their turn, would hide themselves and hold parties out of his sight, so as not to sadden him still more.

✓ ✓ ✓

Chuang Tzu said: "At the present time the whole world is under a delusion, and though I may wish to go in a certain direction how can I succeed in doing so? Knowing that I cannot go that way, to force my way would be another delusion. Therefore my best course is to let my purpose go and no more pursue it. If I do not pursue it, whom shall I have to share my sorrow?"

✓ ✓ ✓

From Jean Giono, *Le Poids du Ciel* (Paris, Gallimard):

"Industrial society can live on war, and soon it will be able to live on war alone. Peasant society can live on peace. . . . In peasant life the true greatness of man manifests itself: not national, not class greatness, individual greatness. All the elements of that greatness are found in *work that accords with the measure of man and is within the reach of his hands.* In spite of all the bloody sacrifices that it demands, national greatness, mass greatness, is nothing but assembled littleness of a multitude of rascals, who, bit by bit, rot it away, destroy it, drive it on to ever greater sacrifices in order to maintain itself in existence. It is an illusory greatness, the bitterest hoax of those moralities that have been termed 'constructive.' There is no hoax about the individual greatness of the peasant.

"It would seem by some chemical kind of justice, nature, when driven to self-contradiction and the anti-natural, makes its offshoots work for their own destruction."

Giono is a passionate and articulate defender of the human scale, the human measure. And in the long run, without this measure, God Himself cannot be known, for He revealed Himself scaled down to our dimensions. Giono has a wonderful essay about walking the roads of Provençe, from village to village. He says that this is the only way to really "know" a region. He is, of course, perfectly right. On all the journeys I have made in trains and planes (not so many) I remember mostly being tired and buffeted by impressions. Even though walking is an exertion, one does not remember it as tiring, but only as a joy.

✓ ✓ ✓

From moment to moment I remember with astonishment that I am at the same time empty and full, and satisfied because I am empty. I lack nothing. The Lord rules me.

✓ ✓ ✓

Much more to the point: the prayer that struggles toward God in obscurity, in trial, beating down the phantoms.

✓ ✓ ✓

"A vigorous defender of the family, of freedom, or of socialism may be further from the spirit of those values than another person who seems to be opposing them, but in fact is only incensed against the hardened and decadent forms they have assumed."                                   —Emmanuel Mounier

Obviously the same is true about those who defend and who attack religion.

✼ ✼ ✼

Gandhi once asked: "How can he who thinks he possesses absolute truth be fraternal?"

Let us be frank about it: the history of Christianity raises this question again and again.

The problem: God has revealed himself to men in Christ, but He has revealed Himself first of all as love. Absolute truth is then grasped as love: therefore not in such a way that it excludes love in certain limited situations. Only he who loves can be sure that he is still in contact with the truth, which is in fact too absolute to be grasped by his mind. Hence, he who holds to the gospel truth is afraid that he may lose the truth by a failure of love, not by a failure of knowledge. In that case he is humble, and therefore he is wise. But *scientia inflat*. Knowledge expands a man like a balloon, and gives him a precarious wholeness in which he thinks that he holds in himself all the dimensions of a truth the totality of which is denied to others. It then becomes his duty, he thinks, by virtue of his superior knowledge, to punish those who do not share his truth. How can he "love" others, he thinks, except by imposing on them the truth which they would otherwise insult and neglect? This is the temptation.

In the refectory a tendentious book about Communism is being read. Communism is insidious. We should hate all that is insidious, especially this ultimate diabolical insidiousness which is Communism. If we truly hate it with all the power of our being, then we can be sure that we ourselves are, and will remain, righteous, free, sincere, honest, open. Today, then (we are told) hatred of Communism is the test of a good Christian. The pledge of all truth is our political hate. Hate Castro. Hate Khrushchev. Hate Mao. All this in the same breath as "God's merciful love" and the "beatings of the Sacred Heart." There seems to be some other dimension we have not discovered. . . .

Chrysostom has some fine things to say about sheep and wolves in the III Nocturn of St. Barnabas' Day. "As long as we remain sheep, we overcome. Even though we may be surrounded by a thousand wolves, we overcome and are victori-

ous. But as soon as we are wolves, we are beaten: for then
we lose the support from the Shepherd who feeds not wolves,
but only sheep."                   —from Homily 34 on St. Matthew

𝟄  𝟄  𝟄

A sweet summer afternoon. Cool breezes and a clear sky.
This day will not come again.
The young bulls lie under a tree in the corner of their field.
Quiet afternoon. Blue hills. Day lilies nod in the wind.
This day will not come again.

𝟄  𝟄  𝟄

Christianity and the world: this is a matter about which
suddenly, one must have an approved answer. I have none.
The traditional monastic answer is certainly not the "approved" one. It is being quietly and discretely forgotten by
monks, as a matter of fact, and is being taken over by poets.
Brendan Behan, for example, has declared that for all he
cares the whole world can go to the devil. This is not exactly
the monastic formula either (though I suppose there have
been monks who would not have used it because they would
have felt it to be quite otiose to do so: the world having gone
to the devil long since).

The point is, there is in Christianity, or Christendom, and in
Buddhism, and in many other religions, a tradition of *contemptus mundi* which needs to be re-examined and understood. Originally, no doubt, it was intended to give the believer a certain freedom of action, a distance, a detachment,
a liberation from care without which any question of love
for the people in the world would be completely irrelevant.

Unfortunately, this *contemptus mundi* became a formality
of religious organizations that were, in their own way, quite
worldly. The ascetic concept of *contemptus mundi* has been
radically transformed since the theoretical distinction of "spiritual" and "secular" power was worked out during the medieval struggle over lay investitures. *Contemptus mundi* became more and more an asceticism of obedience in the
service of "spiritual" power—or the Church's side in politics.

It was taken for granted that one contemned "the world" while seeking the same ends as the world, but with a different set of motives. Hence, what one contemned was in reality not "the world" as such, but a rival power structure or simply "our competitor." Contempt for the world became not contempt for the objectives of the world, but competition with the world on its own ground and for the same power, with contempt for its motives. Thus, in time, the "opposition" of "spiritual" and "secular" power has become in fact no more than the spirit of fraternal rivalry that exists (I presume) between Ford and General Motors. And now this has come to be seen for what it is: as a pose which has little meaning. The approved answer? At present everyone seems to think the best thing would be a merger that would make all *contemptus* useless—especially since now all the power is secular anyway!

As a matter of fact, however, the problem is not as simple as all that. One finds a general agreement that the Church had better acquire a healthy and articulate respect for the modern world—otherwise she will have no place in it, except to be reduced to the level of fringe groups like Jehovah's Witnesses. But in what does this respect for the world consist?

The conservative position retains a certain element of traditional *contemptus mundi*. We keep up our cohesion and morale by fulminating against certain typical issues—especially lax sexual morals, birth control, divorce, pornography, which are not only obvious but also typological—that embody in themselves all that we mean by "the world" and "sin." (Here we tend to forget that they typify the "flesh" rather than "the world." The world, in the triad world-flesh-devil, represents greed for wealth and prestige, and this is seldom attacked. As a matter of fact, it is precisely here that, having "satisfied" the Christian conscience by anathemas directed at the flesh, we can come to terms with the world which, let us admit it, offers us a prestige which we believe to be essential for the dissemination of the Gospel. The message of the priest who drives an Oldsmobile is surely more credible than that of one who rides in the bus!)

The liberal attitude, on the other hand, makes a different choice of symbols. Less exercised on the problems of the flesh, it concerns itself more with symbolic social issues, and having taken an edifying stand (somewhat late) in questions of civil rights (in the United States) or labor (Europe) it explicitly declares that the Church has much to learn from "the world" in these matters, and that the insights of the most modern and advanced social thought are more relevant to Christianity than the platitudes of a theology that has still not caught up with the twentieth century.

For the liberal, the message of the Church will become credible to the modern world if the priest is seen on the assembly line—or if he is arrested in a sit-in. There is no question that this position is somewhat more relevant to the times and implies a more real sense of man's need than the position of those who reduce *contemptus mundi* to anti-Communism and the readiness to shower Russia with H-bombs in the name of Christ.

But does the ancient, ascetic idea of renunciation of the world have no meaning at all in the present context?

*✓ ✓ ✓*

As usual, one comes back to the old question: what do you mean by "the world" anyway? In this, I don't think an abstract answer makes too much sense. My concrete answer is: what did I leave when I entered the monastery? As far as I can see, what I abandoned when I "left the world" and came to the monastery was the *understanding of myself* that I had developed in the context of civil society—my identification with what appeared to me to be its aims. Certainly, in the concrete, "the world" did not mean for me either riches (I was poor) or a life of luxury, certainly not the ambition to get somewhere in business or in anything else except writing. But it did mean a certain set of servitudes that I could no longer accept—servitudes to certain standards of value which to me were idiotic and repugnant and still are. Many of these were trivial, some of them were onerous, all are closely related. The image of a society that is happy because it drinks Coca-Cola or Seagrams or both and is protected by the bomb.

The society that is imaged in the mass media and in advertising, in the movies, in TV, in best-sellers, in current fads, in all the pompous and trifling masks with which it hides callousness, sensuality, hypocrisy, cruelty, and fear. Is this "the world?" Yes. It is the same wherever you have mass man. The basic pattern is identical in Russia, the United States, Germany, France. The materials and appearances differ, and in Western Europe perhaps the cut is a little more sophisticated. But it is the same suit of clothes, and same pair of ready-made pants, the same spiritual cretinism which in fact makes Christians and atheists indistinguishable.

All this is obviously irreversible. Whether one is "with" it or "against" it makes not the slightest difference. And perhaps that is why "believers" are tired of pretending that their "belief" somehow distinguishes them from others who are completely committed to these values. In fact, belief makes no earthly difference. For my own part, I am by my whole life committed to a certain protest and nonacquiescence, and that is why I am a monk. Yet I know that protest is not enough—is perhaps meaningless. Yet that is also why protest and nonacquiescence must extend to certain conceptions of monasticism which seem to me to be simply a fancy-dress adaptation of what we are claiming we have renounced.

As if, for instance, "leaving the world" were adequately summed up by those pictures of "the Trappist" with his cowl over his head and his back to the camera, looking at a lake.

✓  ✓  ✓

A Tibetan student on his way out to Washington stopped here and I had a talk with him. He told me something of his life. How as a boy he was brought (by the government) to Lhasa to learn how to dance. How he hated it and tried to run away. How he made some money in business and escaped to India on pilgrimage when the Reds came. He is obsessed with getting an education and has been going from college to college in this country with scholarships and grants of various kinds.

Naturally I asked him about the Tibetan monks. He spoke of the good and the bad. The various orders which I can

never get straight. The hermits, who have renounced everything are, he says, "the best." He spoke of Mila Repa and
says that this is the Tibetan I must read.

He says there is a Mongolian monk now in New Jersey
setting up a little community, and plans are being made to
send several Tibetan monks now in India to this monastery in
New Jersey. He says the Dalai Lama is very anxious to have
the monks that are with him in India trained in knowledge
of Western culture and religion.

*✓  ✓  ✓*

Don R——, prominent in Italian Catholic Action and editor
of a rather lavish magazine, writes a pleasant breezy note,
asking for an article on "The Holiness of the Church": just
like that! People are now convinced that I secrete articles
like perspiration. This is clearly more my fault than theirs,
and something has to be done about it. And yet, if people
were to really *read* me, they might not take it for granted that
I could simply reach into the back of my mind for a dish of
ready-to-serve Catholic answers about everything under the
sun. It seems to me that one of the reasons why my writing
appeals to many people is precisely that I am not so sure of
myself and do not claim to have all the answers. In fact, I
often wonder quite openly about these "answers," and about
the habit of always having them ready. The best I can do is
to look for some of the questions.

What about the holiness of the Church, for example. Is
this simply a matter of declaring that the Church is Christ
made visibly present in the world—that in her the holiness of
Christ radiates for all to see? And should this be declared in
such a way that no distinction is made between the Church
as a community of persons united in love, and as an institution
in which individuals are organized by law—so that their obedience to law becomes, in fact, an epiphany of the holiness
of Christ? And should this imply that this itself is plain to all
the elect, and that no further evidence of holiness is required?
That the correctness of those who obey the laws is in fact a
pledge at once of holiness and happiness? That their disci-

pline is joy? That those who do not see it are blind because
of ill will and sin? That the proof of the holiness of the Church
is perhaps that the holy see that blind obedience is holy, and
the unholy do not? Such curious hesitations are obviously
not what the Father is asking for.

*✓  ✓  ✓*

Again: the Church and the world. The main ambiguity in
this "opposition" which is to be reconciled is the conscious
sense of guilt over the Church's former resistance to science.

This is essentially a medieval problem. We are facing it five
hundred years late. In my opinion the problem is sociological
even more than religious.

The medieval Church made a theoretical separation between the sacred and secular spheres. This separation was in
reality pragmatic and political. It was inseparable from the
Church's struggle to preserve her liberty from secular power
in the investiture conflict.

At the same time it was an affirmation of a certain supremacy even in secular affairs. In all that concerned man's social,
intellectual, and cultural life, the last word belonged to the
clerical specialist trained in a theology which was indifferent
to "the world" (in theory) and indeed retained something of
the old ascetic *"contemptus mundi."*

But it is one thing to cultivate a *contemptus mundi* that
implies a sense of liberation and unconcern because one has
completely abandoned the cares of the world by a life of poverty and renunciation, and quite another thing to remain
very much in the world as a *decisive influence* upon all its
affairs, and to bring this influence to bear with "contempt"
—while at the same time, in practice, loving worldly power
and wealth oneself.

The particular form taken by *contemptus mundi* in this
case was the assumption that theology had nothing to learn
from the world and everything to teach the world. That theology was a store of static and eternal truths which were un-
affected by any conceivable change in the world, so that if

the world wanted to remain in touch with eternal truth it would do well to renounce all thought of changing. This *contemptus mundi* amounted, in a word, to the assumption that the world must accommodate itself to the systems of Scholastics and should cease to develop. History should simply *stop*. In no circumstances did it occur to anyone that perhaps the theologian might have to question the world, even if only to make sure he was still in contact with it. . . .

It is here that the real failure of the clerks was manifest. New movements in thought, especially in science, which developed independently of the closed professional circle of theologians and jurists, were regarded with profound distrust as a secular threat, and were seen in a context of power struggle, not love for truth. Thus, a traditionally spiritual and ascetic concept of liberation *from* the world, now used as a weapon for domination and suppression, becomes in fact a *contempt for truth*. (This refusal to "see" scientific truth was of course justified by an appeal to a presumably "higher truth." But the appeal was suspect.)

This is the great scandal and shame of the Church's opposition to science down to the nineteenth century. Because of this shame, many Christians are now acutely conscious that their ancestors sinned against truth by their "contempt of the world"—they ignored new truths which were discovered precisely by and in the world.

The enormous success of Teilhard de Chardin is due to the universal relief that Christians now feel: they are all at once able to acknowledge their collective guilt and make a gesture of *reconciliation* with "the world" to which, it turns out, they belong anyway. Teilhard has enabled Christians to believe in themselves as men in the world to which they obviously and necessarily belong, and toward which any attitude of *"contemptus"* in theology would be a meaningless pose. His phenomenal success is due to the fact that he has enabled thousands of Christians to become reconciled *with themselves*. In doing this, of course, he has accomplished a providential task, essential for genuine contemporary renewal of religion.

✓ ✓ ✓

There is also the question of the great secular hopes of a hundred and fifty years ago. With the enlightenment and the industrial revolution it was taken for granted that a "better world" was now at hand, and that what had for centuries stood in the way of its discovery was the obscurantism of faith. Now the new, aggressive secular faith in progress took hold on everybody. Even Christians adopted this faith as part of their own, but it took them more than a century to identify the world of technology with the "new creation" spoken of in the New Testament.

Yet this hope was not altogether new. Since the thirteenth century Europe had already been fermenting obscurely with a new sense of eschatology: not the traditional hope of the second coming of Christ *at the end,* but of the revelation of eschatological finality *worked out within history* itself. Joachim of Flora, a Cistercian prophet, was perhaps in some ways an ancestor of Teilhard de Chardin—not that he was a scientist, but that he called for recognition of a new and definitive age of perfect human and Christian fulfillment, the "Third Kingdom," that of the Holy Spirit. It was to be a kingdom in which the world would be totally transformed by Franciscans living in absolute poverty—a thing which the established powers saw to be impracticable.

The chief effect Joachimism had in the Church was to make zeal for complete poverty seem suspect and devotion to the Holy Spirit sound dangerous.

Meanwhile, just at the point where eschatology in the old sense seems more credible than ever, Christians are turning to the hope of a technological golden age!

✓ ✓ ✓

The word "layman" has come to mean, among other things, "one who lacks specialized knowledge." In medicine, in engineering, in ethnology, etc. "I am a layman." That is to say I do not belong to the esoteric group of specialists who have done professional research in these fields. I can even say this now though in fact I am a cleric and they are "laymen." It

is a way of saying that they are "clerics"—a high compliment
in the language that is supposed to be mine but now is theirs.
Except, of course, they too will admit that with regard to
some other field than their own, they too are "laymen."

✓ ✓ ✓

"Since Augustine's time and particularly after Charlemagne's oversimplified interpretation of his thought, Western
Christianity has been convinced of the possibility of promot-
ing the Kingdom of God on earth by direct means."
—Mirgeler, *Mutations of Western Christianity*

The anguish, the ambiguity, and even, one might say, the
existential absurdity of the problem of the Church in the
world today is rooted in this unadmitted assumption. If one
is conservative, then the Kingdom of God on earth is the
Church as a sociological entity, an established institution with
a divine mandate to guide the destinies of culture, science,
politics, etc., as well as religion. If one is a liberal or radical,
then one admits that the progressives and revolutionaries of
"the world" have unconsciously hit upon the right answers
and are building the Kingdom of God where the Church has
failed to do so. Hence, the Christian must throw in his lot
with revolution—and thus guarantee that Christianity will survive and rediscover itself in a transformed society.

Before we can properly estimate our place in the world, we
have to get back to the fundamental Christian respect for
the *transiency* of both the world and the institutional structure of the Church.

True *contemptus mundi* is rather a *compassion* for the
transient world and a humility which refuses arrogantly to set
up the Church as an "eternal" institution in the world. But if
we despise the transient world of secularism in terms which
suggest an ecclesiastical *world* that is not itself transient, there
is no way to avoid disaster and absurdity.

✓ ✓ ✓

Meister Eckhart may have limitations, but I am entranced
with him nevertheless. I like the brevity, the incisiveness of

his sermons, his way of piercing straight to the heart of the
inner life, the awakened spark, the creative and redeeming
Word, God born in us. He is a great man who was pulled
down by a lot of little men who thought they could destroy
him: who thought they could drag him to Avignon and have
him utterly discredited. And indeed he was ruined, after his
death in twenty-eight propositions which might doubtless be
found somewhere in him, but which had none of his joy, his
energy, his freedom. They were not "his" in the sense that
they were not at all what he intended. But they could be
made to coincide with words that had been spoken. And I
suppose one must take such things into account. Eckhart did
not have the kind of mind that wasted time being cautious
about every comma: he trusted men to recognize that what
he saw was worth seeing because it brought obvious fruits
of life and joy. For him, that was what mattered. But these
others had other things in mind. They were concerned with
what the words might mean to someone who had no interest
in Eckhart's kind of religious *experience*.

The first step in identifying "heresy" is to refuse all identi-
fications with the subjective intuitions and experience of the
"heretic," and to see his words *only* in an impersonal realm in
which there is no dialogue—in which dialogue is denied *a
priori*.

✓  ✓  ✓

A chance phrase in Romain Rolland shows me, again, why
I am quite impressed by his book on India. *"Tout m'est
fermé en France; et je n'ai pas où aller."* When the doors are
closed in one's own country, then one goes everywhere. This
is the condition for true universality. But if one penetrates
everywhere, one still reaches only a few.

✓  ✓  ✓

Gandhi said (according to Romain Rolland): "To refuse
military service when the time has come for it to be necessary, is to act *after* the time to combat the evil has run out."
Compulsory military service is only a symptom of a deeper

evil. All who support the state in its organizing for war or in policies that imply the willingness to organize for war, and all who profit by privileges in such a state, have no business refusing military service. The refusal must be much more radical and much more sacrificial. It implies the refusal of privileges and benefits as well as of cooperation in a few policies with which one does not agree.

✓ ✓ ✓

I agree with the following ideas in Christopher Dawson's *Historic Reality of Christian Culture*.

"Christians stand to gain more in the long run by accepting their minority position and looking for quality rather than quantity."—

Here the question of Christian education comes in. And the question of propaganda. Is it possible that if we become too obsessed with quantity we will end up with a "Christian" mentality that is no longer even superficially Christian?

Christian education at the university level remains important if we believe that we stand to gain something by keeping alive the Christian cultural tradition of the West. I can accept this but I would add that we should broaden our view to include all the religious wisdom of the other traditional religious cultures as well: whether Asian, or primitive American, or African. (Father Daniélou was here the other day and we talked about this. He recommended a book by Father Placide Tempels on Bantu philosophy.)

The Christian, according to Dawson, still remains responsible for communicating something of traditional Christian wisdom and culture to a subreligious and neopagan world. He believes that the subrational and rational levels of social life need to be coordinated and brought to focus in a spiritual experience which transcends them both, and is entirely lacking in modern technological culture. And recovery of this experience, this outlook, is the task of Christian education.

Yes. But not the only task, or even the most important task. Back to the old problem of humanism and eschatology!

✓   ✓   ✓

Someone has come out with the theory that racial injustice is the product of *individualism*. There may be something to it, in the sense that individualism is a component in the lawlessness and irresponsibility of a society that has no care whatever to treat other human beings as if *they* might conceivably have human needs, and rights. In a sense, even Nazism was a "result of individualism." Mass society is indeed made up of individuals who, left to themselves, know they are zero, and who, added together in a multitude of zeroes, seem to themselves to acquire reality and power. But this is the negative individualism of the man who thinks he establishes himself as real by comparing himself with everything that is "not-I." (When you count up enough things that are not-I, you end up by discovering that even I is not-I.) But, meanwhile, what is to blame is not individualism but collectivism. Reinhold Niebuhr says rightly: "Racial pride is revealed today as man's primary *collective* sin."

✓   ✓   ✓

Why can we not be content with an ordinary, secret, personal happiness that does not need to be explained or justified? We feel guilty if we are not happy in some publically approved way, if we do not imagine that we are meeting some standard of happiness that is recognized by all. God gives us the gift and the capacity to make our own happiness out of our own situation. And it is not hard to be happy, simply by accepting what is within reach, and making of it what we can. But if we do this, and I find that I do, we still wonder if there is not something wrong. Are we getting something that others cannot have (a private and personal happiness!)? Obviously my happiness is not somebody else's—until I share it. And in sharing it I am happier than I was before.

Or we ask if we are failing to meet a general level which alone is authentic. (For instance, can a happiness that is absolutely free, costs nothing at all, has never been advertised in *Life*, be genuine? It turns out to be the only kind that *is* genuine!)

It is all there, yet we worry about it a little, as if it were not allowed. As if we could not be happy without the sanction of Madison Avenue. Or Washington, or the FBI, or somebody. And yet this, of all things, is precisely that for which no permission is needed.

I have used secular examples: but the case is just as evident in the realm of official and approved spirituality.

✓ ✓ ✓

January 22, 1961: President Kennedy's inauguration speech has just been read in the refectory. It was clear and intelligent. The country obviously has a good president. It remains to be seen what the country will do about it. I suspect our standard gestures of cooperation—they are not quite enough.

✓ ✓ ✓

While I was being tonsured this morning I watched the novices milling around getting ready for work—standing in their patched coveralls, with their white woolen hoods, some taking pains to be recollected, some being very businesslike, most of them quite happy. I was moved by the sight of them and at the thought that we get so much in our own way and try to carry so much useless baggage in the spiritual life. And how difficult it is to help them without unconsciously adding much more useless baggage to the load they already carry, instead of relieving them of it (which is what I try to do). I can at least love them in simplicity and thus preserve the climate in which the Holy Spirit unbinds the impossible and futile burdens. . . .

✓ ✓ ✓

The Dark Face of Wisdom: war, famine, pestilence. Quasimodo's quiet and profound poem on Auschwitz sees this. A great classic poem of compassion and reason, not devoid of horror, but contemplative, detached and yet profoundly committed. Auschwitz, a sign of the depraved wisdom of men who judge by the measure of the weapon: *"sapienza dell'-*

*uomo che si fa misura d'armi."* The sad, dirty myths and relics: but the dark side of the divine wisdom was not this garbage-wisdom of man the exterminator. Auschwitz itself is the judgment upon those who said "yes" to a philosophy which held such implications. Power judges itself by its own impotence and its own incapacity to bestow anything but death: this is the dark side of God's wisdom. The other side is mercy. Both are seen on the Cross.

Auschwitz is a sign of judgment, a sign of the Cross—and also, inscrutably, of mercy. But who can read it? Not I.

✓ ✓ ✓

Every time Kennedy sneezes or blows his nose an article is read about it in the refectory.

✓ ✓ ✓

The superb moral and poetic beauty of the *Phaedo.*

One does not have to agree with Plato, but one must hear him. Not to listen to such a voice would be unpardonable: like not listening to conscience, or to nature itself. I love this great poem, this purifying music of which my spirit has need, and with which mind does not agree.

I think the same may be said also for Gandhi. One does not have to agree with everything (for instance the spinning wheel) but one must hear him, one must listen with respect, one must see why it was in many ways right and inevitable that he should express the truth he knew in this special way.

Certainly we all have need to do more than hear him, on nonviolence. We also have to learn from him. Again, not slavishly. We do not have to make a cult of Gandhi, or follow his nonviolent teaching as a kind of party line. All party lines deform the doctrine which they claim to preserve.

But because we are so little capable of understanding Gandhian nonviolence, our lives have become a moral debacle, an enslavement to half truths, in which we are the passive prey of totalitarian forces. We are ruled, and resign to let ourselves be ruled, by our own weakness and by the prejudices of those who, more guilty and more frustrated than ourselves, need to exercise great power. We let them. And we excuse our cowardice by letting ourselves be driven to violence under "obedience" to tyrants. Thus, we think ourselves noble, dutiful, and brave. There is no truth in this. It is a betrayal of God, of humanity, and of our own selves. Auschwitz was built and managed by dutiful, obedient men who loved their country, and who proved to themselves they were good citizens by hating their country's enemies.

But were they enemies?

✓ ✓ ✓

"A person who realizes the particular evil of his time and finds that it overwhelms him, dives deep in his own heart for inspiration, and when he gets it he presents it to others."

—Gandhi

✓ ✓ ✓

"Even if we sin, we are thine, knowing thy power.
But we will not sin, because we know that we are accounted thine." —Wisdom 15:2

✓ ✓ ✓

In the midst of reciting the *Benedicite* I saw the great presence of the sun, which had just risen behind the cedar trees. And now under the pines the sun has made a great golden basilica of fire and water.

Perspective: crows making a racket in the east, dogs making a racket in the west, yet over all, the majestic peace of Sunday. Is this, after all, the real picture of our world? *Deus cujus providentia in sui dispositione non fallitur.* . . .

This is the great truth: Christ has indeed conquered the world and it does indeed belong to Him alone. This cannot help but be rejected even in a world where all men ignore Him and misunderstand His kingship. Society cannot be left entirely to the forces of evil. But that does not mean, either, that we must expect the eventual triumph of our own small, prejudiced self-complacent idea of the *civitas Christiana.* Certainly not if this involves some kind of clerical fascism!

On the other hand, there is a temptation to false Christian optimism, the facile optimism which we offer as a contrast to the Marxist cult of progress.

Christianity stands accused by the Marxists of having divided and alienated man, of leaving him miserable, pretending to save him and really leaving him utterly lost, alienated even from himself, divided against himself, empty, hollow, mournful, waiting to be taken up in the great warm arms of the Soviet state.

To refute this at all costs, we try to get rid of anything resembling *angst* and dark night. Whatever you do, don't look *sad,* especially if there is a Communist in the audience. Don't say gloomy things. Don't suggest that anything might ever go wrong. Don't refer to the Last Judgment! We are happy, happy, happy. We are not and cannot be sick. *Epanouissement!* Come brethren, joy, victory, alleluia.

Personally, I don't intend to sing alleluias with sidelong glances at Karl Marx. Alleluias are not meant to carry political convictions, or a social message.

There is alienation among us, and there is still more among the Marxists. In either case it is due not to religion or to pseudoreligion. It is due to technology and to the moral collapse of a materialist world. And, yes, when ideologies try to spirit this alienation off into thin air, then ideologies aggravate the problem.

There is no sickness in the world that can be cured by propaganda.

On my forty-sixth birthday they put an ape into space. They shot him farther than they intended. They recovered him alive. He flew through space at a fabulous speed, pressing buttons, pulling levers, eating banana-flavored pills. He signaled with faultless regularity, just as he had been trained to do. He did not complain of space. He did not complain of time. He did not complain either of earth or heaven.

He was bothered by no metaphysical problems. He felt no guilt. At least it is not reported that he felt any guilt.

Why should an ape in space feel guilt? Space is where there is no more weight and no more guilt. And an ape does not feel guilt even on earth, for that matter.

Would that we on earth did not feel guilt! Perhaps if we can all get into space we will not feel any more guilt. We will pull levers, press buttons, and eat banana-flavored pills. No, pardon me. We are not quite apes yet.

We will not feel guilt in space. We will not feel guilt on the moon. Maybe we will feel just a *little* guilt on the moon, but when we get to Mars we will feel no guilt at all.

From Mars or the moon we will blow up the world, perhaps. If we blow up the world from the moon we may feel a little guilt. If we blow it up from Mars we will feel no guilt at all. No guilt at all. We will blow up the world with no guilt at all. Tra la. Push the buttons, press the levers! As soon as they get a factory on Mars for banana-colored apes there will be no guilt at all.

I am forty-six years old. Let's be quite serious. Civilization has deigned to grace my forty-sixth birthday with this marvelous feat, and I should get ribald about it? Let me learn from this contented ape. He pressed buttons. He pulled levers. They shot him too far. Never mind. They fished him out of the Atlantic and he shook hands with the Navy.

# PART TWO

## Truth and Violence: An Interesting Era

AN *oriental wise man always used to ask the Divinity in his prayers to be so kind as to spare him from living in an interesting era. As we are not wise, the Divinity has not spared us, and we are living in an interesting era.*

—Albert Camus

ONE *is distressed by the failure of reasonable people to perceive either the depths of evil or the depth of the holy. With the best of intentions they believe that a little reason will suffice them to clamp together the parting timbers of the building. They are so blind in their desire to see justice done to both sides they are crushed between the two clashing forces and end by achieving nothing. . . . The news that God has become man strikes at the very heart of an age in which the good and the wicked regard either scorn for man or the idolization of man as the highest attainable wisdom.*

—Dietrich Bonhoeffer

SHORT *dayes, sharpe dayes, long nights come on apace*
*Ah, who shall hide us from the winter's face?*

—T. Nashe

*Alas we*
*Who wished to lay the foundations of kindness*
*Could not ourselves be kind.*   —Bertolt Brecht

This is no longer a time of systematic ethical speculation, for such speculation implies time to reason, and the power to bring social and individual action under the concerted control of reasoned principles upon which most men agree.

There is no time to reason out, calmly and objectively, the moral implications of technical developments which are perhaps already superseded by the time one knows enough to reason about them.

Action is not governed by moral reason but by political expediency and the demands of technology—translated into the simple abstract formulas of propaganda. These formulas have nothing to do with reasoned moral action, even though they may appeal to apparent moral values—they simply condition the mass of men to react in a desired way to certain stimuli.

Men do not agree in moral reasoning. They concur in the emotional use of slogans and political formulas. There is no persuasion but that of power, of quantity, of pressure, of fear, of desire. Such is our present condition—and it is critical!

Bonhoeffer wrote, shortly before his death at the hands of the Nazis, that moral theorizing was outdated in such a time of crisis—a time of villains and saints, and of Shakespearian characters. "The villain and the saint have little to do with systematic ethical studies. They emerge from the primeval depths and by their appearance they tear open the infernal or the divine abyss from which they come and enable us to see for a moment into mysteries of which they had never dreamed."

And the peculiar evil of our time, Bonhoeffer continues, is to be sought not in the sins of the good, but in apparent virtues of the evil. A time of confirmed liars who tell the truth in the interest of what they themselves are—liars. A hive of murderers who love their children and are kind to their pets. A hive of cheats and gangsters who are loyal in pacts to do evil. Ours is a time of evil which is so evil that it can do good without prejudice to its own iniquity—it is no longer threatened by goodness. Such is Bonhoeffer's judgment of a world in which evil appears in the form of probity and righteousness. In such a time the moral theorist proves himself a perfect fool by taking the "light" at its face value and ignoring the abyss of evil underneath it. For him, as long as evil takes a form that is theoretically "permitted," it is good. He responds mentally to the abstract moral equation. His heart does not detect the ominous existential stink of moral death.

"It is not by astuteness, by knowing the tricks, but by simple steadfastness in the truth of God, by training the eye upon this truth until it is simple and wise, that there comes the experience and knowledge of the ethical reality."
—Bonhoeffer, *Ethics*

✓   ✓   ✓

We live in crisis, and perhaps we find it interesting to do so. Yet we also feel guilty about it, as if we *ought not to be* in crisis. As if we were so wise, so able, so kind, so reasonable, that crisis ought at all times to be unthinkable. It is doubtless this "ought," this "should" that makes our era so interesting that it cannot possibly be a time of wisdom, or even of reason. We think we know what we ought to be doing, and we see ourselves move, with the inexorable deliberation of a machine that has gone wrong, to do the opposite. A most absorbing phenomenon which we cannot stop watching, measuring, discussing, analyzing, and perhaps deploring! But it goes on. And, as Christ said over Jerusalem, we do not know the things that are for our peace.

✓   ✓   ✓

We are living in the greatest revolution in history—a huge spontaneous upheaval of the entire human race: not the revolution planned and carried out by any particular party, race, or nation, but a deep elemental boiling over of all the inner contradictions that have ever been in man, a revelation of the chaotic forces inside everybody. This is not something we have chosen, nor is it something we are free to avoid.

This revolution is a profound spiritual crisis of the whole world, manifested largely in desperation, cynicism, violence, conflict, self-contradiction, ambivalence, fear and hope, doubt and belief, creation and destructiveness, progress and regression, obsessive attachments to images, idols, slogans, programs that only dull the general anguish for a moment until it bursts out everywhere in a still more acute and terrifying form. We do not know if we are building a fabulously wonderful world or destroying all that we have ever had, all that we have achieved!

All the inner force of man is boiling and bursting out, the good together with the evil, the good poisoned by evil and fighting it, the evil pretending to be good and revealing itself in the most dreadful crimes, justified and rationalized by the purest and most innocent intentions.

Man is all ready to become a god, and instead he appears at times to be a zombie. And so we fear to recognize our *kairos* and accept it.

*  *  *

Our times manifest in us a basic distortion, a deep-rooted moral disharmony against which laws, sermons, philosophies, authority, inspiration, creativity, and apparently even love itself would seem to have no power. On the contrary, if man turns in desperate hope to all these things, they seem to leave him more empty, more frustrated, and more anguished than before. Our sickness is the sickness of disordered love, of the self-love that realizes itself simultaneously to be self-hate and instantly becomes a source of universal, indiscriminate destructiveness. This is the other side of the coin that was current in the nineteenth century: the belief in indefinite progress, in the supreme goodness of man and of all his appetites. What passes for optimism, even Christian optimism, is the indefectible hope that eighteenth- and nineteenth-century attitudes can continue valid, can be *kept* valid just by the determination to smile, even though the whole world may fall to pieces. Our smiles are symptoms of the sickness.

✓ ✓ ✓

We are living under a tyranny of untruth which confirms itself in power and establishes a more and more total control over men in proportion as they convince themselves they are resisting error.

Our submission to plausible and useful lies involves us in greater and more obvious contradictions, and to hide these from ourselves we need greater and ever less plausible lies. The basic falsehood is the lie that we are totally dedicated to truth, and that we can remain dedicated to truth in a manner that is at the same time honest and exclusive: that we have the monopoly of all truth, just as our adversary of the moment has the monopoly of all error.

We then convince ourselves that we cannot preserve our purity of vision and our inner sincerity if we enter into dialogue with the enemy, for he will corrupt us with his error. We believe, finally, that truth cannot be preserved except by the destruction of the enemy—for, since we have identified him with error, to destroy him is to destroy error. The adversary, of course, has exactly the same thoughts about us and exactly the same basic policy by which he defends the "truth." He has identified us with dishonesty, insincerity, and untruth. He believes that, if we are destroyed, nothing will be left but truth.

✓ ✓ ✓

If we really sought truth we would begin slowly and laboriously to divest ourselves one by one of all our coverings of fiction and delusion: or at least we would desire to do so, for mere willing cannot enable us to effect it. On the contrary, the one who can best point out our error, and help us to see it, is the adversary whom we wish to destroy. This is perhaps why we wish to destroy him. So, too, we can help him to see his error, and that is why he wants to destroy us.

In the long run, no one can show another the error that is within him, unless the other is convinced that his critic first sees and loves the good that is within him. So while we are perfectly willing to tell our adversary he is wrong, we will never be able to do so effectively until we can ourselves appreciate where he is right. And we can never accept his judgment on our errors until he gives evidence that he really appreciates our own peculiar truth. Love, love only, love of our deluded fellow man as he actually is, in his delusion and in his sin: this alone can open the door to truth. As long as we do not have this love, as long as this love is not active and effective in our lives (for words and good wishes will never suffice) we have no real access to the truth. At least not to moral truth.

✓ ✓ ✓

There are religious people who fear socialism, because they fear the revelation of their own injustice, egoism, and inertia. Socialists who fear religion, because they fear the unmasking of their own complacent sophistries, the puerile, pragmatic games they have played with truth, their own pseudoreligion, which is far more foolish and superstitious than the spiritual religions they claim to have exploded.

✓ ✓ ✓

The crisis of the present moment in history is the crisis of Western civilization: more precisely of European civilization, the civilization that was founded on the Greco-Roman culture of the Mediterranean, and built up by the gradual incorporation of the barbarian invaders into the Judeo-Roman-Christian religious culture of the fallen Roman Empire. Into this crisis I was born. By this crisis my whole life has been shaped. In this crisis my life will be consumed—but not, I hope, meaninglessly!

✓ ✓ ✓

We have hated our need for compassion and have suppressed it as a "weakness," and our cruelty has far outstripped

our sense of mercy. Our humanity is sinking under the waves
of hatred and desperation, and we are carried away by a
storm that would never have been so terrible if we were not
capable of such feelings of guilt about it! That is why the
intellectuals of the nineteenth and twentieth centuries have
willed at any price to throw off the Nessus shirt of Christianity
with its burning remorse of conscience. And that is why I
sought refuge in compunction and in conscience, even though
this has meant living in anguish, in hesitation, and in frequent questioning. Europe indeed stands for independence
precisely because it stands for questioning, free inquiry. Europe learned long ago to be free from the foregone conclusion. This is by no means un-Christian. For the first Europeans
who became Christians had to doubt the old, dead, cosmic
religions, the nature philosophies, the saving power of the
mysteries, or the sanctifying force of the Jewish Law before
they could have faith in Christ. This is why they seemed to
be "atheists" to the Romans.

We too often forget that Christian faith is a principle of
questioning and struggle before it becomes a principle of certitude and of peace. One has to doubt and reject everything
else in order to believe firmly in Christ, and after one has
begun to believe, one's faith itself must be tested and purified.
Christianity is not merely a set of foregone conclusions. The
Christian mind is a mind that risks intolerable purifications,
and sometimes, indeed very often, the risk turns out to be too
great to be tolerated. Faith tends to be defeated by the burning presence of God in mystery, and seeks refuge from him,
flying to comfortable social forms and safe conventions in
which purification is no longer an inner battle but a matter of
outward gesture.

✓ ✓ ✓

Europe stands for freedom, diversity, self-knowledge, sophistication, personalism, creativity. The European mind is
active, subtle, critical, proud, resourceful, adventurous. It is
at the same time romantic and cynical, wild and disciplined,
tender and unscrupulous.

And in the end the European, with all his love of certainty, free investigation, and liberal truth, becomes a first-class liar lying to all others after having first lied to himself. Yet he is perhaps readier than any other to admit his own lie when the time comes to do so. At least he is ready to do this if he is English, because all that is best in Europe remains alive in England—along with some of the worst.

*1   *1   *1*

There remains, however, one most embarrassing truth about Western civilization that must be recognized, at least by the Christian, in spite of the confusion and guilt which this recognition must inevitably bring with it: the world of Christendom, that is to say the world of the West, Europe, Russia, America, is the world into whose history the revelation of God as man broke through, profoundly modifying all human structures and cultural developments. This does not mean that all other cultures are, as regards this revelation, completely insignificant—quite the contrary. They all point to it in their own way. But it was into *our* history that God came, revealing Himself as man, and it was to *us* that was entrusted the task of bearing His revelation of Himself to other cultures. It may be said at once that, in so far as this meant more than a unilateral imposition of our interpretation of God's message upon others, in so far as it demanded a close, attentive, and humble awareness of the way those other traditions were already open to the possibility of God in Man, the Western mission to the rest of the world has largely failed.

The point is not to praise Western culture as perfectly Christian (which it obviously is not, and has never really been) or to blame it as a betrayal of Christianity. More important, and far more difficult, is the actual Christian task, the disconcerting task, of accepting ourselves as we are, in our confusion, infidelity, disruption, ferment and even desperation, as the civilization that developed out of the revelation of God in Man.

As Bonhoeffer says: our history has a special seriousness and our heritage is not like that of other peoples because, whether we like it or not, admit it or not, "our forefathers are the witnesses of the entry of God into history." And we may add, others of our forefathers have been unfaithful to this revelation, so unfaithful that we are now involved in a situation that would be utterly tragic but for the fact that the promises of God do not change, and the humanity He accepted was, and remains, in all truth, *our* humanity.

In one word: the only way in which I can make sense in the unparalleled confusion and absurdity of the breakdown of Western culture is to recognize myself as part of a society both sentenced and redeemed: a society which, if it can accept sentence and redemption, will live. A society which has received the mercy of Christ and been unfaithful to Him. And if my society cannot face this truth, it will destroy itself and perhaps everyone else besides.

√  √  √

Once again, let me be clear about this word "breakdown." It is bound to be taken as an incomprehensible affront by all those who are firmly convinced that the technological power of our society represents the highest development of man, the beginning of the golden age of plenty and of perfect freedom. I am as ready as the next man to admire the astonishing achievements of technology. Taken by themselves, they are magnificent. But taken in the context of *unbalance* with the other aspects of human existence in the world, the very splendor and rapidity of technological development is a factor of disintegration.

The Greeks believed that when a man had too much power for his own good the gods ruined him by helping him increase his power at the expense of wisdom, prudence, temperance, and humanity until it led automatically to his own destruction.

Suppose a hundred men who in a former age would have died of typhoid fever today crash to their deaths in a supersonic jet plane. Does the fact that typhus is controllable and that supersonic flight is possible make any difference in their deaths? Or, if technology means safety, and if life is easily and surely prolonged, travel safer, and so on: what difference does this make if, in the congested, irrational, frustrated and

bored society that results, everyone nurses an acute and pathological death wish, and if weapons are at hand that might
conceivably implement that wish in drastic fashion?

What I am saying is, then, that it does us no good to make
fantastic progress if we do not know how to live with it, if
we cannot make good use of it, and if, in fact, our technology
becomes nothing more than an expensive and complicated
way of cultural disintegration. It is bad form to say such
things, to recognize such possibilities. But they are possibilities, and they are not often intelligently taken into account.
People get emotional about them from time to time, and then
try to sweep them aside into forgetfulness. The fact remains
that we have created for ourselves a culture which is not yet
livable for mankind as a whole.

Never before has there been such a distance between the
abject misery of the poor (still the great majority of mankind)
and the absurd affluence of the rich. Our gestures at remedy-
ing this situation are well meant but *almost totally* ineffec-
tive. In many ways they only make matters worse (when for
instance those who are supposed to be receiving aid realize
that in fact most of it goes into the pockets of corrupt politicians who maintain the *status quo*, of which the misery of
the poor is an essential part).

The problem of racism—by no means confined to the south-
ern United States, South Africa, or Nazi Germany—is becoming a universal symptom of homicidal paranoia. The desperation of man who finds existence incomprehensible and
intolerable, and who is only maddened by the insignificance
of the means taken to alleviate his condition.

The fact that most men believe, as an article of faith, that
we are now in a position to solve all our problems does not
prove that this is so. On the contrary, this belief is so un-
founded that it is itself one of our greatest problems.

*   *   *

Bonhoeffer was so convinced that the *historical* unity of the
West is based on Christ that he even went so far as to assert
that for this reason no European war could be a total war.
Doubtless he wrote that before the beginning of World War

II. Doubtless, also, this passage is not perfectly clear, because in other places, focusing on the apostasy of the West from Christ as the apocalyptic problem of our time, he implies that this infidelity does open the way infallibly to total war. In any event he lived to see that total war was not impossible in the West! In fact the history of the West in the twentieth century hinges entirely on the ever-present possibility of total war between nations that have a Christian heritage. Not only that, but an appeal is even made to Christianity itself to justify total war against total evil. And Communist eschatology —which justifies the Russian view of total war—is itself rooted in hidden Christian assumptions. What has happened is not that the bond of *historical* unity holds the formerly Christian West together, but that new forms of irrationality and fanaticism, making use of distorted notions borrowed from their common Christian heritage, appeal to the final and total use of force as the way to definitive unity—by the elimination of the one adversary who is the source of all division and disruption. For the West, this one Antichrist is Communism. For the Communists it is capitalist imperialism. Not even the obvious divisions within the two camps can persuade men to drop this paranoid obsession with *one* presumed source of all evil!

✓ ✓ ✓

Certainly America seems to have lost much in World War II. It has come out a bloated, suspicious, truculent militarist and one who is not without paranoid tendencies: yet there are in America also, fully alive and fully creative, some of the best tendencies of European independence and liberal thought. No matter how we may criticize Europe and America, they are still in full strength, and in their liberal minority the hope of the future still lies.

Our ability to see ourselves objectively and to criticize our own actions, our own failings, is the source of a very real strength. But to those who fear truth, who have begun to forget the genuine Western heritage and to become immersed in crude materialism without spirit, this critical tendency presents the greatest danger. Indeed it must seem perilous to those who cultivate a simultaneous complacent certitude of might and right in order to destroy without hesitation the ideological enemy. Wait until we have completely lost our European humor (from which American humor is derived) and we will be in a posture to blast Russia or China quite seriously off the face of the earth, unable to see the grim joke that in so doing we are also destroying ourselves and anything good that was left for us to "save" by war. It is precisely the dogmatic *humorlessness* of the self-designated realists that is the greatest danger. They are the ones who have shrugged off practically all that was left of Europe in our society. I for one mean to preserve all the Europe that is in me as long as I live, and above all I will keep laughing until they close my mouth with fallout.

↗ ↗ ↗

The central problem of the modern world is the complete emancipation and autonomy of the technological mind at a time when unlimited possibilities lie open to it and all the resources seem to be at hand. Indeed, the mere fact of questioning this emancipation, this autonomy, is the number-one blasphemy, the unforgivable sin in the eyes of modern man, whose faith begins with this: science can do everything, science must be permitted to do everything it likes, science is infallible and impeccable, all that is done by science is right. No matter how monstrous, no matter how criminal an act may be, if it is justified by science it is unassailable.

The consequence of this is that technology and science are now responsible to no power and submit to no control other than their own. Needless to say, the demands of ethics no longer have any meaning if they come in conflict with these autonomous powers. Technology has its own ethic of expediency and efficiency. What *can* be done efficiently *must* be done in the most efficient way—even if what is done happens, for example, to be genocide or the devastation of a country by total war. Even the long-term economic interests of society, or the basic needs of man himself, are not considered when they get in the way of technology. We waste our natural resources, as well as those of undeveloped countries,

iron, oil, etc., in order to fill our cities and roads with a con-
gestion of traffic that is in fact largely useless, and is a symptom of the meaningless and futile agitation of our own minds.

The attachment of the modern American to his automobile,
and the *symbolic* role played by his car, with its aggressive
and lubric design, its useless power, its otiose gadgetry, its
consumption of fuel, which is advertised as having almost
supernatural power . . . this is where the study of American
mythology should begin.

Meditation on the automobile, what it is used for, what it
stands for—the automobile as weapon, as self-advertisement,
as brothel, as a means of suicide, etc.—might lead us at once
right into the heart of all contemporary American problems:
race, war, the crisis of marriage, the flight from reality into
myth and fanaticism, the growing brutality and irrationality
of American mores.

I thoroughly agree with Bonhoeffer when he says:

The demand for absolute liberty brings men to the depths of
slavery. The master of the machine becomes its slave. The
machine becomes the enemy of men. The creature turns
against its creator in a strange reenactment of the Fall. The
emancipation of the masses leads to the reign of terror of
the guillotine. Nationalism leads inevitably to war. The liberation of man as an absolute ideal leads only to man's self-
destruction.                                   —*Ethics*

If technology really represented the rule of reason, there
would be much less to regret about our present situation. Actually, technology represents the rule of *quantity*, not the rule
of reason (quality=value=relation of means to authentic
human ends). It is by means of technology that man the
person, the subject of qualified and perfectible freedom, becomes *quantified*, that is, becomes part of a mass—mass man
—whose only function is to enter anonymously into the process of production and consumption. He becomes on one side
an implement, a "hand," or better, a "bio-physical link" between machines: on the other side he is a mouth, a digestive
system and an anus, something *through which* pass the products of his technological world, leaving a transient and mean-

ingless sense of enjoyment. The effect of a totally emancipated technology is the regression of man to a climate of moral infancy, in total dependence not on "mother nature" (such a dependence would be partly tolerable and human) but on the pseudonature of technology, which has replaced nature by a closed system of mechanisms with no purpose but that of keeping themselves going.

If technology remained in the service of what is higher than itself—reason, man, God—it might indeed fulfill some of the functions that are now mythically attributed to it. But becoming autonomous, existing only for itself, it imposes upon man its own irrational demands, and threatens to destroy him. Let us hope it is not too late for man to regain control.

✓ ✓ ✓

The greatest need of our time is to clean out the enormous mass of mental and emotional rubbish that clutters our minds and makes of all political and social life a mass illness. Without this housecleaning we cannot begin to *see*. Unless we *see* we cannot think. The purification must begin with the mass media. How?

✓ ✓ ✓

A pharisee is a righteous man whose righteousness is nourished by the blood of sinners.

*How to be a pharisee in politics:* At every moment display righteous indignation over the means (whether good or evil) which your opponent has used to attain the same corrupt end which you are trying to achieve. Point to the means he is using as evidence that your own purposes are righteous—even though they are the same as his. If the means he makes use of are successful, then show that his success itself is proof that he has used corrupt methods. But in your own case, success is proof of righteousness.

In politics, as in everything else, pharisaism is not self-righteousness only, but the conviction that, in order to be right, it is sufficient to prove that somebody else is wrong. As long as there is one sinner left for you to condemn, then you are justified! Once you can point to a wrongdoer, you become justified in doing anything you like, however dishonest, however cruel, however evil!

*   *   *

We are all convinced that we desire the truth above all. Nothing strange about this. It is natural to man, an intelligent being, to desire the truth. (I still dare to speak of man as "an intelligent being"!) But actually, what we desire is not "the truth" so much as "to be in the right." To seek the pure truth for its own sake may be natural to us, but we are not able to act always in this respect according to our nature. What we seek is not the pure truth, but the partial truth that justifies our prejudices, our limitations, our selfishness. This is not "the truth." It is only an argument strong enough to prove us "right." And usually our desire to be right is correlative to our conviction that somebody else (perhaps everybody else) is wrong.

Why do we want to prove them wrong? Because we need them to be wrong. For if they are wrong, and we are right, then our untruth becomes truth: our selfishness becomes justice and virtue: our cruelty and lust cannot be fairly condemned. We can rest secure in the fiction we have determined to embrace as "truth." What we desire is not the truth, but rather that our lie should be proved "right," and our iniquity be vindicated as "just." This is what we have done to pervert our natural, instinctive appetite for truth.

No wonder we hate. No wonder we are violent. No wonder we exhaust ourselves in preparing for war! And in doing so, of course, we offer the enemy another reason to believe that *he* is right, that he must arm, that he must get ready to destroy us. Our own lie provides the foundation of truth on which he erects his own lie, and the two lies together react to produce hatred, murder, disaster.

*   *   *

Is there any vestige of truth left in our declaration that we think for ourselves? Or do we even trouble to declare this any more? Perhaps the man who says he "thinks for himself" is simply one who does not think at all. Because he has no fully articulate thoughts, he thinks he has his own incommunicable ideas. Or thinks that, if he once set his mind to it, he could have his own thoughts. But he just has not got around to doing this. I wonder if "democracies" are made up entirely of people who "think for themselves" in the sense of going around with blank minds which they imagine they *could* fill with their own thoughts if need be.

Well, the need has been desperately urgent, not for one year or ten, but for fifty, sixty, seventy, a hundred years. If, when thought is needed, nobody does any thinking, if everyone assumes that someone else is thinking, then it is clear that no one is thinking either for himself or for anybody else. Instead of thought, there is a vast, inhuman void full of words, formulas, slogans, declarations, echoes—ideologies! You can always reach out and help yourself to some of them. You don't even have to reach at all. Appropriate echoes already rise up in your mind—they are "yours." You realize of course that these are not yet "thoughts." Yet we "think" these formulas, with which the void in our hearts is provisionally entertained, can for the time being "take the place of thoughts"— while the computers make decisions for us.

Nothing can take the place of thoughts. If we do not think, we cannot act freely. If we do not act freely, we are at the mercy of forces which we never understand, forces which are arbitrary, destructive, blind, fatal to us and to our world. If we do not use our minds to think with, we are heading for extinction, like the dinosaur: for the massive physical strength of the dinosaur became useless, purposeless. It led to his destruction. Our intellectual power can likewise become useless, purposeless. When it does, it will serve only to destroy us. It will devise instruments for our destruction, and will inexorably proceed to use them. . . . It has already devised them.

✓ ✓ ✓

Thinking men. Better still, *right-thinking* men! Who are they? The right-thinking man has an instinctive flair for the words and formulas that are most acceptable to his group: and in fact he is partly responsible for making them acceptable. He is indeed a man of timely ideas, opportune ideas.

He is the man whose formulas are replacing the outworn formulas of the year before. And no doubt the formulas of the year before were his also: they were the ones with which he supplanted the formulas of two years ago, which perhaps were his too. The right-thinking man has a knack of expressing, and indeed of discovering, the attitudes that everyone else is unconsciously beginning to adopt. He is the first one to become conscious of the new attitude, and he helps others to become aware of it in themselves. They are grateful to him. They respect him. They listen to his utterances. He is their prophet, their medicine man, their shaman. They talk like him, they act like him, they dress like him, they look like him. And all this brings them good luck. They despise and secretly fear others who have different formulas, dress differently, act differently, speak differently.

Fortunately, though, all right-thinking men think the same these days. At least all who belong to the same tribal society. Even those who do not conform are in their own way a justification of the right-thinking man: the beatnik is necessary to make the square unimpeachably respectable.

The right-thinking men are managers, leaders, but not eggheads. Hence they can be believed. They can justify any wrong road, and make it seem the *only* road. They can justify everything, even the destruction of the world.

✦ ✦ ✦

Gandhi saw that Western democracy was *on trial*. On trial for what? On trial to be judged by its own claims to be the rule of the people by themselves. Not realizing itself to be on trial, assuming its own infallibility and perfection, Western democracy has resented every attempt to question these things. The mere idea that it might come under judgment has seemed absurd, unjust, diabolical. Our democracy is now being judged, not by man but by God. It is not simply being judged by the enemies of the West and of "democracy." When anyone is judged by God, he receives, in the very hour of judgment, a gift from God. The gift that is offered him, in his judgment, is *truth*. He can receive the truth or reject it; but in any case truth is being offered silently, mercifully, in the very crisis by which democracy is put to the test. For instance, the problem of integration.

When one is on trial in this life, he is at the same time receiving mercy: the merciful opportunity to anticipate God's decision by receiving the light of truth, judging himself, changing his life. Democracy has been on trial in Berlin, in Alabama, in Hiroshima. In World War II. In World War I. In the Boer War. In the American Civil War. In the Opium War. What have we learned about ourselves? What have we seen? What have we admitted? What is the truth about us? Perhaps we still have time, still have a little light to see by. But the judgment is getting very dark. . . . The truth is too enormous, too ominous, to be seen in comfort. Yet it is a great mercy of God that so many of us can recognize this fact, and that we are still allowed to *say* it.

✓ · ✓ · ✓

We have got ourselves into a position where, because of our misunderstanding of theoretical distinctions between the "natural and the supernatural," we tend to think that nothing in man's ordinary life is really supernatural except saying prayers and performing pious acts of one sort or another, pious acts which derive their value precisely from the fact that they rescue us, momentarily, from the ordinary routine of life. And therefore we imagine that Christian social action is not Christian *in itself*, but only because it is a kind of escalator to unworldliness and devotion. This is because we apparently cannot conceive material and worldly things seriously as having any capacity to be "spiritual." But Christian social action, on the contrary, conceives man's work itself as a *spiritual* reality, or rather it envisages those conditions under which man's work can *recover* a certain spiritual and holy quality, so that it becomes for man a source of spiritual renewal, as well as of material livelihood.

Christian social action is first of all action that discovers religion in politics, religion in work, religion in social programs for better wages, Social Security, etc., not at all to "win the worker for the Church," but because God became man, because every man is potentially Christ, because Christ is our brother, and because we have no right to let our brother live in want, or in degradation, or in any form of squalor whether physical or spiritual. In a word, if we really understood the meaning of Christianity in social life we would see it as part of the redemptive work of Christ, liberating man from misery, squalor, subhuman living conditions, economic or political slavery, ignorance, alienation.

✓   ✓   ✓

Once this has been said, we understand what it might mean to transform the world by political principles spiritualized by the Gospel. It is an attempt to *elevate man*, whether professedly Christian or not, to a level consonant with his dignity as a son of God, redeemed by Christ, liberated from the powers that keep him in subjection, the old dark gods of war, lust, power, and greed. In such a context, political action itself is a kind of spiritual action, an expression of spiritual responsibility, and a witness to Christ. But never merely by the insertion of religious clichés into political programs.

Such social action implies three great emphases. First, emphasis on the *human* as distinct from the merely collective, the technological. Affirmation of *man* and not of the process of production. Saving man from becoming a cog in an enormous machine, a mere utensil for production. Liberation of man from the tyranny of the faceless mass in which he is submerged without thoughts, desires, or judgments of his own, a creature without will or without light, the instrument of the power politician.

Second, emphasis on the *personal*—for if we merely respect man's nature, and *we must respect that nature*, we still do not go far enough. The personal values are those that are spiritual and incommunicable, and hence they evade analysis.

To respect the personal aspect in man is to respect his solitude, his right to think for himself, his need to learn this, his need for love and acceptance by other persons like himself. Here we are in the realm of freedom and of friendship, of creativity and of love. And it is here that religion begins to have a meaning: for a mass religion of faceless ones delivers men over to the demons.

Third, emphasis on *wisdom* and *love*—a sapiential view of society is less activistic, more contemplative; it enables men and institutions to see life in its wholeness, with stability and purpose, though not necessarily in a politically conservative sense. This is the view which prevailed in the ancient traditional cultures that lasted for centuries because they were rooted in the patterns of the cosmos itself, and enabled man to live according to the light of wisdom immanent in the world and in the society of which he formed a part.

✦ ✦ ✦

Christian social action must liberate man from all forms of servitude, whether economical, political, or psychological. The words are easily said. Anyone can say them, and everyone does in some way or other. And yet in the name of liberty, man is enslaved. He frees himself from one kind of servitude and enters into another. This is because freedom is bought by obligations, and obligations are bonds. We do not sufficiently distinguish the nature of the bonds we take upon ourselves in order to be free.

If I obligate myself spiritually in order to be free economically, then I buy a lower freedom at the price of a higher one, and in fact I enslave myself. (In ordinary words, this is called selling my soul for the sake of money, and what money can buy.)

Today, as a matter of fact, there is very little real freedom anywhere because everyone is willing to sacrifice his spiritual liberty for some lower kind. He will compromise his personal integrity (spiritual liberty) for the sake of security, or ambition, or pleasure, or just to be left in peace.

✦ ✦ ✦

The signals have been changed. The United States has become a great power in the world precisely at the moment when a wholly new political language has been instituted. And our statesmen have not learned the new language. They are generally unable to interpret the new signals. They have eyes and see not, ears and hear not. What they say no longer really makes sense. There have been new words coined, new kinds of meaning, new ways of doing things. Opportunistic, mysterious signs and symbols for action different from our kind of action. When will we learn the signals?

Instead of learning them, we devise our own concept of political realities and try to make international conflicts fit our *a priori* dogmatic declarations. We decide that Cuba is all ready to throw off the yoke of Castro, and this brings on the fiasco of the Bay of Pigs. After we have made fools of ourselves we discover that the men providing us with information have, instead, fed us our own propaganda! Let us at least learn that even the best and most starry-eyed of ideologies is no substitute for a humble attention to concrete and unacceptable *fact*.

✓ ✓ ✓

Here is a statement of Gandhi that sums up clearly and concisely the whole doctrine of nonviolence: "The way of peace is the way of truth." "Truthfulness is even more important than peacefulness. Indeed, *lying is the mother of violence*. A truthful man cannot long remain violent. He will perceive in the course of his research that he has no need to be violent, and he will further discover that so long as there is the slightest trace of violence in him, he will fail to find the truth he is searching." Why can we not believe this immediately? Why do we doubt it? Why does it seem impossible? Simply because we are all, to some extent, liars.

✓ ✓ ✓

The mother of all other lies is the lie we persist in telling ourselves about ourselves. And since we are not brazen enough liars to make ourselves believe our own lie individually, we pool all our lies together and believe them because they have become the big lie uttered by the *vox populi*, and this kind of lie we accept as ultimate truth. "A truthful man cannot long remain violent." But a violent man cannot begin to look for the truth. To start with, he wants to rest assured that his enemy is violent, and that he himself is peaceful.

For then his violence is justified. How can he face the desperate labor of coming to recognize the great evil that needs to be healed in himself? It is much easier to set things right by seeing one's own evil incarnate in a scapegoat, and to destroy both the goat and the evil together.

↗ ↗ ↗

Gandhi does not mean that everyone may expect to become nonviolent by wishing to do so. But that all who dimly realize their need for truth should seek it by the way of nonviolence, since there is really no other way. They may not fully succeed. Their success may be in fact very slight. But for a small measure of good will they will at least *begin* to attain the truth. Because of them there will be at least a little truth in the darkness of a violent world. This idea of Gandhi cannot, however, be understood unless we remember his basic optimism about human nature. He believed that in the hidden depths of our being, depths which are too often completely sealed off from our conscious and immoral way of life, we are more truly nonviolent than violent. He believed that love is more natural to us than hatred. That "truth is the law of our being."

If this were not so, then "lying" would not be the "mother of violence." The lie brings violence and disorder into our nature itself. It divides us against ourselves, alienates us from ourselves, makes us enemies of ourselves, and of the truth that is in us. From this division hatred and violence arise. We hate others because we cannot stand the disorder, the intolerable division in ourselves. We are violent to others because we are already divided by the inner violence of our infidelity to our own truth. Hatred projects this division outside ourselves into society.

This is not so far from the traditional doctrine of the Fathers of the Church concerning original sin! Note of course that the doctrine of original sin, properly understood, is *optimistic*. It does not teach that man is by nature evil, but that evil in him is unnatural, a disorder, a sin. If evil, lying, and hatred were natural to man, all men would be perfectly at home, perfectly happy in evil. Perhaps a few seem to find contentment in an unnatural state of falsity, hatred, and greed. They are not happy. Or if they are, they are unnatural.

✓ ✓ ✓

Berdyaev pointed out that in the old days we used to read of utopias and lament the fact that they could not be actualized. Now we have awakened to the far greater problem: how to prevent utopias from being actualized.

✓ ✓ ✓

Douglas Steere remarks very perceptively that there is a pervasive form of contemporary violence to which the idealist fighting for peace by nonviolent methods most easily succumbs: activism and overwork. The rush and pressure of modern life are a form, perhaps the most common form, of its innate violence. To allow oneself to be carried away by a multitude of conflicting concerns, to surrender to too many demands, to commit oneself to too many projects, to want to help everyone in everything is to succumb to violence. More than that, it is cooperation in violence. The frenzy of the activist neutralizes his work for peace. It destroys his own inner capacity for peace. It destroys the fruitfulness of his own work, because it kills the root of inner wisdom which makes work fruitful.

✓ ✓ ✓

The tactic of nonviolence is a tactic of love that seeks the salvation and redemption of the opponent, not his castigation, humiliation, and defeat. A pretended nonviolence that seeks to defeat and humiliate the adversary by spiritual instead of physical attack is little more than a confession of weakness. True nonviolence is totally different from this, and much more difficult. It strives to operate without hatred, without hostility, and without resentment. It works without aggression, taking the side of the good that it is able to find already present in the adversary. This may be easy to talk about in theory. It is not easy in practice, especially when the adversary is aroused to a bitter and violent defense of an injustice which he believes to be just. We must therefore be careful how we talk about our opponents, and still more careful how we regulate our differences with our collaborators. It is possible for the most bitter arguments, the most virulent hatreds, to arise among those who are supposed to be working together for the noblest of causes. Nothing is better calculated to ruin and discredit a holy ideal than a fratricidal war among "saints."

✓ ✓ ✓

American Catholics pray, no doubt sincerely, for the "conversion of Russia."\* Is this simply a desire that the Russians will stop menacing us, will stop being different from us, will stop challenging us, will stop trying to get ahead of us? Is it for this that we pray and do penance? That the Russians may all suddenly embrace the very same kind of Catholicism that is prevalent in the United States, along with all the social attitudes of American Catholics, all their customs, their religious clichés, and even their prejudices? This is a dream, and not even a very good one. It would indeed harm us greatly if all the rest of the world suddenly enclosed itself within our own limitations. Who would then challenge and complete us?

Until we recognize the right of other nations, races, and societies to be different from us and to stay different, to have different ideas and to open up new horizons, our prayer for their conversion will be meaningless. It will be no better and no worse, perhaps, than the Russian Communist's idea that we will someday become *exactly like him*. And if we are not prepared to do so . . . he will destroy us. For he wants us to have all his attitudes, his prejudices, and his limitations. Until we feel in our own hearts the sufferings, the desires, the needs, the fears of the Russians and Chinese as if they were our own, in spite of political differences, until we *want* their problems to be solved in much the same way as we

---

\* At this time, for instance, prayers were still said after each Mass for the conversion of Russia.

want our own to be solved: until then it is useless to talk
about "conversion"—it is a word without significance.

*    *    *

The realm of politics is the realm of waste. The Pharaohs
at least built pyramids. With the labor of hundreds and thousands of slaves, they built temples, and they built pyramids.
Perhaps in a certain sense this labor was wasted: yet it has
meaning, and its meaning remains powerful and eloquent, if
mysterious, after centuries. The work of the slaves was forced,
it was cruel, but it was work. It still had a kind of human
dimension. There was something of grandeur about it. The
slaves lived, and saw "their" pyramids grow. Our century is
not a century of pyramids, but of extermination camps: in
which man himself is purely and deliberately wasted, and the
sardonic gesture, saving the hair, the teeth, and the clothes
of the victims, is simply a way of pointing to the *wasting of
humanity*.

It was a way of saying: "These people, whom you think to
be persons, whom you are tempted to value as having souls,
as being spiritual, these are nothing, less than nothing. The
detritus, the facts and chemicals that can be derived from
them, the gold fillings in their teeth, their hair and skin, are
more important than they. We are so much better and more
human than they that we can afford to destroy a whole man
in order to make a lampshade out of his skin. He is nothing!"

*    *    *

Religious belief, on the deepest level, is inevitably also a
principle of freedom. To defend one's faith is to defend one's
own freedom, and at least implicitly the freedom of everyone
else. Freedom from what, and for what? Freedom from control that is not in some way immanent and personal, a power
of love. Religious belief in this higher sense is then always a
liberation from control by what is less than man, or entirely
exterior to man. He who receives the grace of this kind of
religious illumination is given a freedom and an experience
which leave him no longer fully and completely subject to

the forces of nature, to his own bodily and emotional needs, to the merely external and human dictates of society, the tyranny of dictatorships. This is to say that his attitude to life is independent of the power inevitably exercised over him, exteriorly, by natural forces, by the trials and accidents of life, by the pressures of a not always rational collectivity.

↗ ↗ ↗

Since I am a Catholic, I believe, of course, that my Church guarantees for me the highest spiritual freedom. I would not be a Catholic if I did not believe this. I would not be a Catholic if the Church were merely an organization, a collective institution, with rules and laws demanding external conformity from its members. I see the laws of the Church, and all the various ways in which she exercises her teaching authority and her jurisdiction, as subordinate to the Holy Spirit and to the law of love. I know that my Church does not look like this to those who are outside her; to them the Church acts on a principle of authority but not of freedom. They are mistaken. It is in Christ and in His Spirit that true freedom is found, and the Church is His Body, living by His Spirit.

At the same time, this aspiration to spiritual, interior, and personal freedom is not foreign to the other branches of Christianity and to the other great religions of the world. It is one thing that all the higher religions have in common (though doubtless on different levels), and it would be no advantage to a Catholic to try to deny this: for what brings out the dignity and grandeur of all religion is by that very fact a point in favor of Catholicism also. It is true that in the Catholic Church we believe that we have truly received the Spirit of God, the Spirit of Sonship which makes us free with the freedom of the sons of God. It is true that Protestants make this claim no less firmly, and perhaps indeed it is characteristic of them to make it with greatest emphasis. I am not the one to judge each individual and sincere Protestant as wrong when he says this of himself. How do I know what grace God can and does give to the sincere evangelical Christian who obeys the light of his conscience and follows Christ according to the faith and love he has received? I am persuaded that he would have greater security and clearer light if he were in my Church, but he does not see this as I do, and for this there are deeper and more complex reasons than either he or I can understand. Let us try to understand them, but meanwhile let us continue each in his own way, seeking the light with all sincerity.

The Jews, too: the promise to Abraham is a promise of freedom, of independence under God, and the passage through the Red Sea was the passage out of Egyptian slavery into the liberty of the people God had formed and chosen for Himself, to be His own people, to live in fidelity to a covenant, which is a free agreement and a bond of liberty and love.

The fidelity of Israel to the covenant meant refusing to be enslaved by the fascination and lure of the cosmic nature cults, refusing to surrender to the blind cycle of nature and to the domination of the forces of the earth. What did the prophets protest against more than the infidelity by which Israel forfeited her freedom and her espousal to Yahweh in liberty and in love?

This same intransigeance is found in Islam: a freedom which lifts the believer above the limitations dictated by nature, by race, by society: incorporation in a higher community, delivered from the fascination of idols, even idols of the mind, and set free to travel in a realm of white-hot faith as bare and grand as the desert itself, faith in the One God, the compassionate and the merciful. What are compassion and mercy but the gifts of freedom to freedom? What are they but deliverance from limitation, slavery, doubt, subservience to passion and to prejudice?

Whatever may be said of the great Oriental religions and their "cosmic" character, they aim ultimately at liberation from the unending natural round, at freedom of spirit, at emptiness, and they all give man a principle of liberty by which he can rise above domination by necessity and process, study and judge the world around him, study and judge the forces of passion and delusion that go into operation when he confronts the world in his own isolated ego.

✓ ✓ ✓

Freedom from domination, freedom to live one's own spiritual life, freedom to seek the highest truth, unabashed by any human pressure or any collective demand, the ability to say one's own "yes" and one's own "no" and not merely to echo the "yes" and the "no" of state, party, corporation, army, or system. This is inseparable from authentic religion. It is one of the deepest and most fundamental needs of man, perhaps the deepest and most crucial need of the human person as such: for without recognizing the challenge of this need no man can truly be a person, and therefore without it he cannot fully be a man either. The frustration of this deep need by irreligion, by secular and political pseudoreligion, by the mystiques and superstitions of totalitarianism, have made man morally sick in the very depths of his being. They have wounded and corrupted his freedom, they have filled his love with rottenness, decayed it into hatred. They have made man a machine geared for his own destruction.

✓ ✓ ✓

It is because religion is a principle and source of the deepest freedom that all totalitarian systems, whether overt or implicit, must necessarily attack it. Yet at the same time the situation is very complex, because those who attack religion rarely do so except in the name of the same values which religion itself protects. All attacks on religious belief are to some extent to be seen as partial judgments passed by history on organized religion. The slightest failure in fidelity, in inner freedom, in integrity, in truth warrants an instant criticism and attack by those who wish to destroy religion by proving that it is not and has never been what it claims to be. The cult of the Absolute is attacked in the name of the Absolute. Truth is destroyed in the name of truth. But the fact that these attacks on religion generally lack understanding, and lack it because they lack compassion, and lack compassion because they do not know man, means that even the most sincere attack on religion always has in it some culpable blindness. This I do not say blaming men who, in attacking religion, have perhaps had more integrity than I have had in practicing it. But it is essential above all to understand that the basic principle of all spiritual freedom, all freedom from what is less than man, means first of all submission to what is more than man. And this submission begins with the recognition of our own limitation.

Hence, to attack religion because human beings have human limitations, and seek to be liberated from them, is a kind of pharisaism. But this pharisaism in turn is perhaps due in large measure to the pharisaism of religious people themselves who, once they have embraced a spiritual ideal as credible and worthy of admiration, at once begin to speak and act as if they had attained it.

✓ ✓ ✓

We are afflicted, hesitant, dubious in our speech, above all where we know we are *obliged* to speak. Language has been so misused that we fear and mistrust it. We do not mind playing with words, manipulating them, but when the game gets serious we lose courage. And we lose courage for the silliest possible reason: our inborn natural sense of the *logos*, our love for reasonable expression, our healthy delight in it, shames us with a false sense of guilt. We are drawn to the logos with a strong and noble attraction, but at the same time held back by unnatural fear. The more earnestly we hope to tell the truth, the more secretly we are convinced that we will only add another lie to all the others told by our contemporaries. We doubt our words because we doubt our very selves—and woe to us if we do not doubt our words and ourselves!

There have been so many words uttered in contempt of truth, in despite of love, honor, justice, and of all that is good. Even these concepts themselves (truth, honor, goodness) have become sick and rotten to us, not because they are defiled, but because we are. Nevertheless, we must risk falsity, we must take courage and speak, we must use noble instruments of which we have become ashamed because we no longer trust ourselves to use them worthily. We must dare to think what we mean, and simply make clear statements of what we intend. This is our only serious protection against repeated spiritual defilement by the slogans and programs of the unscrupulous.

Clement of Alexandria remarks that Christ our Lord, taking bread, first spoke, blessing the bread, then broke it and gave it to His disciples, for He willed them to know what it was that He was giving them. The word, therefore, was as important as the act, and in both the Lord, Himself the Word of God, gave Himself to us.

Clement says: "Reasonable speech, logos, regenerates the soul and orients it towards the noble and beautiful act [Kalokagathia]. Blessed is he who is adept in both word and work. . . . That which the act presents to our sight, is made intelligible by the word. The word prepares the way for action and disposes the hearers to the practice of virtue. There is a saving word just as there is a saving work. And justice does not take shape without *logos*."

*—Stromateis I*, 10, n. 46

✓ ✓ ✓

Shall I say that we are confronted with a choice: either to live by the truth or be destroyed? (Pilate said: "What is truth?")

Shall I say that we are being given one last chance to be Christians, and that if we do not accept it, then we are done for? And not only we the "Christians," but also everybody in our society, the society once based on Christian principles?

Shall I say that we are offered one last opportunity to work out in practice the social implications of the Gospel, and that if we fail we shall have an earthly hell, and either be completely wiped out or doomed to a future of psychopathic horror in the new barbarism that must emerge from the ruins we have brought down upon our own heads?

Why should I use tired expressions like these: "The social implications of the Gospel?" Such words arouse no response. They no longer penetrate the mind of the hearer. But you see, we must begin at last to take to heart the words that mean something, and not simply those that awaken a reflex of some sort, a jolt, a shudder, a twitching of the head in the people who hear us.

Is it possible to transform the world on Christian principles? (And some people will wonder if it is even possible to ask this question with a straight face.)

What do you mean "Christian principles?"

Certainly *Mater et Magistra* and *Pacem in Terris* are clear enough statements of them. A society built on Christian principles is one in which every man has the right and opportunity to live in peace, to support himself by meaningful, decent, and productive work, work in which he has a considerable share of responsibility, work which is his contribution to the balance and order of a society in which a reasonable happiness is not impossible.

A Christian society? Such a society is not one that is run by priests, not even necessarily one in which everybody has to go to Church: it is one in which work is for production and not for profit, and production is not for its own sake, not merely for the sake of those who own the means of production, but for all who contribute in a constructive way to the process of production. A Christian society is one in which men give their share of labor and intelligence and receive their share of the fruits of the labor of all, and in which all this is seen in relation to a transcendental purpose, the "history of salvation," the Kingdom of God, a society centered upon the divine truth and the divine mercy.

Sometimes there may be a little truth in the suspicion that Christian social action lacks seriousness because it may be exploited for the sake of *something else* of an entirely different essence, something otherworldly that has nothing at all to do with things like wages and work, or with politics, war, and peace.

That is the trouble. We have got ourselves into a position where, because of our misunderstanding of theoretical distinctions between the "natural and the supernatural" we tend to think that nothing in man's ordinary life is really supernatural except saying prayers and performing pious acts of one sort or another, pious acts which derive their value precisely from the fact that they rescue us, momentarily, from the ordinary routine of life.

✶ ✶ ✶

Since I am a man, my destiny depends on my human behavior: that is to say upon my decisions. I must first of all appreciate this fact, and weigh the risks and difficulties it entails. I must therefore know myself, and know both the good and the evil that are in me. It will not do to know only one and not the other: only the good, or only the evil. I must then be able to love the life God has given me, living it fully and fruitfully, and making good use even of the evil that is in it. Why should I love an ideal good in such a way that my life becomes more deeply embedded in misery and evil?

To live well myself is my first and essential contribution to the well-being of all mankind and to the fulfillment of man's collective destiny. If I do not live happily myself how can I help anyone else to be happy, or free, or wise? Yet to seek happiness is not to live happily. Perhaps it is more true to say that one finds happiness by not seeking it. The wisdom that teaches us deliberately to restrain our desire for happiness enables us to discover that we are already happy without realizing the fact.

To live well myself means for me to know and appreciate something of the secret, the mystery in myself: that which is incommunicable, which is at once myself and not myself, at once in me and above me. From this sanctuary I must seek humbly and patiently to ward off all the intrusions of violence and self-assertion. These intrusions cannot really penetrate the sanctuary, but they can draw me forth from it and slay me before the secret doorway.

If I can understand something of myself and something of others, I can begin to share with them the work of building the foundations for spiritual unity. But first we must work together at dissipating the more absurd fictions which make unity impossible.

✓ ✓ ✓

How glad, how grateful men are when they can learn from another what they have already determined, in their hearts, to believe for themselves.

They do not realize that they have already promised their assent to this or that proposition: that they are committed to it in advance. When it comes to them from another they think they have made a discovery. They enjoy something of the excitement of discovery. They have, indeed, discovered a little of what was hidden in themselves: a legitimate joy.

Yet perhaps the other one only told them this because he, in turn, *sensed that it was what they wanted to hear from him.* He himself divined it in them: though of course it was also in himself. This, too, seemed a "discovery" to him.

Thus we encourage one another to cling firmly and blindly to prejudice.

✓ ✓ ✓

The terrible thing about our time is precisely the ease with which theories can be put into practice. The more perfect, the more idealistic the theories, the more dreadful is their realization. We are at last beginning to rediscover what perhaps men knew better in very ancient times, in primitive times before utopias were thought of: that liberty is bound up with imperfection, and that limitations, imperfections, errors are not only unavoidable but also salutary.

The best is not the ideal. Where what is theoretically best is imposed on everyone as the *norm*, then there is no longer any room even to be good. The best, imposed as a norm, becomes evil.

One might argue that the best, the highest, is imposed on all in monasteries. Far from it: St. Benedict's principle is that the Rule should be moderate, so that the strong may desire to do more and the weak may not be overwhelmed and driven out of the cloister.

You must be free, and not involved. Solitude is to be preserved, not as a luxury but as a necessity: not for "perfection" so much as for simple "survival" in the life God has given you.

Hence, you must know when, how, and to whom you must say "no." This involves considerable difficulty at times. You must not hurt people, or want to hurt them, yet you must not placate them at the price of infidelity to higher and more essential values.

People are constantly trying to use you to help them create the particular illusions by which they live. This is particularly true of the collective illusions which sometimes are accepted as ideologies. You must renounce and sacrifice the approval that is only a bribe enlisting your support of a collective illusion. You must not allow yourself to be represented as someone in whom a few of the favorite daydreams of the public have come true. You must be willing, if necessary, to become a disturbing and therefore an undesired person, one who is not wanted because he upsets the general dream. But be careful that you do not do this in the service of some other dream that is only a little less general and therefore seems to you to be more real because it is more exclusive!

✓ ✓ ✓

A distinction: to be "thought of" kindly by many and to "think of" them kindly is only a diluted benevolence, a collective illusion of friendship. Its function is not the sharing of love but complicity in a mutual reassurance that is based on nothing. Instead of cultivating this diffuse aura of benevolence, you should enter with trepidation into the deep and genuine concern for those few persons God has committed to your care—your family, your students, your employees, your parishioners. This concern is an involvement, a distraction, and it is vitally urgent. You are not allowed to evade it even though it may often disturb your "peace of mind." It is good and right that your peace should be thus disturbed, that you should suffer and bear the small burden of these cares that cannot usually be told to anyone. There is no special glory in this, it is only duty. But in the long run it brings with it the best of all gifts: it gives life.

Unlike the great benevolent and public movements, full of
noisy and shared concern, it is not foggy, diffuse, devouring,
and absurd. Only a personal concern of this kind leads to love.

✓ ✓ ✓

There are various ways of being happy, and every man has
the capacity to make his life what it needs to be for him to
have a reasonable amount of peace in it. Why then do we
persecute ourselves with illusory demands, never content until we feel we have conformed to some standard of happiness
that is not good for us only, but for *everyone*? Why can we
not be content with the secret gift of the happiness that God
offers us, without consulting the rest of the world? Why do
we insist, rather, on a happiness that is approved by the
magazines and TV? Perhaps because we do not believe in a
happiness that is given to us for nothing. We do not think we
can be happy with a happiness that has no price tag on it.

If we are fools enough to remain at the mercy of the people
who want to sell us happiness, it will be impossible for us
ever to be content with anything. How would they profit if
we became content? We would no longer need their new
product.

The last thing the salesman wants is for the buyer to become content. You are of no use in our affluent society unless
you are always just about to grasp what you never have.

The Greeks were not as smart as we are. In their primitive
way they put Tantalus in hell. Madison Avenue, on the contrary, would convince us that Tantalus is in heaven.

God gives us freedom to make our own lives within the
situation which is the gift of His love to us, and by means of
the power His love grants us. But we feel guilty about it.
We are quite capable of being happy in the life He has provided for us, in which we can contentedly make our own
way, helped by His grace. We are ashamed to do so. For we
need one thing more than happiness: we need approval. And
the need for approval destroys our capacity for happiness.
"How can you believe, who seek glory one from another?"

For in the United States, approval has to be bought—not
once, not ten times, but a thousand times over every day.

Leon Bloy remarked on this characteristic of our society: A businessman will say of someone that he *knows* him if he *knows he has money*.

To say of someone "I do not know him" means, in business, "I am not so sure that he will pay."

But if he has money, and proves it, then "I know him."

So we have to get money and keep spending it in order to be known, recognized as human. Otherwise we are excommunicated.

✓ ✓ ✓

Einstein was a great prophet of the now dead age of liberalism. He emerged with the disconcerting kindness and innocence of the liberal, came forth from the confusions of his day to produce for us all a little moment of clarity, and also, as an afterthought, he left us the atomic bomb. But we cannot take the bomb as a pretext for looking down on his liberalism, or doubting his benevolence.

✓ ✓ ✓

Our thought should not merely be an answer to what someone else has just said. Or what someone else might have said. Our interior word must be more than an echo of the words of someone else. There is no point in being a moon to somebody else's sun, still less is there any justification for our being moons of one another, and hence darkness to one another, not one of us being a true sun.

It may seem that a child begins by *answering* his parents. This is not true. What is important in the child is his primal utterance, his response to *being*, his own free cries and signs, his admiration.

It is true that he has to learn language. Unfortunately in learning to speak, he also learns to answer *as expected*. Thus he learns more than language: he acquires, with words themselves, a kind of servitude. He gives out the words that are asked of him, that evoke a pleasant or approving response. He ceases to acclaim reality and responds to demands, or evades punishment, or engineers consent. He does not merely answer: he conforms, or he resists. He is already involved in public relations.

Would that we could remember how to answer or to keep silence. To learn this, we must learn even to go without answering. One may say: "But to answer is to love." Certainly there is no love without response. But merely to submit one's intelligence, to make a deal, to conciliate, to compromise with error or injustice is not love. Silence, too, is a response. It can at times be the response of a greater love, and of a love that does not endanger truth or sacrifice reason in order to placate a too demanding or too needy lover.

St. Alphonsus Rodriguez said: "Answer nothing, nothing, nothing."

✓    ✓    ✓

It is no exaggeration to say that democratic society is founded on a kind of faith: on the conviction that each citizen is capable of, and assumes, complete political responsibility. Each one not only broadly understands the problems of government but is willing and ready to take part in their solution. In a word, democracy assumes that the citizen knows what is going on, understands the difficulties of the situation, and has worked out for himself an answer that can help him to contribute, intelligently and constructively, to the common work (or "liturgy") of running his society.

For this to be true, there must be a considerable amount of solid educational preparation. A real training of the mind. A genuine formation in those intellectual and spiritual disciplines without which freedom is impossible.

There must be a completely free exchange of ideas. Minority opinions, even opinions which may appear to be dangerous, must be given a hearing, clearly understood and seriously evaluated on their own merits, not merely suppressed. Religious beliefs and disciplines must be respected. The rights of the individual conscience must be protected against every kind of open or occult encroachment.

Democracy cannot exist when men prefer ideas and opinions that are fabricated for them. The actions and statements of the citizen must not be mere automatic "reactions"—mere mechanical salutes, gesticulations signifying passive conformity with the dictates of those in power.

To be truthful, we will have to admit that one cannot expect this to be realized in *all* the citizens of a democracy. But if it is not realized in a significant proportion to them, democracy ceases to be an objective fact and becomes nothing but an emotionally loaded word.

What is the situation in the United States today?

✦ ✦ ✦

Christianity overcame pagan Rome by nonviolence.

But when Christianity became the religion of the Empire, then the stoic and political virtues of the Empire began to supplant the original theological virtues of the first Christians. The heroism of the soldier supplanted the heroism of the martyr—though there was still a consecrated minority, the monks, who kept the ideal of charity and martyrdom in first place.

The ideal of self-sacrifice was never altogether set aside—on the contrary! But it was transferred to a new sphere. Now the supreme sacrifice was to die fighting under the Christian emperor. The supreme self-immolation was to fall in battle under the standard of the Cross. In the twelfth century even monks took up the sword, and consummated their sacrifice of obedience by dying in battle against infidels, against heretics. . . .

Unfortunately, they also fought other monks, and this was not necessarily regarded as virtue. But it does show what comes of living by the sword!

Christian chivalry was the fruit of a union between Christian faith and Roman, Frankish, or Germanic valor. In other words, Christians did here what they also did elsewhere: they adopted certain non-Christian values and "baptized" them, consecrating them to God. Christianity might just as well have turned to the East and "baptized" the nonmilitant, contemplative, detached, and hieratic institutions of the Orient. But by the time Christianity was ready to meet Asia and the New World, the Cross and the sword were so identified with one another that the sword itself was a cross. It was the only kind of cross some conquistadores understood.

There was no further thought of Christianizing the ideals and institutions of these ancient civilizations: only of destroying them, and bringing their people into subjection to the militant Christianity of Europe. Hence the strange paradox that certain spiritual and largely nonviolent ideologies which were in fact quite close to the Gospel were attacked and coerced in the name of Christ by the Christian soldier who was often no longer a Christian except in name: for he was violent, greedy, self-complacent, and supremely contemptuous of anything that was not a perfect reflection of himself.

*   *   *

We need to understand the Communist mentality. To ignore it is dangerous as well as absurd. It is one of the keys to the mystery of Providence in our time. It is the mentality of over half the world, or soon will be. At least it wants to be, strives to be.

We need to be as keenly interested in history, as obsessed with history as Marxism is supposed to be.

For the Marxian idea that the key to everything is found in history is, curiously enough, the basic idea of the Bible. We, the Christians, have forgotten this. We have reduced our religious thought to the consideration of static essences and abstract moral values. We have lost the dynamic sense of God's revelation of Himself in history. Have we lost the sense of the movement of history toward the final, eschatological fulfillment of revelation, by which all our strivings are to be measured? Have we lost the sense of responsibility, of ability to "answer" the summons of history, in the challenge of our own time?

Let us not overestimate the Communists. Since Stalin, they, too, have bogged down in their own falsification of history. In practice, for Stalin as for Ford, history was bunk.

Not that the Reds admit as much. But history is for them a creature of their own imagination. It is alive as long as it has not taken place. Once it has happened it is a corpse, embalmed like Lenin and entombed in Red Square, or in an official pronouncement. A corpse that is dressed up this way and that, interred, disinterred, dressed up again, perhaps finally put away altogether: like the article on Berea in the Soviet Encyclopedia, which disappeared when he was shot. (All the subscribers were instructed to tear out the pages and replace them with an equal number of fully authoritative columns on the Bering Sea.)

And now the corpse of Stalin also has been moved out of the monument. He who rewrote history to suit himself has been written out of the place he assigned to himself in history. His history was already dead when he thought it was alive and growing in his heart. Moving the dead body is nothing, adds nothing, takes away nothing.

We need, then, to know *true* history, and not history as corrupted by propaganda.

✦ ✦ ✦

The use of pharisaical arguments by modern power politics: point to the Inquisition, and then go ahead and do anything you like. Because the Inquisition was tyrannical, because it implied an abuse of power, because it was violent and extreme, then *you* are justified in destroying your opponents by *terrorism.* But the Inquisition was not terrorism.

Specific charges were made, a judicial process was followed. One who knew what the charges were, and what the process was, had ways of avoiding them. True, the charges might be unjust and tyrannical: but one could tell what they would be. In terrorism nothing is predictable, everything is arbitrary, there are no standards, there is no process: victims are selected at random, tortured and put to death according to the caprice of the political police, without reason, without specific charges, simply because they are presumed to be against those in power, or because they might conceivably at some time or other harbor thoughts contrary to those in power, or for no real reason at all except to strike terror into everybody.

The very essence of terrorism is that it is *lawless and absolute* power.

Indeed terrorism often aims directly and purposely at the innocent, the helpless, the docile, as a calculated exercise of power against which there can be no hope of appeal.

(See Hannah Arendt, *Totalitarianism*)

✦ ✦ ✦

The Inquisition (which itself punished nobody, but which turned over its victims to the secular arm for punishment) claimed to strike at man's body in order to save his soul.

Totalitarian terrorism demands ruthless sacrifice in the present for the sake of the future. In either case authority is improperly understood: its brutality claims to be justified by the fallacy that *power saves man.* That servile submission to power is necessary either for the salvation of man's soul or for the creation of a just society. What matters is not man, but power. When Kirov was murdered (this was the beginning of the great purges under Stalin: a victim is immolated and then terror is let loose on a grand scale). When Kirov I say, was murdered, all the jails in Leningrad had to be emptied in order to accommodate the hundreds and thousands of suspects in the new case.

More men were killed, without reason, uselessly, without trial, *in one night and in one city* (Leningrad), than were killed in four hundred years of Inquisition in the whole of Latin America: and simply to make room for more victims for more terror than the world had ever seen in any previous century. The ruthlessness and cruelty of Stalinist terror was exceeded only by the even greater horror of Nazi terrorism. Yet people still speak of the Inquisition as though its cruelty were something fabulous.

✦ ✦ ✦

Soviet idealization of the Tsarist General Suvarov, who took the Cossack leader Pugachev, and put him in a cage, and sent him to Catherine the Great to be executed in 1775!

The nineteenth-century Russian intellectual Belinsky was prepared to destroy half the earth with fire and sword "in order that mankind might be happy."

He did not have the means to do this, but we have. And now his philosophy is accepted not only in Russia but everywhere. He started with a hypothesis: *"If* by destroying half the earth, mankind could be made happy . . ."* Today we have come to act as if the destruction of half the earth were *necessary* to make mankind happy: and this when it is clearly evident to everyone that to destroy half the earth quickly by fire and explosion means also to leave the other half to perish slowly by radiation.

Men of power are generally convinced that man is corrupt, that he will not make the effort to become happy. Others have to make the effort for him. Power must *compel* him to be happy. Forced labor camps are places where one "learns to be happy": either you lose all desire to survive, and you let yourself die, or else you yearn so ardently for release that any fate at all, after your release, seems by comparison to be "happiness."

We should not need so much austerity to learn to be content with ordinary life!

✦    ✦    ✦

It is a familiar truth to say that Marxist-Leninist thought has a purely theological pattern. Not that it rests on a revelation of God, but it rests nevertheless on premises whose absolute authority is never questioned. Lenin reached what we might call "theological conclusions" by reasoning from the absolute and infallible premises drawn from Marx and Engels.

✦    ✦    ✦

Is dialectical thinking anything more than a grandiose word for political opportunism? Does not every clever politician think, in practice, "dialectically" when, not allowing ideals and principles to confuse his mind, he seizes now one and now another occasion to advance his interests, even when he appears to contradict himself? No good politician is ever caught contradicting himself. He is always consistently opportunistic. Unfortunately, in democratic politics, the politician is hampered by the fact that he has promised so many rewards (I almost said bribes) in return for favors done to him and to his cause. The power politicians have eliminated all this, and their dialectic runs, in consequence, much more smoothly.

✓  ✓  ✓

In moments that appear to be lucid, I tell myself that in times like these there has to be something for which one is willing to get shot, and for which, in all probability, one is actually going to get shot. What is this? A principle? Faith? Virtue? God? The question is not easy to answer and perhaps it has no answer that can be put into words. Perhaps this is no longer something communicable, or even thinkable. To be executed today (and death by execution is not at all uncommon) one has no need to commit a political crime, to express opposition to a tyrant, or even to hold an objectionable opinion. Indeed most political deaths under tyrannical regimes are motiveless, arbitrary, absurd. You are shot, or beaten to death, or starved, or worked until you drop, not because of anything you have done, not because of anything you believe in, not because of anything you stand for, but arbitrarily: your death is demanded by something or someone undefined. Your death is necessary to give apparent meaning to a meaningless political process which you have never quite managed to understand. Your death is necessary to exercise a hypothetical influence on a hypothetical person who might conceivably be opposed to something you may or may not know or understand or like or hate.

Your death is necessary not because you yourself are opposed to anything, or in favor of anything, but simply because people have to keep dying in order to make clear that opposition to those in power is neither practical nor even thinkable. Your death is necessary as a kind of exorcism of the abstract specter of opposition in the minds of leaders whose dishonesty makes them well enough aware that they ought to be opposed. Two thousand years ago the death of a Christian martyr was a supreme affirmation not only of faith, but of liberty. The Christian proved by martyrdom that he had reached a degree of independence in which it no longer mattered to him whether he lived on earth and that it was not necessary for him to save his life by paying official religious homage to the emperor. He was beyond life and death. He had attained to a condition in which all things were "one" and equal to him. *Cela lui était égal.*

Now, by a reverse procedure, we have arrived at the same "oneness," yet at an opposite extreme. All has become one, all has become indifferent, all has been leveled to equal meaninglessness. But it is not quite the same. It is not that all is "one" but all is "zero." Everything adds up to zero. Indeed, even the state, in the end, is zero. Freedom is then to live and die for zero. Is that what I want: to be beaten, imprisoned, or shot for zero? But to be shot for zero is not a matter of choice. It is not something one is required either to "want" or "not want." It is not even something one is able to foresee.

Zero swallows hundreds of thousands of victims every year, and the police take care of the details. Suddenly, mysteriously, without reason, your time comes, and while you are still desperately trying to make up your own mind what you imagine you might possibly be dying for, you are swallowed up by zero. Perhaps, subjectively, you have tried to convince *yourself* and have not wasted time convincing others. Nobody else is interested. What I have said so far concerns execution for a "political crime." But death in war is, in the same way, a kind of execution for nothing, a meaningless extinction, a swallowing up by zero.

✓ ✓ ✓

*Signing the confession.* When everything else has been turned upside down, when my whole moral being has been gutted, there remains one last vestige of order, of reality, of clarity. Every other reality has been distorted, smashed to pieces, whisked out of sight, buried in oblivion. One normal, recognizable, feasible human act remains within reach. Its possibility has been consistently presented to me, while everything else became impossible, fell apart. Finally I grasp at one last apparently sane act: I reach for the pen, I sign the paper. This is something that is done in the world of human beings to which I once belonged. They sign papers. They affirm themselves, they say they exist, they act. As if an ani-

mal, when nearly beaten to death, should grasp with his teeth
the stick that is beating him; not out of anger, but simply as
a last contact with the world of reality. . . . One last, beautiful sacrificial act by which I am incorporated in a system,
I no longer know how or why: the system wants me to sign.
There must, after all, be a reason. "A lying world of con-
sistency which is more adequate to the human mind than
reality itself."          —Hannah Arendt, *Totalitarianism*

How to resist? Perhaps to cling with love to some living
human being who I know to be outside the system: to some
person who is not part of the system. Love perhaps can give
me strength to resist this final dissolution of my moral being.
Love for my friend.

They show me the document that has already been signed
by my friend.

*✓    ✓    ✓*

*Violation of the individual person by torture* (see Hannah
Arendt). Suffering is a private and incommunicable experience in which one is more and more subjected to "necessity,"
to the domination of pure natural needs. He who is tortured
is reduced to a condition in which nature speaks instead of
freedom, instead of conscience. Pain speaks, not the person.
Torture is the instrument of those who fear personality, fear
responsibility, and wish to convince themselves again and
again that personality does not really exist. That freedom is
weaker than natural necessity. That the *person* can be si-
lenced by the demands of *nature*.

In the calculated use of torture there is also a special evil.
The person is pitted against the *process* in such a way that
the process infallibly wins. From the inmost sanctuary of the
individual person there is extracted, by means of torture, not
the voice of the person, but the voice of the process. The
tortured one does not merely *echo* the process, but he finally
utters, from his own inmost self, the "confession of faith"
which bears witness to the reality of the process, and to the
abdication of his own spiritual freedom. This is a way of saying: "You see, your conviction of your own worth as a person
is the worst of illusions. The inmost reality in you is not a 'self'

but simply the social process which you have tried to reject and to resist." The process is then a Moloch which feeds on individuals. Every person must ultimately be fed to it. Every person must pass through fire, and come out "healed," that is to say destroyed. A nonperson, a being without identity. O merciful therapy! He will no longer have to worry about himself: there is nobody there!

*   *   *

A young priest was sent to preach one Sunday in a "white" Catholic parish in New Orleans. He based his sermon on the Gospel of the Sunday, in which Christ spoke of the twofold commandment, love of God and love of one's brother, which is the essence of Christian morality.

The priest, in his sermon, took occasion to point out that this commandment applied to the problem of racial segregation, and that white people and Negroes ought certainly to love one another to the extent of accepting one another in an integrated society.

He was halfway through the sermon, and the gist of his remarks was becoming abundantly clear, when a man stood up in the middle of the congregation and shouted angrily: "I didn't come here to listen to this kind of junk, I came to hear Mass."

The priest stopped and waited. This exasperated the man even more, and he demanded that the sermon be brought to an end at once, otherwise he would leave.

The priest continued to wait in silence, and another man in the congregation, amid the murmuring support of many voices, got up and protested against this doctrine to which he saw fit to refer to as "crap."

As the priest still said nothing, the two men left the church followed by about fifty other solid Christians in the congregation. As he went out, the first of them shouted over his shoulder at the priest: "If I miss Mass today *it's your fault.*"

Incidents like this have a meaning.

This meaning is simple and objective. Quite apart from the subjective dispositions, the probable sincerity of the warped consciences of the people involved, there is an objective fact

manifested here. That fact is that one can think himself a
"good Catholic" and be thought one by his neighbors, and be,
in effect, an apostate from the Christian faith.

Not only do we see in these men a flat refusal to listen to
the plain meaning of the word of God as preached by a min-
ister of the Church, speaking in the name of God, but also
there is a complete moral and spiritual insensitivity to the
meaning of the Mass as the Christian *Agape*, the union of
brothers in Christ, a union from which no believer is to be
excluded. To exclude a brother in Christ from this union is
to fail to "judge the Body of Christ" and hence to "eat and
drink judgment to oneself."                    (I Corinthians)

Doubtless not one of the men who left church that morning
would subscribe formally to such propositions. Doubtless they
believe that they have in their hearts what they think can
pass muster as "charity" for all men. But is it not an abstract
and legalistic charity? Is not their attendance at Mass a legal
formality? Formalities, abstractions, are not enough. Gestures
of conformity do not make a man a Christian, and when
one's actual conduct obviously belies the whole meaning of
the gesture, it is an objective statement that one's Christianity
has lost its meaning.

I write these sentences realizing fully how repugnant they
will be to many conscientious souls and tender hearts. They
will find these remarks of mine "uncharitable." They will
want me to emend them over and over again so that there
is no longer the slightest suspicion of an adverse judgment
upon these plain men, these simple men of good will, men
like you and me, *hypocrite lecteur, mon semblable, mon
frère!*

Why do we have to be so tenderhearted toward people
like this? Why do we go to any length to excuse them, to
find escape clauses for them, to justify them by their "good
intentions?" We say: "out of charity."

We are so concerned with "charity" that we will find every
possible excuse for men who have no respect for the law of
love, who angrily and rudely separate themselves from the
community of the faithful assembled for the Eucharistic feast
of Christian charity, and who do so in defense of a society

whose customs admit and palliate repeated acts of cruelty, of injustice, of inhumanity which gravely violate the Law of Christ, and crucify Christ in His members.

To excuse such men entirely would be to participate in their violation of charity. Their sin must be pointed out quite clearly for what it is. The pseudocharity that shrinks from this truth is responsible for an awful proliferation of injustice and untruth, under the guise of Christianity. The best that can be said of these poor men is "they know not what they do."

Yet to castigate them, to work off our own aggressions on them in the name of justice, is not permitted.

How often it happens that a person secure in his own enlightenment and in his righteousness provokes the weaker and more violent man to sin, and then with all the greater security, condemns him.

We who claim to love peace and justice must always be careful that we do not use our righteousness to provoke the violent, and in this way bring about the conflict for which we, too, like other men, are hungering in secret, and with suppressed barbarity.

✓ ✓ ✓

Notes on the race situation before the violence began— 1962.

In their struggle for integration into American society, the Negroes not only have to contend with the hostility and opposition of the whites, who are tormented by unconscious guilt and fear, but above all they have to face guilt, fear, inertia, and passivity in themselves. Perhaps the very fact that they know so well the evil that is in the whites, all the evil, the cruelty, the injustice, restrains them from acting in their own defense.

They know this evil. They have seen it, kept silent about it, borne it for generations. Already the silent witness of the Negro is torment enough to the whites who are not able to be fully conscious of it. But when the Negro protests, and when by protesting he must inevitably bring out into the open some of that deadly evil . . . then the white man will hate the Negro all the more because the Negro makes him struggle openly with the deadly fear of hating himself: who can blame the Negro for keeping quiet?

To me one of the most moving of all the things the Negro has ever done has been the sweetness, the patience, the delicacy, the self-restraint with which he has so far refused to call names, refused to condemn his white persecutor (1962!). And the white man despises him all the more for it. For the Negro has the goods on him, all the goods!

What is worse, the Negro perhaps despises himself. Perhaps the very sweetness which I admire in him, and can never imitate because I am not a Negro, is the worst element in his ambivalence. Maybe it is what he secretly hates in himself, thinking that he ought to, after all, cut loose and give the white man what he has coming to him.

But, of course, he could not succeed. Not yet! And let us hope he will not burden himself with all the white man's evil by answering cruelty with more cruelty, when the day comes that he can.

Meanwhile, perhaps it is most difficult for the Negro to admit to himself quite fully, in his heart, what he certainly knows intellectually without a doubt: that he is in the right, completely in the right.

Fortunately the Negroes have a leader who is a man of grace, who understands the law of love, who understands the mystery of the greatest secret grace that has been *given to the Negro and to no other*. The grace which the people who first created the spirituals well knew about: the grace of election that made them God's chosen, the grace that elevated them above the meaningless and trivial things of life, even in the midst of terrible and unjust suffering.

There are things the Negro knows that the white man can never know. Things which belong to the pure, unique, spiritual destiny of America, and which have been denied to the white man, will be denied to him forever because of his brutality to the Negro and to the Indian. So, too, there are things the Jew alone can know, things closed forever to the gentile, even to the best of Christians.

Yet, unfortunately, this secret heritage, this most precious revelation of God, which one senses in the singing of Mahalia Jackson as well as in some of the very great, obscure artists of jazz can also be lost. The mere fact of being a Negro does not guarantee that one is worthy of this precious inheritance.

✦  ✦  ✦

Perhaps the chief reason why there was at one time so much opposition, on the part of religious people, to psychoanalysis is that it completely undermines a complacent and evasive ethic of good intentions. The cultivation of "good intentions" and of a "good conscience" (in the sense of a complacent and undisturbed conscience) is about all many people have in lieu of morality. This inevitably implies that for them psychoanalysis means simply the destruction of all morality.

As a matter of fact, by showing that the righteous "conscience" may in actual fact be the mask of a brutal, selfish, cruelly unjust, greedy, and murderous unconscious, and by challenging man to bring his *whole* house in order by the humble acknowledgment of reality in all its depths, psychoanalysis can in fact do Christianity a real service. Not, of course, that it has not been abused by quacks: but the principle remains—we must seek to eradicate the unconscious roots of sin, and these roots go very deep. Christianity sees more in this eradication than mere psychological catharsis and reintegration (useful though these may sometimes be). The power of the Cross alone is capable of purifying these deep springs poisoned by self-worship, dread, and hate.

The crisis of Christianity today is most acute precisely in those circles where fundamentalist and conservative superstitions seek at all cost to defend the shallow and subjective "good intentions" and conformity to the superficial legal demand against all deeper understandings of one's real hidden motivations. One must face the fact that "good intentions" are only good as long as they are faithfully re-examined in the light of new knowledge, and in the light of their fruits.

More and more we see how in reality the "good," "kind," "humane," and "loving" intention bears fruit in real evil, cruelty, inhumanity, and hate. The experience of each day makes this more and more clear.

The ethic of subjective "good intentions" has been judged and found wanting. We must refocus on the objective results of our decisions!

✓ ✓ ✓

The Christian faith takes hold on each one of us when each one sees himself no longer in the persepctive of individual fulfillment and satisfaction, but in the light of the Cross. This implies the renunciation of one attitude toward sin and death, and a completely new understanding of these realities. In the first case, you implicitly accept death as an inevitable but incomprehensible fact, from which you resolutely turn away in order to make the best you can out of time, and to live as if, in fact, you were never going to die. This implies a firm will to ignore death, and it may also imply an equally firm will to ignore sin and guilt. You come to terms with life and with your society, and you make the most effective possible use of the means which are offered, here and now, to achieve a relative happiness, a relative sense that you are a real and meaningful being.

The Christian faith on the other hand demands a recognition that this view of life is in reality a delusive form of wilfulness and of despair, since in fact it cannot make the moral effort to confront the most important and inscrutable realities of life. Christianity recognizes that these realities cannot be understood by reason alone, but it accepts from God, on faith, a revelation of their true import. Death and sin are inextricably involved in one another: they are in fact two aspects of the same mystery—man's separation from God by the wilful assertion of his individuality as ultimate, and by the determination to live as if, in fact, it were ultimate. In the end, this false view tends to assert, at least implicitly, the *complete* autonomy of the individual, who is no longer responsible to anyone, who is able to choose for himself any one of an unlimited number and quality of possibilities, and who is, in fact, free to do exactly as he pleases without rendering an account to anyone and without taking into consideration the moral and physical consequences of any of his acts.

This implicit claim to complete autonomy for man, dressed

in various mythical trappings, constitutes the various beliefs by which modern man attempts to explain his existence.

An essential and obviously characteristic element of the Christian faith is the admission that this claim to autonomy is in fact rooted in despair and death. While appearing to be an affirmation of life and hope, it is actually a fallacious construction of the mind of man, by which he hopes to create for himself some kind of meaning in a life which will be resolved into meaninglessness by death. Furthermore, Christianity sees that a society that justifies its behavior and bases its existence on this supposed autonomy of man does, in fact, devote to destruction and death the very resources and energies which it claims to be using for the affirmation and improvement of life.

The ways in which, historically and sociologically, this inner contradiction becomes manifest are regarded, by Christianity, as silent expressions of the "judgment of God" upon such societies: they are a form of quiet and definitive comment upon the real nature of the society and upon the validity of its ethical claims. It was the task of the prophets, for instance, to discover this kind of meaning in the events of the history of Israel. And it remains the prophetic task of the Church to interpret events of our own time in this same kind of way.

But supposing that Christians themselves, while claiming to remain Christians, themselves apostatize from this basic faith?

The basic Christian faith is that he who renounces his delusive, individual autonomy in order to receive his true being and freedom in and by Christ is "justified" by the mercy of God in the Cross of Christ. His "sins are forgiven" in so far as the root of guilt is torn up in the surrender which faith makes to Christ. Instead of my own delusive autonomy I surrender to Christ all rights over me in the hope that by His Spirit, which is the Spirit and Life of His Church, He will live and act in me, and, having become one with Him, having found my true identity in Him, I will act only as a member of His Body and a faithful citizen of His Kingdom.

The Church is the place in which this surrender of individ-

116 CONJECTURES OF A GUILTY BYSTANDER

ual autonomy becomes real, guaranteed by the truth of the Spirit and by His love, and by the pardon of sins: for the Church herself takes upon herself all man's sin. The Church at once confesses the sins of all men as her own, and receives in herself the mercy that is offered to all men.

But now, supposing that, instead of confessing the sins of the world which she has taken upon herself, the Church—or a group of Christians who arrogate to themselves the name of "Church"—becomes a social mechanism for self-justification? Supposing this "Church," which is in reality no church at all, takes to herself the function of declaring that everyone else is guilty and rationalizing the sins of her members as acts of virtue? Suppose that she becomes a perfect and faultless machine for declaring herself not guilty? Suppose that she provides men with a convenient method of deciding when they do or do not need to accuse themselves of anything before God? Supposing that, instead of conscience, she provides men with the support of unanimous group approval or disapproval?

This is what explains the fact that some men can commit murder in the name of Christ and believe themselves guiltless, indeed congratulate themselves on having served Him well. For them, the function of "the Church" is to provide a milieu in which one can decide what is and is not guilty, what is or is not sinful. The "Church" becomes simply a place where men gather to decree that others are guilty and they themselves are innocent. The fact that others then accuse them of hypocrisy and of flagrant infidelity to truth only confirms them in their own self-assured righteousness. The "Church" in such an event becomes a machine for setting the unquiet conscience at rest. It is a perfectly efficient machine for the manufacture of self-complacency and inner peace!

It is characteristic of pseudo-Christianity that, while claiming to be justified by God, by faith, or by the works of faith and love, it merely operates a machine for excusing sin instead of confessing and pardoning it—a machine for producing the feeling that one is right and that everyone else is wrong. If it becomes expedient to commit murder, whether by lynch law or by inquisitorial tyranny, then murder becomes an act of holy justice. To oppress and persecute others becomes an affirmation of one's own religious freedom and courage before God, a mark of Christian strength. And how does one strengthen this faith? How does one confirm the brethren in their witness? By repetition of these thrilling, violent, and momentous acts which outsiders denounce as crimes and acts of guilt. The way to prove to oneself that one is virtuous and not a criminal is to renew the act, renew it over and over, and if necessary to be tried and acquitted for it by a jury of one's peers, thus proving that the act was not criminal but right and holy. Thus gradually the determination to pervert the Christian conscience becomes a function of the "Church" —perhaps even its prime function. And this becomes, inevitably, the sign of God's judgment upon that "Church." The awful innocence of these "just men" stands on their forehead like the mark of Cain—the mark of the one no man can touch because he is set apart for hell.

*  *  *

"The business of every God-fearing man," says Gandhi, "is to dissociate himself from evil in *total disregard of the consequences*. He must have faith in a good deed producing only a good result . . . He follows the truth though the following of it may endanger his very life. He knows that it is better to die in the way of God than to live in the way of Satan."

—*My Non-violence*

This is precisely the attitude that we have lost in the West, because we have lost our fundamentally religious view of reality, of being and of truth. And that is what Gandhi retained. We have sacrificed the power to apprehend and respect what man is, what truth is, what love is, and have replaced them with a vague confusion of pragmatic notions about what can be done with this or that, what is permissable, what is feasible, how things can be used, irrespective of any definite meaning or finality contained in their very nature, expressing the truth and value of that nature.

We are concerned only with "practicality"—"efficiency": that is, with means, not with ends. And therefore we are

more and more concerned only with *immediate consequences.* We are the prisoners of every urgency. In this way
we so completely lose all perspective and sense of values that
we are no longer able to estimate correctly what even the
most immediate consequences of our actions may turn out to
be. We know well enough that if we do certain things, certain
definite reactions will follow: but we lose all capacity to grasp
the significance of those reactions, and hence we cannot see
further than the next automatic response. Having lost our
ability to see life as a whole, to evaluate conduct as a whole,
we no longer have any relevant context into which our actions
are to be fitted, and therefore all our actions become erratic,
arbitrary, and insignificant. To the man who concerns himself
only with consequences everything soon becomes inconsequential, nothing "follows from" anything else, all is haphaz-
ard, futile, and absurd. For it is not humanly possible to live
a life without significance and remain healthy. A human
life has to have a human meaning, or else it becomes morally
corrupt.

Hence we come to be forced into evil in order to avoid
what seem to us evil consequences. We find ourselves more
and more backed into a corner in which there seems to be no
choice but that of a "lesser evil" for the sake of some urgency,
some imaginary or desperately hoped for good. But an evil
choice can never have wholly good consequences. And a
good choice can never have wholly evil consequences. But
when one chooses to do *good irrespective of the consequences,* it is a paradox that the consequences will ultimately
be good, and the good that is in them will far outweigh the
possible evil.

Gandhi's standard is the standard of the New Testament:
to do all things in the name of Christ, in the name of the
truth, that is to say for the sake of the truth in them which is
a manifestation of Christ. To act out of love for truth, "doing
the truth in charity" is to act for truth alone, and without
regard for consequences. Not that one recklessly does what
seems to be good without care for possible disaster, but that
one carefully chooses what one believes to be good and then
leaves the good itself to produce its own good consequences
in its own good time.

Of one thing we must be persuaded: good action is not by any means a mere arbitrary conformity to artificial social norms. To conform is not to act well, but only to "look good." There is an objective moral good, a good which corresponds to the real value of being, which brings out and confirms the inner significance of our life when we obey its norms. Such an act integrates us into the whole living movement and development of the cosmos, it brings us into harmony with all the rest of the world, it situates us in our place, it helps us fulfill our task and to participate fruitfully in the whole world's work and its history, as it reaches out for its ultimate meaning and fulfillment. In a word, it is an act of obedience to God. Sometimes it may be necessary for us to go against social norms in order to obey real norms of objective good on the direct word of God. For when the norms of conduct in a society become arbitrary, capricious, and pragmatic there is great danger that one will passively enter into cooperation with injustice and evil, and refuse to listen to God's preemptory command.

In times like ours, it is more than ever necessary for the individual to train himself, or be trained, according to objective norms of good, and learn to distinguish these from the purely pragmatic norms current in his society. Thus he will come to know the difference between the "ways of God and the ways of Satan." We cannot trust our society to tell us this difference. Everything is confused, and the men of our time blindly follow now God and now Satan, blown this way and that by every changing wind of urgency and opportunity, judging only by what seem to them to be the immediate consequences. We must recover our inner faith not only in God but in the good, in reality, and in the power of the good to take care of itself and us as well, if only we attend to it, observe, listen, choose, and obey.

Gandhi pointed out very wisely that our feeling of helplessness in the presence of injustice and aggression arises from "our deliberate dismissal of God from our common affairs." Those who relinquish God as the center of their moral orbit lose all direction and by that very fact lose and betray their manhood. They become blindly dependent on circumstances, and upon those who are astute enough or powerful enough to use every circumstance for their own ends. Those who renounce God immediately become victims of the nearest brute that is a little more powerful than they. They have to live in submission to this gangster, and pay him dearly for their safety. It doesn't matter much whether the "power" thus exercised is physical or moral, whether it is a matter of force or money or cleverness. Those who renounce God have to fall back on force when they get sick of their state of dependence on other men. Yet force alone can never deliver them completely. Indeed, to rely on the military power of stronger allies is the sure way to national suicide. The prophets taught this lesson tirelessly for centuries—without success.

Reliance on God, of course, does not mean passivity. On the contrary, it liberates man for a clearly defined activity, "the will of God." This is, in Gandhi's words, "intelligent action in a detached manner." God wills that we act humanly, therefore intelligently. He wills that we act for His sake, for love of the truth, not out of concern for immediate material interest: therefore He wills that we act in a "detached manner." Detachment is not pure indifference, but again only a concentration of attention on the subject of the act itself, not on the results or the consequences. We are not responsible for more than our own action, but for this we should take *complete responsibility*. Then the results will follow of themselves, in a manner we may not always be able to foresee.

But the point is that we do not always have to foresee every possibility. We have only to judge whether the act is right, just, and accords with truth and love here and now, because we "believe in the good" and are therefore convinced that, whatever consequences may follow, they will certainly be good ones, beneficial to ourselves and to society.

✓ ✓ ✓

The Law of Love.

We still speak of the Law of Love. The first and greatest commandment. And the second like unto the first. What is this Law of Love?

We tend to think of it uneasily as a dictate which interferes with our ordinary, natural, human existence. The interference is of course salutary, indeed "salvific." We do not regret this interruption of our ordinary pursuits. Still, it is a nuisance!

Yet the "Law of Love" (supernatural) tends to break into the Law of Nature, which we assume is contrary to it. With a sigh we renounce that to which we are spontaneously inclined and turn away to "duty"—the duty of love, imposed for some inscrutable reason by God in order to "save us." Well, of course, we do want to be saved, don't we?

Because the Law of Love is presented in this gray light, fewer and fewer people are able to keep alive a genuine interest in salvation.

Let us forget this travesty, and try to understand the Christian view of love.

First of all, the Law of Love *is the deepest law of our nature*, not something extraneous and alien to our nature. Our nature itself inclines us to love, and to love freely.

The deepest and most fundamental exigency of the divine law in our hearts is that we should reach our fulfillment by loving. It is not enough for us to possess human nature, we have to act as humans, we have to exercise all the deepest capacities of our nature. More than this, we have to act as persons—freely! As soon as we come into existence we begin to obey the Law of Love.

The demands of the Law of Love are progressive. We begin by loving life itself, by loving survival at any price. Hence, we must first of all love ourselves. But as we grow we must love others. We must love them as our own fulfillment. Then we must come to love them in order to fulfill them, to develop their capacity to love, and finally we must love others and ourselves in and for God.

But the most fundamental demand of the Law of Love is that we should love *freely*. We are commanded to choose our own object of love, and not simply to love any object that is placed before us.

Yet at the same time our choice is bounded by certain limitations—for our time, our place, our society, our state of life determine for us a certain limited number of friends and enemies. We are not entirely free to say who precisely shall be our friend and who shall be our enemy. Our choice is limited to certain definite possibilities. But, still, we can and must choose to love the men we actually encounter, whether as friends or as men loved in spite of their hostility.

The Law of Love then is not a law commanding that we wallow in sentimental consolation or in condescending official benevolence. It is a command to commit ourselves to the use of this deep power that is in us, to choose to commit ourselves even in situations where the power does not go into action instinctively.

In a word, the command to love is a command to rise above the mechanisms of natural instinct, to use a natural force freely and deliberately, instead of permitting ourselves to be led by it, and carried away by it blindly.

Only this free use elevates the natural drive to a personal and spiritual level. But freedom does not necessarily deny and frustrate nature altogether. The choice of a partner in marriage is obedience to this high spiritual law. Married love can be a fulfillment of this profound love, a spiritual act of obedience to God in freedom and in joy.

✓ ✓ ✓

Beware of the temptation to refuse love, to reject love, for ostensibly "spiritual motives." Consider the awful sterility of those who, claiming to love God, have in reality dispensed themselves from all obligations to love anyone, and have remained inert and stunted in a little circle of abstract, petty concerns involving themselves and a few others as sterile as themselves!

✓ ✓ ✓

Beware also of the temptation of the "omnipotent choice." Choice alone is not magic, and the power to choose is no guarantee that any choice, provided only that it is a deeply convinced choice, will always be the right choice. Here choosing is not obedience to the Law of Love. One may choose not to love. One may choose to love in a way that defeats and frustrates love. Love does not seek its own defeat. Nor does it seek mere victory in conquest. Love is beyond conquest, beyond victory and defeat. Hence the Law of Love is not the mere Law of Will. Development is not the mere development of will. Mere wilfulness, pretending to be love, has no power except the power of delusion and madness.

Love is at once *dependent and free*. It depends on objective values, and it also freely creates new values within itself.

The Law of Love is the law that commands us to add new values to the world given us by God, through the creative power that He has placed in us—the power of joy in response, in gratitude, and in the giving of self.

✓ ✓ ✓

"Thy Kingdom Come."

The question of the Parousia remains *the* great question of Christianity: and of course in itself it is no question at all. The Kingdom is already established, but not yet definitively manifest—we remain in a time of development, of choice, and of preparation.

We remain in a time of decision.

A Christian is, or should be, one who has "decided for" the Parousia, for the final coming of the Kingdom. His life is oriented by this decision. His existence has meaning in so far as the Parousia is crucial to him.

But the Parousia is, it seems, indefinitely delayed.

This is no accident either. It must be taken as part of the question. The Parousia by itself is no question. The delay of the Parousia is not the whole question. This delay raises the question. The question is as follows.

As Christians we are men who have based all our hopes on the Kingdom of Christ, to be definitively manifest by final victory in the Parousia—this is the final victory of life over death.

The Parousia having been "delayed," we have been for two thousand years left to construct for ourselves in the world a kind of kingdom, a cultural-religious-political Christendom, which is admittedly not all one would have looked for, but which has its advantages.

Now the question is—if the Parousia means the end and destruction of this provisional structure, indeed its judgment,

should we really desire the Parousia? Should we not in all
earnestness *pray for the Parousia to be delayed indefinitely*,
and indeed, with all the power given to us over the will of
God, by prayer, should we not rather attempt to change His
plan, and forget the whole business?

Should we not rather make it our duty to ask Him to let
us build the Kingdom in our own way, a kingdom consistent
with what we have begun, a Kingdom of God that is at once
a sacred enclave in the world and also politically in collabora-
tion with the world? Should we not insist that the Parousia
should simply be regarded as our social, cultural, religious,
and political triumph in the world, so that we are no longer an
enclave, but have finally succeeded in *taking it all over*? We
tried it once, beginning in the eighth century and going on
through the Middle Ages—it was a good attempt, but some
important points were overlooked. Can we not get ourselves
into a position to make a better try? And this time to succeed?

Thus we find ourselves, in effect, *deciding against* the Parousia. "Thy Kingdom come"—but not now, not in that distressing way—but in *our* time and *our* way.

Thus the Christian has learned to pray against judgment,
and for an eternity that is an indefinite prolongation of time,
because time is what we need: time to try it over and over
again.

Suggested emendation in the Lord's Prayer: Take out "Thy
Kingdom come" and substitute "Give us time!"

✦ ✦ ✦

But then what? What are we going to do with "time?"
Make deductions from past history, devise a system—a Christian system—and put it to work? Or rather consider carefully
the systems devised by others and baptize *their* systems, making them suddenly Christian, and discovering in them the
unexpected Kingdom?

✦ ✦ ✦

Mirgeler* shows how the Stoic concept of "Natural Law"
became extremely convenient for a Christianity which was

* See A. Mirgeler, *Mutations of Western Christianity*, pp. 17–18.

reconciled to settling down in the world of late antiquity and getting along without the Parousia.

✓ ✓ ✓

"The Church confesses that she has taken in vain the name of Jesus Christ, for she has been ashamed of his name before the world and she has not striven forcefully enough against the misuse of this name for an evil purpose. She has stood by while violence and wrong were being committed under cover of this name."                                                        —Bonhoeffer

Curious that in the United States, particularly the South, at the height of the struggle for Civil Rights, the (Protestant) churches were swept with a wave of glossolalia—"speaking in tongues." Naturally this "charism" had nothing to do with the current violence—anything but! Though it was perhaps an outlet, in some cases, for inarticulate and apocalyptic fears. I don't know what they were saying, in their tongues. The irony of it is that it seems to have been an ultimate protest against the inacceptable realities and challenges of the historical situation—a convenient resort to immediate inspiration rather than the difficult and humiliating business of hearing and obeying the Word of God in the need of one's fellow man.

In the whole question of the (Catholic) Church and the world, we come again and again to the various ways in which adaptation to "the world" can in fact be an expression of shame and fear—guilt at having failed to "hold" the modern world and to charm it with spectacles, pageantry, lively new debates, and other contrivances. To be dominated by the fear of losing our "hold" on men, especially on youth, is implicitly to confront the world in abject shame at the name and power of Christ. We do not preach Christ, we preach our own modernity, our own cleverness, our liveliness, our fashionableness, and our charm; or (if we are conservatives) our unshakable security and unchangeable rightness, our inviolable respectability (and God knows *that* is no attraction for the youth of the world!).

Bonhoeffer, writing in the time of the *Hitler Jugend*,

wrote: "The Church offered no resistance to contempt for age and the idolization of youth, for she was afraid of losing youth and with it the future. As though her future belonged to youth!"

The last thing in the world that should concern a Christian or the Church is *survival* in a temporal and worldly sense: to be concerned with this is an implicit denial of the Victory of Christ and of the Resurrection.

Yet this is what seems to concern most Christians. It is this fear of destruction and of suffering that has reduced the "Christianity" of so many Christians to mere anti-Communism and little else. It is this mortal terror of not "surviving," or indeed of not having a privileged place in society, that makes Christians willing and eager to destroy Communism with H-bombs. Or, in the case of liberals, the same fear takes another form: the fear of falling behind the intellectuals and the radicals who seem to make more sense than anyone else, and who seem to know the way into the future. The same fear of not surviving, of not being acceptable any more, of not having any place in the world of the future!

Anything that a Christian does under the impulsion of this fear is bound to be, in some way, an evasive repudiation of the name of Christ, whose death has "overcome the world" and whose resurrection is the only pledge of a real future that anyone can possibly have!

✓ ✓ ✓

"The time is fully come, and the Reign of God is at hand: repent and believe in the good news."    —Mark 1:15

The greatest temptation that assails Christians is that in effect, for most of us, the Gospel has ceased to be news. And if it is not news it is not Gospel: for the Gospel is the proclamation of something absolutely new, everlastingly new, not a message that was once new but is now two thousand years old. And yet for many of us the Gospel is precisely the announcement of something that is not new: the truths of the Gospel are old, deep-rooted, firmly established, unchanging and in some sense a refuge against all that is disturbing be-

cause it is new. . . . The message of the Gospel when it was
first preached was profoundly disturbing to those who wanted
to cling to well-established religious patterns, the ancient and
accepted ways, the ways that were not dangerous and which
contained no surprises.

Repentance is at the same time a complete renewal, a discovery, a new life, and a return to the old, to that which is
before everything else that is old. But the old and the new
meet in the metanoia, the inner change, that is accomplished
by the hearing of God's word and the keeping of it. That
which is oldest is also newest because it is the beginning. "I
am the Beginning, and I speak to you." "I am the Alpha and
the Omega, the first and the last, the beginning and the end."
The Jews were scandalized at Christ, who spoke as if He
were already known to Abraham. *"Thou art not yet forty
years old."* Christ replied: "Before Abraham was made, I
*am."* The new is within the old because it is the perennial
beginning of everything, and emerges from the old, transcending it, having no part in it, eternally renewing its own
life. The Gospel is handed down from generation to generation *but it must reach each one of us brand new, or not at all.*
If it is merely "tradition" and not news, it has not been
preached or not heard—it is not Gospel.

Any word that comes from God is news!

But our ideas of news, the newspapers' idea of news, might
lead us to believe that any word *except* what came from God
was news. As if what was said by God had to be so fixed,
so determined, so rigid in its set form that it could never be
anything new, never unpredictable, never astonishing, never
frightening. If there is no risk in revelation, if there is no
fear in it, if there is no challenge in it, if it is not a word
which creates whole new worlds, and new beings, if it does
not call into existence a new creature, our new self, then
religion is dead and God is dead. Those for whom the Gospel is old, and old *only,* have killed it for the rest of men.
The life of the Gospel is its newness.

Those who preach the Gospel as if it were not and could
not be news, as if it never could be news again, are saying
in their own way, and much more terribly than Nietzsche,

that "God is dead." They are declaring it officially, they are proclaiming it not just as the paradox of an eccentric, but as the doctrine of their church.

What makes the Gospel news? The faith, which is created in us by God and with which we hear it as news. This acceptance of faith, this new birth in the Spirit, opens up a new dimension in which time and eternity meet, in which all things are made new: eternity, time, our own self, the world around us.

But also the news of the Gospel is more than a personal, subjective discovery, my own individual realization here and now of a universal message. It is true that what is known to all who have believed becomes known to me also, in praise, in wonder, in the creative light and peace of interior prayer. And my discovery must in some sense enrich the light and the joy of all. But more than that: the Gospel looks to a future event that is still not fulfilled—the full revelation of the Glory and the Reign of Christ. He reigns already, but His reign is not yet manifested as it will be. Yet this brings with it another temptation: the false news of those who have too much of a message, too clear a message—"Lo, here is Christ, precisely *here. And we are the ones who have found Him for you.*" They have the date and the hour of His coming, and they are themselves the main part of the news. A very important part, indeed. The second coming is *their* news.

Such news is not to be believed. The Gospel itself is much simpler. *Now* is the judgment of the world, and the newest of all the news, because it is the simple and inscrutable heart of every now, the life and the heartbeat of every history of every man and every race and every nation.

The Gospel is the news that, if I will, I can respond now in perfect freedom to the redemptive love of God for man in Christ, that I can *now* rise above the forces of necessity and evil in order to say "yes" to the mysterious action of Spirit that is transforming the world even in the midst of the violence and confusion and destruction that seem to proclaim His absence and His "death."

Let us not underestimate our era, the era of disaster and fulfillment, by calling it "interesting."

# PART THREE

## *The Night Spirit and the Dawn Air*

*We must love them both, those whose opinions we share and those whose opinions we reject. For both have labored in the search for truth and both have helped us in the finding of it.* —St. Thomas Aquinas

> *When devils drive the reasonable wild*
> *They strip the adult century so bare,*
> *Love must be regrown from the sensual child.*
> —W. H. Auden

How the valley awakes. At two-fifteen in the morning there are no sounds except in the monastery: the bells ring, the office begins. Outside, nothing, except perhaps a bullfrog saying "Om" in the creek or in the guesthouse pond. Some nights he is in Samadhi; there is not even "Om." The mysterious and uninterrupted whooping of the whippoorwill begins about three, these mornings. He is not always near. Sometimes there are two whooping together, perhaps a mile away in the woods in the east.

The first chirps of the waking day birds mark the *"point vierge"* of the dawn under a sky as yet without real light, a moment of awe and inexpressible innocence, when the Father in perfect silence opens their eyes. They begin to speak to Him, not with fluent song, but with an awakening question that is their dawn state, their state at the *"point vierge."* Their condition asks if it is time for them to "be." He answers "yes." Then, they one by one wake up, and become birds. They manifest themselves as birds, beginning to sing. Presently they will be fully themselves, and will even fly.

Meanwhile, the most wonderful moment of the day is that when creation in its innocence asks permission to "be" once again, as it did on the first morning that ever was.

All wisdom seeks to collect and manifest itself at that blind sweet point. Man's wisdom does not succeed, for we are fallen into self-mastery and cannot ask permission of anyone. We face our mornings as men of undaunted purpose. We know the time and we dictate terms. We are in a position to dictate terms, we suppose: we have a clock that proves we are right from the very start. We know what time it is. We are in touch with the hidden inner laws. We will say in advance what kind of day it has to be. Then if necessary we will take steps to make it meet our requirements.

For the birds there is not a time that they tell, but the virgin point between darkness and light, between nonbeing and being. You can tell yourself the time by their waking, if you are experienced. But that is your folly, not theirs. Worse folly still if you think they are telling you something you might consider useful—that it is, for example, four o'clock.

So they wake: first the catbirds and cardinals and some that I do not know. Later the song sparrows and wrens. Last of all the doves and crows.

The waking of crows is most like the waking of men: querulous, noisy, raw.

Here is an unspeakable secret: paradise is all around us and we do not understand. It is wide open. The sword is taken away, but we do not know it: we are off "one to his farm and another to his merchandise." Lights on. Clocks ticking. Thermostats working. Stoves cooking. Electric shavers filling radios with static. "Wisdom," cries the dawn deacon, but we do not attend.

✓ ✓ ✓

We are now in the most perfect days of the Appalachian spring, late April: days of dogwood and redbud blossoms. Cool clear days with every delicate shade of green and red in the thinly budding branches of the oaks and maples. Later, in the burnt haze of summer, Kentucky's soaked green will be monotonous as a jungle, turning brown in the heat. Now it is France, or England. The hills suddenly look like the Cotswolds.

✓ ✓ ✓

Yesterday I got a letter from one of the last Shaker eldresses, at their community in New Hampshire. It was an answer to an inquiry, and she enclosed a rather touching little leaflet about how the Shakers now faced extinction without concern, convinced that they had not been a failure, that they had done what the Lord had asked of them. I find this easy to believe. The Shakers have been something of a sign, a mystery, a strange attempt at utter honesty which, in trying perhaps to be too ideally pure, was nevertheless pure—with moments of absurdity.

They were absolutely loyal to a vision that led nowhere: but which seemed to them to point to a definitive eschatological goal. And perhaps they were not as deceived as one might think. Can such definitive visions really be pure illusion? Even in leading "nowhere," are they perhaps not significant? Could the Shakers do the perfect work they did (in their furniture, for instance) if their vision were not real? The witness of their craftsmanship is certainly most impressive.

✦ ✦ ✦

The poems of Bertolt Brecht are like sackcloth and brown bread. To what extent is their healthy disillusionment itself an artifice? I think he is genuine. But if so, how does he believe what he seems to believe? Or does he believe it? Or is his Marxism a matter of convenience? It would be silly to suppose that a Marxist poet with official backing could not be also a good poet. I don't know how much of a Marxist Brecht really is. But I like him, in any case: and I like his poems better than his plays. I like his poetry better than that of the esoteric American pontiffs of the day. Brecht is a most individual poet, more so than many who are intensely conscious of their individuality.

✦ ✦ ✦

It is curious that the growth of anti-Semitism in medieval Germanic Christendom went hand in hand with a kind of practical Judaizing of Christianity. The consciousness of Germanic Christendom in the eighth to eleventh centuries was increasingly levitical and military. The God of Charlemagne was the Lord of Hosts who anointed him emperor. Liturgy and theology became allegorical and midrashic. Germanic medieval culture appealed spontaneously to the Old Testament rather than to the New to justify its instinctive tendencies. So also in some measure did the Celtic Church, with its penitential tariffs. The altar of the Christian Church became once again the altar of the temple, in the holy of holies, the hidden sanctuary, served by a levitical priesthood. The theology of baptism in this cultural and religious climate turned back to look again at circumcision (says Chenu).

The theology of suffering is strongly tinged with ideas of punishment, and morality becomes a morality of obedience rather than love. In this aggressive, solemn, dark and feudal Christianity in which the emperor is nearer and more real than the Pope, in which the bishop is at once a high priest and a general and monks are fighting Levites, there grows up the hatred and contempt of the Jew, whose role is more and more that of the theological Christ-killer on whom the curse has fallen. But perhaps there was in this a deep unconscious guilt for Christians who did not truly understand Christ. St. Paul was still read, and there must have been something of a consciousness of a return to the Law which is, in the eyes of Paul, the confession that one has failed to understand Christian faith and has secretly abandoned it.

It is interesting to note the creeping anti-Semitism in the Liturgical Easter Trope, which turns into a real drama, with comic characters and villains. This development is seen for example at St. Gall, where an odious and comic Jewish villain, Rufus, comes to play a more and more important part in the Crucifixion scenes, for the Easter play, as we advance into the Middle Ages, becomes more and more a Passion play. It is with the dramatizing of the Passion that the image of the Jew as villain and "Christ-killer" becomes fixed in the European mind.

In the theology of the time, the transition from Old to New Testament was more and more the esoteric privilege of those who, understanding the "mystical sense" of the Old Testament types, were able to see the Charity and the Spirit of Christ in the "carnal figures" of the Old Testament. But since this mystical understanding implied, in fact, not only a very special culture, but also a highly developed spirituality, it was not the affair of many. The fact that in monasteries there were many monks who could not transcend in this way the Old Testament symbolism and ritual of the monasteries constituted something of a problem. Blessed Guerric of Igny, the Cistercian, in his Christmas sermons (which like all his sermons are very Pauline) upbraids these severe and rather pessimistic monks and calls them "the Jews." Thus again there was a renewal of a very bad conscience among those who were thought and supposed to be the best of Christians. If many of these were still "no better than Jews," what about the Jews themselves, down at the bottom of the social scale? (Note, as the Middle Ages went on Cistercian monasteries were often heavily in debt to Jews.

(See Knowles, *Monastic Order in England*)

John of Salisbury, the School of Chartres, and St. Thomas Aquinas, in creating a new climate of philosophy and theology, changed this somewhat. The School of St. Victor at the beginning of the twelfth century returned to the literal interpretation of Scripture with much friendly consultation of rabbis. St. Anselm and his group were open to a more tolerant and reasonable dialogue with the Jew as well as the Muslim. But the Crusades did much to destroy this spirit of openness and toleration.

✓ ✓ ✓

The greatness of the Old Testament is beginning to be fully evident in some of the fine Old Testament theologies written by Protestant scholars like Von Rad, Eichrodt, and others. The universe of the Old Testament is a praising universe, of which man is a living and essential part, standing shoulder to shoulder with the angelic hosts who praise Yahweh: and praise is the surest manifestation of true life. The characteristic of *Scheol*, the realm of the dead, is that there is no praise in it. The Psalms then are the purest expression of the essence of life in this universe: Yahweh is present to His people when the Psalms are sung with triumphant vigor and jubilation (not just muttered and meditated in the individual beard). This presence and communion, this *coming into being* in the act of praise, is the heart of Old Testament worship as it is also of monastic choral praise. Living praise is the fullness of man's being with God and the "mystery of the spirit" (Von Rad). But it also has a historical dimension: faith in the power of Yahweh and in His great works of mercy as well as in His promises makes history present to the singer as a theological reality and fact (again Von Rad). The theological realization of these great acts of the Lord is *felt and experienced in their beauty;* the magnificent power of the radiance of the Lord revealed in His saving acts takes hold entirely on the worshiper. Hence the "transported" quality of the Psalms which we priests miss entirely when we simply mumble our way through the breviary, with no taste left for words like *cantate, jubilate, exultate. . . .* (I remember when Dom Baron came to Gethsemani and was teaching us chant: he finally got us really going in the Introit of the fourth Sunday after Easter and I thought we were going to rock the roof off the Church. But that was only once—no, we nearly did it again on the following Ascension Day. The text was perfect for it: *Jubilate Deo omnis terra,* "Sing your joy to God all the earth.") *Jubilate:* it is a joy one *cannot contain.* Where is that in our liturgy today? This is the true liturgical shout of triumph, the triumph we know when divine and angelic beauty possess our whole being, in the joy of the risen Christ!

Returning to my previous section on the "Old Testament" quality of early Germanic Christendom and monasticism: we must not be too one-sided about it. One cannot read the monastic Fathers, whether you take Paschasius Radbertus, or Rupert of Deutz, or St. Bernard, or Guerric of Igny, or Odo of Cluny, or Peter the Venerable, without realizing that this sense of being transported with praise came to life in the monasteries of the early Middle Ages: but perhaps after the years it was deadened (and then we get the bawdy and despairing songs of the wandering, lost, beat monks, the Goliards).

The beauty of God is best praised by the men who *reach and realize their limit* knowing that their praise cannot attain to God. It is then that the inarticulate, long *jubilus* takes over in Gregorian chant: some of the extended melismatic developments of the alleluia in the Easter Liturgy, particularly those of the seventh tone. Gregorian has a special grace for bringing out this experience of praise that reaches its limit, fails, and yet continues in a new dimension.

In this way praise reaches not only the heart of God but also the heart of creation itself, finding everywhere the beauty of the righteousness of Yahweh.

❧ ❧ ❧

Bishop Nanayakkara of Kandy in Ceylon was here last week. He said that he got to know St. John of the Cross when the books were sent to him as a present by a poor working woman in the United States. He is glad to have the Little Brothers of Jesus in his diocese, and says he told one of them, who is a shoemaker, that if the other shoemakers have a party and invite him, he ought to go: for if he is not able to go he is betraying his vocation!

❧ ❧ ❧

The Ox Mountain parable of Mencius: Note the importance of the "night spirit" and the "dawn breath" in restoring to life the forest that has been cut down.

Even though the Ox Mountain forest has been cut to the ground, if the mountain is left to rest and recuperate in the night and the dawn, the trees will return. But men cut them down, cattle browse on the new shoots: no night spirit, no dawn breath—no rest, no renewal—and finally one is convinced that there never were any woods on the Ox Mountain. So, Mencius concludes, with human nature. Without the night spirit, the dawn breath, silence, passivity, rest, man's nature cannot be itself. In its barrenness it is no longer *natura*: nothing grows from it, nothing is born of it any more.

❧ ❧ ❧

Lewis Mumford says, in his *City in History*, that the earliest cities were cities of the dead. The necropolis, the cemetery, antedates the city of the living. This is clear in Genesis. Abraham lives in tents and is on the move all the time—until he dies. There is one fixed place only: the place where you finally stop and "rest" or "sleep with the Fathers." This place may be selected (or indeed hallowed by the tombs of generations), and one may die far from it: but one's body must then be transported there. The beginning of the world as we know it is the beginning of fixed cities for the living, growing up next to the cities of the dead, under the shadow of the ancestors. The metropolis. But the metropolis, with all its affluence and all its bursting pride of apparent life, is a center for death. Even the architecture of a city like modern Washington is the architecture of a necropolis (compare the even more tomblike government buildings erected by Hitler, Mussolini, Stalin). Among the big white tombs, vast dark areas of slums, through which one travels without seeing them: the permanence of death, sickness, vice in the world of the poor who remain imprisoned in their poverty, nailed to one place by it!

Why all this? In spite of our myths about him, Stone Age man was not a man of war. He was concerned with hunting, agriculture, domesticating animals, the home. The city is the place where the mythology of power and war develop, the center from which the magic of power reaches out to destroy the enemy and to perpetuate one's own life and riches—interminably if only it were possible. But it is never possible. Hence, the desperate need to placate the gods, to have the gods on our side, to win: for this, the most drastic and "effective method" is human sacrifice. Wars have to be won in order to keep the gods of the city supplied with the blood of conquered victims. The dead also demand the blood of the living. This is the answer of Minerva justifying the war of Troy (Simone Weil). Once you have four dead heroes you have four unanswerable reasons why a whole army must shed its blood until the enemy is destroyed and the heroes are avenged. Urban culture is then committed to war "as to the elixir of sovereign power and the most effective purgation of sovereign discontent with that power" (Mumford).

We live, of course, in the most advanced of all urban cultures.

✝ ✝ ✝

Czeslaw Milosz has sent some of his translations of Zbigniew Herbert—a fantastically good poet—along with a letter in which he challenges me on my love of nature, my optimistic attitude toward it, my not reflecting how cruel nature is, and so on. In other words, he thinks I am not Manichaean enough: do I have a right at a time like this to be, (or to imagine myself), immune to certain poisons? (Others are convinced that I am too Manichaean, but I have never taken them seriously.)

Should I really experience nature as *alien* and *heartless*? Should I be prepared to imagine that this alienation from nature is real, and that an attitude of sympathy, of oneness with it, is only imaginary? On the contrary—we have a choice of projections. Our attitude toward nature is simply an extension of our attitude toward ourselves, and toward one another. We are free to be at peace with ourselves and others, and also with nature.

Or are we?

There is this problem: it was the swine in the SS who most loved nature, and who turned to "her" as a relief from their orgies, to keep themselves, after all, human in the midst of the hell they had created for themselves by creating it for others. They would torture others, and then turn around and be at peace with nature! The problem is this: that since in fact it is those who are most beastly who often tend to speak in the simplest and most innocent terms of the happiness of life, does it follow that one should not permit himself to be happy in such a time as ours, because the mere fact of enjoying life, or any aspect of life, automatically puts one in connivance with those who are systematically ruining it?

In any case, there is certainly a trite and completely false naturalism that is part of the totalitarian myth—or simply part of the mentality of mass society (campers, national parks, driving to the beach, etc., etc.). But does that mean that one cannot retain any claim to honesty and authenticity without making a cult of the ugly, the irrelevant?

Sartre's meditation on the root in *La Nausée* seems to me to be just as forced and just as trite as any romantic effusion of Lamartine on a moonlit landscape . . . just as pitiable as the cry of a kid on the waterfront promenade at Bouville when the lighthouse turned on: this cry which made the hero of *La Nausée* turn in disgust from the Sunday crowd.

(Where I meet Roquentin, the dour hero of *La Nausée*, is in the cafe, listening to "Some of These Days!" Here I identify with him. I wonder if Sartre realized the full impact of this voice of the distant Negro singer *abolishing* the absolute loneliness of Roquentin by making it universal and showing it to be shared by all!)

✦ ✦ ✦

I wonder if it is a sin against poverty to read St. John Perse. His poems abound in all kinds of magnificence, in every sort of rich words. To read such poems is to live and move in splendor. Your heart becomes a tropical palace, opening out on the seven seas and all the continents, with spice ships coming to you from everywhere, and the soft voices of the Antilles speaking from the heart of the sun.

✦ ✦ ✦

The democratic primaries are coming up. There is a man running for jailer who ought to know the job well. He has been in jail four times as a moonshiner. He is a "good Catholic" too. Everything recommends him for the office.

✦ ✦ ✦

Flycatchers, shaking their wings after the rain.

✦ ✦ ✦

This morning there was a theological conference in Chapter. Father A—— came slowly out with a dignity befitting his years and, after a very long silence, began reading what he had written on the backs of envelopes. As the general tittering subsided and everyone sank into a blank, clock-watching resignation, Father A—— went on persistently and almost unintelligibly, developing his chosen theme. I settled back, got myself sitting straight, and started some yoga breathing. Five or six pranayamas. Some square breathing, then concentrated on the stream of air entering my nostrils and followed it in and out of the lungs. The time passed painlessly enough with this and the Jesus prayer. At the end, however, when Father A—— got his envelopes back together again and returned to his place, instead of getting out of there as fast as we decently could we had to sit through a question period. Everyone was so mad that there were very few questions, except one from Father B——, who complained that Father A—— had not quoted from any of the Fathers of the Church. I had not been struck by this oversight myself, and cannot say that I cared. Then Father C—— got up and read two or three authoritative declarations of Councils, Popes, etc., and Father D——, the moderator, as usual, said that the conference was really very good, but he added that he had hoped it would be longer. In any normal gathering this statement would have been unpopular enough to merit boos and catcalls, if not a near riot. We just stood up and chanted the De Profundis.

If you ask me, that was significant enough!

✓ ✓ ✓

A satanic theology—which Rimbaud had learned somewhere, and France and Belgium used to be full of it—hides Christ from us altogether, and makes Him so impossibly beautiful that He must remain infinitely remote from our wretchedness.

"He was a man like you and me: or rather He was a man, but *not like you,* because He was 'The God-Man.' If He suffered, it was almost as if He only seemed to suffer, because He could stop suffering when He wished (which *you* cannot do!) and because even in His suffering He had the beatific vision. God can cheat like that and get away with it. But *you* can't get away with anything.

"On the contrary: His suffering has become *your* condemnation to suffer without reprieve. All sorts of authorities can now point to the Cross as the ultimate reason why you should submit to arbitrary punishment now and forever! Please do not protest or contradict! To do so is now blasphemy!

"He knew He was God. He knew He was *not like you.* He thought of this and was secretly pleased all the time. He thought: I am God, I am *not like them*." (As if He had never preached the parable of the Pharisee and the publican. It is Satan's theology to make Christ the most perfect of all the Pharisees, so that the publicans will all despair while the Pharisees will come to Him and be confirmed in their self-righteousness.)

"All His life long, then, He was looking around at the men He had come to save, knowing He was *not like them*. Death could not hold Him. He did not really have to pray. He just pretended. And by pretending, He set a trap for man. He made all suffering final and inexorable!"

That is a tragedy of Rimbaud's meditations, the brave despair of one forever alienated by the beautiful, satanic hypocrisy of a gnostic incarnation! The despair of one who feels that to be poor and miserable is automatically to be damned: He accepts his poverty and misery fully, he empties himself, in full consciousness of what he is doing, because the only alternative is the self-deception of pretending to come close to the Beautiful Pure One Who is forever inaccessible! With only a little less contempt on his lips, Rimbaud would have the face of a saint, and who is to say what his heart was? Who will say that the bitterness was his fault?

"There is in Him no comeliness." Christ came on earth, not to wear the awful cold beauty of a holy statue, but to be numbered among the wicked, to die as one of them, condemned by the pure, He Who was beyond purity and impurity. If Christ is not really my brother with all my sorrows, with all my burdens on His shoulder and all my poverty and sadness in His heart, then there has been no redemption. Then what happened on the Cross was only magic, and the miracles were magic without purpose. We have trouble understanding the Albigensians? But the world is full of them, Rimbaud, Surrealists, Beats . . . not only poor Simone Weil! Whose fault, I wonder?

*✓ ✓ ✓*

Both in Malraux and in Orwell it is there—the obsession with immortality. You find it everywhere. Orwell comes out with it several times, in essays: He will say, in passing, that this is the "great question." Immortality. "The major problem of our day is the decay of the belief in personal immortality." Such are his words.

The Ministry of Truth has its own way of dealing with that question. Indeed, the great question, among totalitarians. And Berken, in Malraux's *Royal Way* (a poor book), seeking to remain immortal among dead cities in Cambodia!

*    *    *

Julien Green continually asks himself: can a novelist be a saint? Can a novelist save his soul? But perhaps the salvation of his soul depends precisely on his willingness to take that risk, and to be a novelist. And perhaps if he refused to challenge and accepted something that seemed to him more "safe," he would be lost. "He that will save his life must lose it."

*    *    *

I believe, with Diadochos of Photike, that if at the hour of my death my confidence in God's mercy is unfaltering, I will pass the frontier without trouble and get by the dreadful array of my sins as if they were not there, because of God's grace and the Precious Blood of Christ the Lamb of God, and the compunction He gives to the repentant. And I will, by His mercy, leave them behind forever.

*    *    *

"*Des hommes comme Saint Seraphim, Saint François d'Assise et bien d'autres, ont accompli dans leur vie l'union des Eglises.*"

This profound and simple statement of an Orthodox Metropolitan, Eulogius, gives the key to ecumenism for monks, and indeed for everyone.

If I do not have unity in myself, how can I even think, let alone speak, of unity among Christians? Yet, of course, in seeking unity for all Christians, I also attain unity within myself.

The heresy of individualism: thinking oneself a completely self-sufficient unit and asserting this imaginary "unity" against all others. The affirmation of the self as simply "not the other." But when you seek to affirm your unity by denying that you have anything to do with anyone else, by negating everyone else in the universe until you come down to *you*: what is there left to affirm? Even if there were something to affirm, you would have no breath left with which to affirm it.

The true way is just the opposite: the more I am able to affirm others, to say "yes" to them in myself, by discovering them in myself and myself in them, the more real I am. I am fully real if my own heart says *yes* to *everyone*.

I will be a better Catholic, not if I can *refute* every shade of Protestantism, but if I can affirm the truth in it and still go further.

So, too, with the Muslims, the Hindus, the Buddhists, etc. This does not mean syncretism, indifferentism, the vapid and careless friendliness that accepts everything by thinking of nothing. There is much that one cannot "affirm" and "accept," but first one must say "yes" where one really can.

If I affirm myself as a Catholic merely by denying all that is Muslim, Jewish, Protestant, Hindu, Buddhist, etc., in the end I will find that there is not much left for me to affirm as a Catholic: and certainly no breath of the Spirit with which to affirm it.

✓ ✓ ✓

I had been waiting for an opportunity to say Mass for Louis Massignon and for his project for African boys, under the patronage of Blessed Charles Lwanga. I happened in a curious and almost arbitrary manner to pick June 3d, and only today did I discover by accident that June 3d is the Feast of the Uganda Martyrs (and of Blessed Charles Lwanga among them). Meanwhile, Louis Massignon writes that nonviolence is mocked in Paris and opposed by the hierarchy.

✓ ✓ ✓

Festival of a martyr (Saint Antonin, September 2).

Through the martyr in whose town I knew thee, O Christ, whose sanctuary I did not enter, though as a child I danced at his festival.

Through the great merits of this martyr bring me to truth and to the suffering of reality, which is my joy.

Thy martyr, O Christ, has a deep green river, and a limestone bridge of unequal arches, reflected in the placid water.

Thy martyr, O Christ, has cliffs and woods, and, as I understand, no longer any train.

Sometimes, O Lord, I pray best to the saints, and sometimes best of all to this one who had a clarinet and a gramophone. (I was reproved for sticking my head into the horn of the gramophone, which was playing "Tea For Two" and not for one.) The people of the town, O Lord! They have not changed. The Germans probably did not come there, or not very much, though there must have been *maquis* in the forest where the wild boars once were, where we danced at the forester's wedding. Wine barrels, berets, *tabliers, l'accent du midi,* and singing in the stinking dark streets, walking slowly! (Watch your step by the old tannery!)

Thy martyr's town, O Lord, still walks at the pace of the ox cart.

Some charitable and some harsh, some beautiful and some ugly. The smell of the hair lotions from the barbershops, and of rabbit stewed in wine in many houses. How could I forget the people of this martyr, laughing over the wine glasses?

Or the girl in the dark dress, the solemn one, who served me beer in the Hotel Luffaut and told me: "Arnold Bennett slept here."

✓ ✓ ✓

For Marxian humanism, man does not yet exist. Man is alienated by the society he lives in. He does not yet know what he will be when he becomes himself. But alienated man must be wiped out, and then man as he really ought to be will come into existence.

It is both dangerous and easy to hate man as he is because he is not "what he ought to be." If we do not first respect what he *is* we will never suffer him to become what he ought to be: in our impatience we will do away with him altogether. Strange that Marx at first toyed with an idea of what man *is* and then rejected it, confessing the sin of "idealism": he had wasted time thinking about an "essence." For Communism, this is the great philosophical sin.

But if you deny man his essence, you refuse him at the same time the respect that is due to his existence. It is of little avail to deify man if at the same time you do not allow that he is real: if at the same time he remains simply a fluid nonentity, the shadow of the situations into which he is maneuvered by history. What matter if he takes charge of history if history, after all, really determines him anyway? If, in the end, he is only the reflection of his own work?

The great question, then, is the ambivalence of Marxian humanism.

*    *    *

Let us walk along here, says my shadow, and compose a number of sentences, each one of which begins: "You think you are a monk, but . . ."

*    *    *

Perhaps I am stronger than I think.

Perhaps I am even afraid of my strength, and turn it against myself, thus making myself weak. Making myself secure. Making myself guilty.

Perhaps I am most afraid of the strength of God in me. Perhaps I would rather be guilty and weak in myself, than strong in Him whom I cannot understand.

*    *    *

Beauty of sunlight falling on a tall vase of red and white carnations and green leaves on the altar of the novitiate chapel. The light and dark. The darkness of the fresh, crinkled flower: light, warm and red, all around the darkness. The flower is the same color as blood, but it is in no sense whatever "as red as blood." Not at all! It is as red as a carnation. Only that.

This flower, this light, this moment, this silence: *Dominus est.* Eternity. He passes. He remains. We pass. In and out. He passes. We remain. We are nothing. We are everything.

He is in us. He is gone from us. He is not here. We are here in Him.

All these things can be said, but why say them?

The flower is itself. The light is itself. The silence is itself. I am myself. All, perhaps, illusion. But no matter, for illusion is the shadow of reality and reality is the grace and gift that underlies all these lights, these colors, this silence. Underlies? Is that true? They are simply real. They themselves are His gift.

The simplicity that would have kept these flowers off this altar is perhaps less simple than the simplicity which enjoys them there, but does not need them to be there.

And for the rest, whatever is said about it is nothing.

✓ ✓ ✓

Louis Massignon is a man with a rare and important vocation: the dialogue with Islam. Not a dressed-up dialogue over teacups or on TV: but the dialogue as compassion, substitution, identification, taking upon himself the effects of what "our own" have done, knowingly or otherwise, to "them," whether in North Africa, the Near East, or anywhere else.

Better than anyone, Massignon understands the peculiar arrogance of an apostolate which, without seeking to understand in depth the meaning of *Tawhid*, bursts in upon the faith of the Muslim with the accusation that he is inferior, with the demand that he betray his highest conception of the purity and oneness of God the Holy: in favor of what we assert to be more holy. He thinks that we are trying to substitute something for the One God and persuade him that the One God is not yet holy enough! Small wonder that he does not betray a truth that, after all, we ourselves are supposed to die for.

✓ ✓ ✓

Heavy snow. It is a cold winter and there is a flu epidemic. There was one warm moment the other day after dinner, in which transient warmth I heard a song sparrow out in the fields beyond the enclosure wall. Sunlight played on the dead yellow grass in the Mill Bottom and lied that spring was coming. Not yet!

There is yellow grass all over the big dirt dam. Behind it, the dark and wooded wall of the Forty Acre Knob.

Flu. People stumble out of the night office and go back to bed. Indulgences in refectory. It is now beginning to get so bad that they are taking sick monks out of the dormitory and putting them, six or eight together, in the big rooms of the old guesthouse. One novice is sleeping in the novitiate typing room, where it is warm. A postulant arrived in the middle of the plague and immediately got it.

Brother Wilfrid, the assistant infirmarian, complains: "All Father Abbot can talk about is temperatures and eggs. I could set fire to the hen house and then we'd have plenty of both."

Room 5 in the old guesthouse is full of novices, therefore full of dissipation, pillow fights, and even some talking, so I am informed.

Brother Lawrence (Cardenal—the Nicaraguan poet) lies in bed with the blanket drawn up to his chin. Asked how he feels he smiles broadly and says: "Very bad."

Two brothers push a wagon up and down the long hall, bringing soup and fruit juice to the victims.

The other night they moved one of the novices, who snores, into a room with some professed. He woke up in the morning and looked around. All the other beds were empty. The wise and prudent had moved to the new guesthouse. Another, with the simplicity of the dove, had gone to sleep on the floor of the scriptorium.

Everyone says the Northern Lights were seen all over the sky early this morning (around three, when we were in choir).

✶ ✶ ✶

Looking out of the novitiate, when the winter sun is rising on the snowy pastures and on the pine woods of the Lake Knob, I am absorbed in the lovely blue and mauve shadows

on the snow and the indescribably delicate color of the sunlit
patches under the trees. All the life and color of the landscape is in the snow and sky, as if the soul of winter had
appeared and animated our world this morning. The green
of the pines is dull, verging on brown. Dead leaves still cling
to the oaks and they also are dull brown. The cold sky is very
blue. The air is dry and frozen. Instead of the mild, ambiva-
lent winter of Kentucky, I breathe again the rugged cold of
upstate New York.

Yang and Yin: the rock and earth, for Chinese artists,
would be *feminine*. The light and austerity of color in the
snow and sky, *masculine*. Yet there is a great deal of pastel
softness in the blue and purple shadows. There is no art that
has anything to say about this and art should not attempt it.
The Chinese came closest to it with their Tao of painting,
and what they painted was not landscapes but Tao. The
nineteenth-century European and American realists were so
realistic that their pictures were totally unlike what they were
supposed to represent. And the first thing wrong with them
was, of course, precisely that they were pictures. In any case,
nothing resembles reality less than the photograph. Nothing
resembles substance less than its shadow. To convey the
meaning of something substantial you have to use not a
shadow but a sign, not the imitation but the image. The
image is a new and different reality, and of course it does
not convey an impression of some object, but the mind of
the subject: and that is something else again.

Man is the image of God, not His shadow. At present, we
have decided that God is dead and that we are his shadow.
. . . Take a picture of that, Jack!

✓  ✓  ✓

A postulant from Colombia, who came to us from the Franciscan seminary, told me about his experiences when Rojas
Pinilla's troops were firing tear gas into the Church of the
Porciuncula in Bogota. Tanks in the crowded street. Crowds
surging out of the church and into the friars' enclosure, for
refuge, everyone of course in tears.

✓ ✓ ✓

Gabriel Marcel says that the artist who labors to produce effects for which he is well known is unfaithful to himself. This may seem obvious enough when it is badly stated: but how differently we act. We are all too ready to believe that the self that we have created out of our more or less inauthentic efforts to be real in the eyes of others is a "real self." We even take it for our identity. Fidelity to such a nonidentity is of course infidelity to our real person, which is hidden in mystery. Who will you find that has enough faith and self-respect to attend to this mystery and to begin by accepting himself as *unknown?* God help the man who thinks he knows all about himself.

✓ ✓ ✓

Today (February 14) is the Feast of the Cistercian hermit, Blessed Conrad—a great embarrassment to the entire Order. I would not be surprised if they did away with him, finally. He even bothered me a bit when I was a novice, and later when I was given the job of writing those absurd lives of saints that, thank God, never got published. Now I find that I have a great love for him. I even think I understand him a little. He is perhaps my favorite saint in the Order—a choice which can only be interpreted as very perverse.

I doubt if I even included him in the "lives" I wrote *in illo tempore.* He seemed to be an odd-ball and a failure. This, of course, is what almost any genuine hermit *must* seem, until such time as he becomes a completely impossible legend (or, more likely, is totally forgotten). Blessed Conrad apparently got nowhere: as if his life, a series of incomprehensible accidents, ended in midair. This last fact is taken, in desperation, by the breviary to justify what was in fact not comprehensible. "He was on his way home because he heard St. Bernard was dying." But of course he did not get home. He died on the way. "In a crypt." He was not even traveling, he was staying in this crypt. Outside Bari, in Italy. It was the people of Bari who venerated him, not the monks (until much later).

Blessed Conrad enjoys the unique distinction of being a monk of the Order who was *permitted by St. Bernard* to become a hermit. This is certainly, in itself, almost a miracle. In addition, it is thought that Blessed Conrad was one of the group that started out for the Holy Land with Abbot Arnold of Morimond, traditionally treated as an apostate. . . .

Obviously none of the really interesting and important things about Conrad are known, except that he was a hermit in Palestine for many years, and then returned, dying as a pilgrim hermit in a crypt outside Bari, dedicated to Our Lady.

But in any event, my Mass on his feast today was certainly festive and splendid. Sun poured in the novitiate chapel onto the altar and a glory of reflected lights from the hammered-silver chalice splashed all over the corporal and all around the Host. Deep and total silence. And the Gospel: "Fear not little flock . . ."

Those who love solitude have a special claim on Providence and must rely on God's love for them even more blindly than anyone else.

✓ ✓ ✓

Massignon has some deeply moving pages in the *Mardis de Dar-es-Salam*: About the desert, the tears of Agar, the Muslims, the *"point vierge"* of the spirit, the center of our nothingness where, in apparent despair, one meets God—and is found completely in His mercy.

✓ ✓ ✓

At the Little Sisters of the Poor in Louisville: the beauty of the Church is evident in the charity of her children, and especially her daughters.

The "Good Mother" is transparent, simple, of no age, both child and mother, and hence something like Mary. Perhaps the complicated names of nuns (which I can never remember) are in the end no names at all, as if nuns could not have names anyway. As if only God could know their names.

Yet how real they are as *persons!* How much more real (often enough) than people who have "big names" in the world. One does not need to idealize the Sisters. They have their problems. Often they have to struggle with a difficult "system." Yet their faith and their love give them greatness.

As for the old people: the beauty of the Church shines also in those who are helped and who have nothing to give except the fact that they can be helped: which is a great gift to the Church! It makes them most important in the Church. Thus, for instance: one old man playing the piano and another old man dancing. The one who danced was turning around and stamping the floor with one foot, apparently unaware that he no longer had the use of the muscles that make for tap dancing. The old man at the piano was banging away with a disastrous abandon and God knows what he was playing, though it was certainly better than rock 'n' roll.

One would certainly have to admit that it was antidancing accompanied by nonmusic. Nor would it be enough to say that one could approve it as a manifestation of "good will"—an expense of effort intended in some way *ad majorem Dei gloriam.* Better than that: I think God was glorified not by the intention, but by the nonmusic itself. Simply by what it was—as a concrete existential fact. Here is where the "beauty of the Church" comes to us: it was she who made this possible. At moments one gets a flash of Zen in the midst of the Church! There should, in reality, be much more. But we frustrate it by reasoning too much about everything.

The old Negro people were especially attractive: a sweet, dignified, and ancient Negro lady told me she had long worked for our doctor in New Haven (now dead). And another old, beat, Negro lady with wisps of white beard, sunk in her blank dream, slowly came out of it, out of some mental ocean, when spoken to. Another old lady who had both legs cut off (it sounds like the title of a child's weird story), and yet another old lady who still thought of herself as a little girl, curtsied and made a speech.

Then in this hierarchic world there were the girl auxiliaries, school girl volunteer helpers in blue and white uniforms, who sang a song about playing the piano and playing the violin and playing the triangle. One of them enters the postulancy this week. I wonder if she will stay.

✵    ✵    ✵

Here is an impressive statement from Vinoba Bhave, in his *Talks on the Gita*. "The action of the person who acts without desire should be much better than that of the person who acts with desire. This is only proper, for the latter is attracted to the fruit and part, much or little, of his time and attention will be spent on thoughts and dreams of the fruit. But all the time and all the strength of the man who has no desire for fruit is devoted to the action." This neatly disposes of the myth that "spirituality" is not practical! But perhaps what some people really mean by spirituality is "spiritual desire"— and that is a worse error than action driven by desire: the awful illusion of a supposed "contemplation" that is nothing but mute desire feeding on itself!

✵    ✵    ✵

There was once a certain Monsignor Hulst, who, before his death, is reported to have said something like this: "I have never denied God a moment of my time: I HOPE HE WILL TAKE THAT INTO ACCOUNT . . . !"

I was comforted to find almost the same thing on the lips of one of Job's friends, in the Bible de Jerusalem:

> Ta piété ne te donne-t-elle pas confiance,
> Ta vie intègre ne fait elle pas ton assurance?

What's the trouble, Job? Aren't you one of us?

I am thoroughly committed to the position that the words of Eliphas are a blasphemy. Even if I had done some good works to trust in, I would not want to trust in them.

✵    ✵    ✵

Julien Green says: "Religion is not understood. Those who wish themselves pious, in order to admire themselves in this state, are made stupid by religion. What is needed is to lose ourselves completely in God; what is needed is perfect silence, supernatural silence. Pious talk has something revolting about it."

There is precisely a revolt against this kind of "religion" even among the most earnest of present-day Christians. The word "religion" itself comes to be used equivocally, since it has been made profoundly ambiguous by religious people themselves.

"Religion," in the sense of something emanating from man's nature and tending to God, does not really change man or save him, but brings him into a false relationship with God: for a religion that starts in man is nothing but man's wish for himself. Man "wishes himself" (magically) to become godly, holy, gentle, pure, etc. His wish terminates not in God but in himself. This is no more than the religion of those who wish themselves to be in a certain state in which they can live with themselves, approve of themselves: for they feel that, when they can approve of themselves, God is at peace with them. How many Christians seriously believe that Christianity itself consists of nothing more than this? Yet it is anathema to true Christianity.

The whole meaning of Paul's anger with "the Law" and with "the elements of this world" is seen here. Such religion is not saved by good intentions: in the end it becomes a caricature. It must. For otherwise we would never see the difference between this and the "religion" which is born in us from God and which perhaps ought not to be called religion, born from the devastation of our trivial "self" and all our plans for "our self," even though they be plans for a holy self, a pure self, a loving, sacrificing self.

This is one of the deep problems that Eliot suggests at the end of *Murder in the Cathedral,* where Thomas is faced with the realization that he may be gladly admitting martyrdom into a political and religiously ambitious scheme for himself: punishing the wicked and making himself a saint by treading down his enemies, stepping upon their heads into heaven. It is in this sense that the fear of the Lord is the beginning of wisdom—and of true religion. This fear questions our own religiosity, our own ambition to be good. It begins to see with horror the complacency of speeches that "know all

about" piety, possess the right method of pleasing God and
infallibly winning Him over to our side, etc. This "fear" is
what imposes silence. It is the beginning of the "supernatural silence" Green asks for.

✐ ✐ ✐

Last night I was on the night watch. It rained heavily. Between rounds I went into the little shelter in the middle of
the cloister court, which is traditionally called by the French
name of *préau* here. Rain poured down on the walls of the
building, on the four big maples, on the roof of the shelter.
I was sleepy, and sat in the chair, nodding in the dark. Hanging on the edge of sleep I could hear the rain around me like
a huge aviary full of parrots: but just as the aviary became
"real" I would wake up, rescue myself from this strange
world of sound, until gradually I would fall into it again. I
did not fall asleep, because I could never sleep in a chair
anyway, no matter how the rain sounded, no matter how
inviting the strange universe of birds created by it!

✐ ✐ ✐

I had to go to Louisville to see about printing the new
postulants' guide. I was driven in by one of the neighbors, a
young man called Yvo who lives up the road and works at
the monastery. Interesting conversation—particularly on the
way home, for when we were in town he went to see "some
kin folks" and came away from them much more voluble
and lively than he had been before. His driving was even
more exciting. He zigzagged madly through traffic, jamming
on his brakes just in time to avoid climbing over the car in
front or flying through red lights. Meanwhile, of course, he
talked about the accidents that other drivers for the monastery have had. Joe Carrol, the family brother, had a historic
one at the bottom of the hill in High Grove, when the brakes
of a dump truck full of cement bags failed and he piled up in
the front yard of one of the houses. He was unhurt, but
entirely covered with cement. The punch line of the story
(which I remember because Yvo repeated it several times)

is the description by the lady of the house, of Joe sitting in the ruins of the truck:

> "He tried to whistle and he couldn't whistle.
> He tried to sing and he couldn't sing.
> He tried to talk and he couldn't talk.
> He couldn't do nothing and he looked like a nigger
>     with all that cement all over him."

I could not match the classic flavor of this with my lame account of Dom Frederic and Senator Dawson skidding off the road into a creek near Mount Washington. I wasn't there. Nobody was there but the angels. It happened in ice and fog when Dom Frederic was supposed to be going to New Melleray for the funeral or the installation of an abbot.

More of Yvo's oracles. Concerning Father Gettlefinger, the pastor in New Haven, he said: "When Father Gettlefinger works in that field he works like he was killing snakes."

Concerning, on the other hand, those who follow a golf ball around a golf course, he had this to say. On the way through Bardstown in the morning, Yvo expressed contempt for golfers, and as we passed the golf club, he said: "You wait, when we come back tonight, *they'll be there.*" Sure enough, when we came back in the evening, they were. "See," said Yvo triumphantly, *"there they are!"* It was as if he had fiercely and rightly predicted in the morning that by evening the town would be completely infiltrated by Communists.

✓ ✓ ✓

In Louisville, at the corner of Fourth and Walnut, in the center of the shopping district, I was suddenly overwhelmed with the realization that I loved all those people, that they were mine and I theirs, that we could not be alien to one another even though we were total strangers. It was like waking from a dream of separateness, of spurious self-isolation in a special world, the world of renunciation and supposed holiness. The whole illusion of a separate holy existence is a dream. Not that I question the reality of my vocation, or of my monastic life: but the conception of "separation from the world" that we have in the monastery too easily presents itself as a complete illusion: the illusion that by making vows we become a different species of being, pseudoangels, "spiritual men," men of interior life, what have you.

Certainly these traditional values are very real, but their reality is not of an order outside everyday existence in a contingent world, nor does it entitle one to despise the secular: though "out of the world" we are in the same world as everybody else, the world of the bomb, the world of race hatred, the world of technology, the world of mass media, big business, revolution, and all the rest. We take a different attitude to all these things, for we belong to God. Yet so does everybody else belong to God. We just happen to be conscious of it, and to make a profession out of this consciousness. But does that entitle us to consider ourselves different, or even *better*, than others? The whole idea is preposterous.

This sense of liberation from an illusory difference was such a relief and such a joy to me that I almost laughed out loud. And I suppose my happiness could have taken form in the words: "Thank God, thank God that I *am* like other men, that I am only a man among others." To think that for sixteen or seventeen years I have been taking seriously this pure illusion that is implicit in so much of our monastic thinking.

It is a glorious destiny to be a member of the human race, though it is a race dedicated to many absurdities and one which makes many terrible mistakes: yet, with all that, God Himself gloried in becoming a member of the human race. A member of the human race! To think that such a commonplace realization should suddenly seem like news that one holds the winning ticket in a cosmic sweepstake.

I have the immense joy of being *man*, a member of a race in which God Himself became incarnate. As if the sorrows and stupidities of the human condition could overwhelm me, now I realize what we all are. And if only everybody could realize this! But it cannot be explained. There is no way of telling people that they are all walking around shining like the sun.

This changes nothing in the sense and value of my solitude, for it is in fact the function of solitude to make one realize such things with a clarity that would be impossible to anyone completely immersed in the other cares, the other illusions, and all the automatisms of a tightly collective existence. My solitude, however, is not my own, for I see now how much it belongs to them—and that I have a responsibility for it in their regard, not just in my own. It is because I am one with them that I owe it to them to be alone, and when I am alone they are not "they" but my own self. There are no strangers!

Then it was as if I suddenly saw the secret beauty of their hearts, the depths of their hearts where neither sin nor desire nor self-knowledge can reach, the core of their reality, the person that each one is in God's eyes. If only they could all see themselves as they really *are*. If only we could see each other that way all the time. There would be no more war, no more hatred, no more cruelty, no more greed. . . . I suppose the big problem would be that we would fall down and worship each other. But this cannot be *seen*, only believed and "understood" by a peculiar gift.

Again, that expression, *le point vierge*, (I cannot translate it) comes in here. At the center of our being is a point of nothingness which is untouched by sin and by illusion, a point of pure truth, a point or spark which belongs entirely to God, which is never at our disposal, from which God disposes of our lives, which is inaccessible to the fantasies of our own mind or the brutalities of our own will. This little point of nothingness and of *absolute poverty* is the pure glory of God in us. It is so to speak His name written in us, as our poverty, as our indigence, as our dependence, as our sonship. It is like a pure diamond, blazing with the invisible light of heaven. It is in everybody, and if we could see it we would see these billions of points of light coming together in the face and blaze of a sun that would make all the darkness and cruelty of life vanish completely. . . . I have no program for this seeing. It is only given. But the gate of heaven is everywhere.

✓ ✓ ✓

Palm Sunday.

Father John of the Cross is one of the few men in this monastery who have anything to say in a sermon. When it is his turn to preach, everybody listens. What he preaches is really the Gospel, not words about the Gospel or knowledge of the Gospel, or yet knowledge of Christ. It is one thing to preach Christ, another to preach that one knows Christ. I know the integrity of this man is very costly to him. He suffers very much in order to be true to his own heart, that is to the heart which God has given him, and which has in it a mysterious command that no one here is able to understand.

Will he be disloyal to this heart? Some will try to make him disloyal, in the name of other kinds of loyalty with which they themselves are more at home: the more comfortable kind. Since in any case he is true to the command that is in him (the command that most of us spend our lives trying not to hear) he does not betray the truth by fitting it into popular and easy formulas. Nor does he trifle with it in any way, to win people to himself in order that they may then hear "his truth." It is not "his" truth that he is preaching, it is just truth.

Speaking of friendship with Christ, he said that in all friendship there is first a stage at which we see the acts of our friend and come, by them, to know who he is. But after we have come to know who he is, then we see his acts differently, only in the light of *who he is*. Then even acts that would otherwise disconcert us and would seem ambiguous in themselves are accepted because we know who he is. The transition point comes when we know the inmost desires of our friend's heart. So, in the Passion of Jesus and in His apparent failure, His yielding to destruction, when He could have saved Himself: the inmost desire of His Heart is to love the Father and to be about the Father's business. Therefore we do not need to know and understand all about the Cross, the Kingdom or the way to the Kingdom. What we need to know is the inmost desire in the heart of Christ, which is that we should come to the Kingdom with Him. He alone knows the way, which is that of the Cross. I would perhaps add, on my own, that the inmost desire in the heart of Christ makes itself somehow present in us in the form of that little point of nothingness and poverty in us which is the "point" or virgin eye by which we know Him!

✓ ✓ ✓

Holy Thursday evening, after the evening Mass and Communion, I was standing in the novitiate garden looking at the gray skies and the hills, when the Colombian postulant came up behind me and said in Spanish that the view without doubt offered poetic inspiration, to which I readily agreed. We talked a little about climates, earthquakes, and what-not, and the "terrible cliffs" along some of the roads in Colombia. (I have heard of them, in Caldas, for example. You look over into the canyons and see the ruins of cars and trucks five hundred feet below.)

Then a moment later he said: "Why would not you, Father Merton, leave here and come to South America and start a totally new kind of monastic order, one that would appeal more to men of modern times?"

I could not tell him how much I would like to try it, or how impossible it would be to make any such attempt without leaving the Order, and how impossible it would be for me to try to leave the Order.

✓ ✓ ✓

I suppose this is a platitude by now, and one that would irritate many: but it represents the area where I disagree with Barth, for instance. I am aware that the Easter Vigil retains many vestiges of primitive nature rites, and I am glad of it. I think this is perfectly proper and Christian. The mystery of fire, the mystery of water. The mystery of spring—*Ver sacrum*. Fire, water, spring, made sacred and explicit by the Resurrection, which finds in them symbols that point to itself. The old creation is made solely for the new creation. The new creation (of life out of death) springs from the old, even though the pattern of the old is the falling away of life in death.

Instead of stamping down the force of the new life rising in us by our very nature (and so turning it into Leviathan, the dragon in the unsanctified waters), let the new life be sweetened, sanctified by the bitterness of the Cross, which destroys death in the waters and makes the waters the laver of life. Water then becomes the dwelling not of Leviathan but of the spirit of life. We are no longer marked like Cain, but signed with the Blood of the Paschal Lamb.

✓ ✓ ✓

A visiting abbot declared in Chapter that the contemplative life consisted in clinging by main force to an idea one had on entering the novitiate. An incredible statement: I mean, incredible that such a statement could be seriously proposed by such a person and in such a place. No one seems to have felt there was anything strange about it. The mere concept of *effort* justifies everything. It doesn't matter what you do so long as you work at it with all your might—I almost said work like the devil.

✓ ✓ ✓

*Audite et intelligite traditiones quas Deus dedi vobis.* There are traditions which God has given us. They are so to speak a *memory* we are born with and into which we are born: a store of meanings, of symbols, of signs. What is born in us is the connatural ability to understand these great buried signs as soon as they are manifested to us. What is given us in society is a more or less authentic manifestation of the signs. If society loses its "memory," if it forgets its language of traditional symbol, then the individuals who make it up become neurotic, because their own memories are corrupted by uninterpreted, unused meanings. Then traditions themselves become mere dead conventions—worse than that, obsessions—collective neuroses. To replace one set of conventions with another, however new, does nothing to revive a truly living sense of meaning and of life. This is our present condition.

✓ ✓ ✓

Saints of the fifteenth century.

In the collapse of medieval society, amid the corruption of the clergy and the decadence of conventual life, there arose men and women of the laity who were *perfectly obedient to God*. Nicholas of Flue, for instance, and Joan of Arc. They were simple and straightforward signs of contradiction in the middle of worldliness, prejudice, cruelty, despair, and greed. They were *not rebels* at all. They were meek and submissive instruments of God who, while being completely opposed to the corrupt norms around them, gave every man and every authority his due. They show clearly and convincingly what it is to be not a rebel, but obedient to God as a sign to men—a sign of mercy, a revelation of truth and power. We are spontaneously drawn to these signs of God with all the love of our hearts. We naturally trust them, believe in their intercession, knowing that they live on in the glory of God and that God would not give us such love for them if they were not still "sacraments" of His mercy to us.

✓ ✓ ✓

"For what, in that world gigantic horror, was tolerable except the slighter gestures of dissent?" So wrote E. M. Forester discussing his satisfaction on reading the early Eliot during World War I.

World War I, that distant, relatively civilized war, in which it took weeks to mobilize the armies, in which it was not yet possible to annihilate entire civilian populations with firestorms and TNT . . . yet that was already and very truly a "gigantic horror." The horror we have come to know in the forty years since then, the even greater horror we have come to anticipate, has made the World War I seem like a very tame brawl.

"The slighter gestures of dissent." For anything slight, we have now only contempt. Indeed dissent itself has come to look like crime, madness, or at least subversion.

Even those strange ones who still see fit to dissent, tend to think now that massive protest is more valid. Yet the more massive a movement is, the more it is doctored and manipulated. The more it tends to be a mass lie, a front. As if protest itself were useless unless supported and patronized by some inhuman power.

Genuine dissent must always keep a human measure. It must be free and spontaneous. The slighter gestures are often the more significant, because they are unpremeditated and they cannot be doctored beforehand by the propagandist.

And so perhaps it is saner and nobler to expect effective protest from the individual, from the small unsponsored group, than from the well-organized mass movement. It is better that the "slighter gestures" never find their way into the big papers or onto the pages of the slick magazines. It is better not to line up with the big, manipulated group.

True, he who dissents alone may confine his dissent to words, to declarations, to attitudes, to symbolic gestures. He may fail to act. Gestures are perhaps not enough. They are perhaps too slight.

On the other hand what seems to be "action" on the mass scale may be nothing more than a political circus, or an organized disaster. Such action is often nothing more than the big absurd lie, the blown-up puerility which, by its own emptiness, ends in a cataclysm of frustration and destructive rage.

Against the empty and debased rhetoric of the giant demonstration, even the smallest, genuine idea, the slightest of sincere and honest protests is not only tolerable but to be admired.

(All this is to be qualified in view of the spontaneous, very effective, very telling power of the Civil Rights movement in America. The thing that it is *not* is what its enemies claim that it is—a front for Communism.)

✶ ✶ ✶

I have great admiration for the simple, austere, Russian figure of Staretz Sylvan, who died on Mount Athos in 1938. He had been a monk of the Rossikon, or St. Panteleimon, since 1892.

He was a tall man with a shaggy beard, and a true Hesychast, avid for solitude and for prayer, humble, outwardly ordinary, a hard worker—in fact he was "steward," or cellarer, of his monastery and had two hundred workmen under him. He identified himself with them in all their troubles and sorrows. They were very aware of this and loved him deeply. His compassion for them was an element in his recollection and in his interior silence. He said: "I became steward as an act of obedience blessed by the Abbot, so I pray better at my task than I prayed at the Old Rossikon [where he had a solitary hut] where I asked to go for the sake of interior silence. If the soul loves and pities the people, prayer is not interrupted."

—from *The Undistorted Image*, biography of Staretz Sylvan, by Archimandrite Sophrony

In his inner conflicts and sorrows he found a strange answer and a still stranger way of prayer. The Lord said to him: "Keep thy soul in hell and despair not." At first it sounds a bit dreadful, or perhaps at best eccentric. Yet to me it is in a strange way comforting. Men still share deeply and silently the anguish of Christ abandoned by His Father (to be abandoned by God is to be "in hell") and they "despair not." How much better and saner it is to face despair and not give in than to work away at keeping up appearances and patching up our conviction that a bogus spirituality is real! That we are not really facing dread! That we are all triumphantly advancing "getting somewhere" (where?), accomplishing great things for Christ, and changing the face of the world!

We can still choose between the way of Job and the way of Job's friends, and we have to have the sense (I say sense, not courage) to choose the way of Job: it takes far more than courage to start out on a way that obviously leads to the far end of nothing, and to walk over the abyss of our own absurdity in order to be found and saved by God, who has called us to walk that way. It takes sense to see that if He calls us, it is the only way. As to courage, He will provide: and of course He will provide it more in the form of *hope* than as plain fortitude. We must not expect to glance at ourselves and see "courage," and take comfort from this. Christ alone, on the Cross and in darkness, but already victorious, is our comfort.

✓   ✓   ✓

"The saints," said Bernanos, "are not resigned, at least in the sense that the world thinks. If they suffer in silence those injustices which upset the mediocre, it is in order better to turn against injustice, against its face of brass, all the strength of their great souls. Angers, daughters of despair, creep and twist like worms. Prayer is, all things considered, the only form of revolt that stays standing up."

This is very true from all points of view. A spirituality that preaches resignation under official brutalities, servile acquiescence in frustration and sterility, and total submission to organized injustice is one which has lost interest in holiness and remains concerned only with a spurious notion of "order." On the other hand, it is so easy to waste oneself in the futilities of that "anger, the daughter of despair," the vain recrimination that takes a perverse joy in blaming everyone else for our failure. We may certainly fail to accomplish what we believed was God's will for us and for the Church: but simply to take revenge by resentment against those who blocked the way is not to turn the strength on one's soul (if any) against the "brass face of injustice." It is another way of yielding to it.

There may be a touch of stoicism in Bernanos' wording here, but that does not matter. A little more stoic strength would not hurt us, and would not necessarily get in the way of grace!

✓   ✓   ✓

Steinmann's book on St. Jerome is interesting and well done, but I am sick of Jerome, sick of his querulous sensitivity, his rage, his politics. And I am sick of Steinmann's anti-Origenism. It is too insistent. I am for John Chrysostom, and especially for Rufinus. These are quarrels about which no monk can be indifferent. We are all implicated in their absurdity.

✓ ✓ ✓

Music is being played to the cows in the milking barn. Rules have been made and confirmed: only sacred music is to be played to the cows, not "classical" music. The music is to make the cows give more milk. The sacred music is to keep the brothers who work in the cow barn recollected. For sometime now sacred music has been played to the cows in the milking barn. They have not given more milk. The brothers have not been any more recollected than usual. I believe the cows will soon be hearing Beethoven. Then we shall have classical, perhaps worldly milk and the monastery will prosper. (Later: It was true. The hills resounded with Beethoven. The monastery has prospered. The brother mainly concerned with the music, however, departed.)

✓ ✓ ✓

If you call one thing vile and another precious, if you praise success and blame failure, you will fill the world with thieves, soldiers, and businessmen. I have praised the saints and I have told at what cost they strove to surpass lesser men. What madness have I not preached in sermons!

✓ ✓ ✓

Is Christian ethics merely a specific set of Christian answers to the question of good and evil, right and wrong? To make it no more than this is to forget that man's fall was a fall *into* the knowledge of good and evil, reinforced by the inexorable knowledge of a condemning law, and that man's restoration in Christ is a restoration to freedom and grace, to a love that needs no law since it knows and does only what is in accord with love and with God. To imprison ethics in the realm of division, of good and evil, right and wrong, is to condemn it to sterility, and rob it of its real reason for existing, which is *love*. Love cannot be reduced to one virtue among many others prescribed by ethical imperatives. When love is only "a virtue" among many, man forgets that "God is love" and becomes incapable of that all-embracing love by which we secretly begin to know God as our Creator and

Redeemer—who has saved us from the limitations of a purely restrictive and aimless existence "under a law."

So Bonhoeffer says very rightly: "In the knowledge of good and evil man does not understand himself in the reality of the destiny appointed in his origin, but rather in his own possibilities, his possibility of being good or evil. He knows himself now as something apart from God, outside God, and this means that he now knows only himself and no longer knows God at all. . . . The knowledge of good and evil is therefore separation from God. Only against God can man know good and evil."

It is clear that an exclusively *ethical* emphasis on right and wrong, good and evil, in Christian education, *breeds doubt and not faith.* The more we insist that Catholicism must consist in the avoidance of sin (especially in the realm of sex), in "being good" and in doing one's duty, the more we make it difficult for men to really believe, and the more we make faith into a mental and spiritual problem, contingent on a certain ethical achievement. The only way faith continues to be humanly possible in such a situation is for it to be understood as a virtue and duty among other virtues and duties. One believes because one is *told to believe,* not because of a living and life-giving aspiration to know the living God. Faith itself becomes shot through with an existential doubt which, nevertheless, one ignores out of duty, while going about one's business of avoiding evil and doing good.

The tension generated by this struggle of doubt and duty eventually seeks a natural release in crusades and in the persecution of heretics, in order that we may prove ourselves "good" and "right" by judging and condemning evil and error in those who are unlike ourselves.

Existentialist ethics, while trying to escape the iron necessity of objective duty imposed by the ethic of law and of good and evil, simply pushes the logic of the fall to its further conclusion. To know good and evil is to know oneself as the subject of choice confronted with indefinite possibilities. The possibilities are meaningless; good and evil are fictitious; all that remains is the subject as the source and origin of his own choices. It is the honesty and authenticity of *the choice* that endows our possibilities with a semblance of "good" (if one would take the trouble to call it that).

The resentment of (atheist) existentialism against the frustrating limits and obstacles imposed by a legalist ethic still imparts no freedom. It tries to transcend good and evil, but it is imprisoned in its own spurious transcendence. *Choice cannot be free from the frustrating, tormenting division between good and evil. Hence subjective choice cannot be an absolute.* There is no way of understanding freedom as long as it is seen only as the power to choose between good and evil. And if one abolishes good and evil, in order to make freedom simply the power to choose, then the difficulty is further compounded by ambiguity and mystification.

✓ ✓ ✓

Then we come around in a full circle: in bourgeois society, the good and respectable were considered *ipso facto* justified. Now it is considered quite sufficient to stand Protestantism on its head and to speak as if all one needed to be justified was to be wicked: the sicker, the more unfaithful, the more revolting your life is, the more justified you are. Thus Sartre's Protestantism in reverse canonizes the good thief Genet since the ability to canonize good thieves puts one automatically in the position of an admittedly secular Christ. This is very entertaining and no one begrudges Sartre his jokes at the expense of conventional Christianity. But things begin to complicate themselves when conventional Christianity itself adopts the gospel of Sartre, and goes around singing that God is dead, alleluia, that we are all alone in the world, that we might as well make the best of it, smoke pot and make our own rules. That is just it: a new set of rules, which we ourselves have decreed! A whole new canon of respectability, a whole new human system of justification, a new ethic that is easy to learn because all it asks is that where the squares say "yes" you say "no" and vice versa.

✓ ✓ ✓

The religious genius of the Protestant Reformation, as I see it, lies in its struggle with the problem of justification in all its depth. The great Christian question is the conversion of man and his restoration to the grace of God in Christ. And this question, in its simplest form, is that of the conversion of the wicked and the sinful to Christ. But Protestantism raised this same question again in its *most radical form*—how about the much more difficult and problematic conversion, that of the pious and the good? It is relatively easy to convert the sinner, but the good are often completely unconvertible simply because they do not see any need for conversion.

Thus the genius of Protestantism focused from the beginning on the ambiguities contained in "being good" and "being saved" or "belonging to Christ." For conversion to Christ is not merely the conversion from bad habits to good habits, but *nova creatura,* becoming a totally new man in Christ and in the Spirit. Obviously the works and habits of the new man will correspond with his new being. There is nothing un-Catholic in this, quite the contrary. Yet Catholic perspectives, in emphasizing good works, sometimes lead to a neglect of the new being, life in Christ, life in the Spirit. And when Protestantism is unfaithful to its gift, it first plays down even the "new being" and the radical depth of conversion, in order to emphasize the pure grace and gift of Christ's pardon (hence we remain essentially wicked), or else, later, forgetting the seriousness of the need to convert the good, bogs down in the satisfied complacency of a rather superficial and suburban goodness—the folksy togetherness, the handshaking fellowship, the garrulous witness of moral platitudes. (In this of course Protestants are often outdistanced by the more complex and sometimes more vulgar inanities of the "good Catholic.")

Here is where *fides sola* may have proved to be dangerous. For the faith that justifies is not just any faith, or even the faith that, at revival time, *feels* itself justified. In the end an insufficient faith is not belief in Christ and obedience to His word, but only a question of believing we believe because we are found acceptable in the eyes of other believers. What matters then is to cultivate this quality of acceptance in a sociological milieu, and then (as in the deep South) even objectively unjust works can be counted virtuous and Christian, since they are approved by those who are locally certified as "good." Truly the great problem is the salvation of those who, being good, think they have no further need to be saved and imagine their task is to make others "good" like themselves!

Those who are faithful to the original grace (I should not say genius) of Protestantism are precisely those who, in all depth, see as Luther saw that the "goodness" of the good may in fact be the greatest religious disaster for a society, and that the crucial problem is the *conversion of the good to Christ*. Kierkegaard sees it, so does Barth, so does Bonhoeffer, so do the Protestant existentialists.

As a Catholic I firmly hold of course to what the Church teaches on justification and grace. One cannot be justified by a faith that does not do the works of love, for love is the witness and evidence of "new being" in Christ. But precisely this love is primarily the work of Christ in me, not simply something that originates in my own will and is then approved and rewarded by God. It is faith that opens my heart to Christ and His Spirit, that He may work in me. No work of mine can be called "love" in the Christian sense, unless it comes from Christ. But "the good" are solely tempted to believe in their own goodness and their own capacity to love, while one who realizes his own poverty and nothingness is much more ready to surrender himself entirely to the gift of love *he knows* cannot come from anything in himself.

It is with this in mind that I will, in the next section, consider the ambiguities of "doing good," knowing that when one is firmly convinced of his own rightness and goodness, he can without qualm perpetrate the most appalling evil. After all, it was the righteous, the holy, the "believers in God" who crucified Christ, and they did so in the name of righteousness, holiness, and even of God (John 10:32).

Note that one of the deep psychological motives of Christian anti-Semitism is, I believe, an attempt to evade this. The Gospel teaches us precisely that human holiness and goodness alone do not prevent us from betraying God and that the "good men" who crucified Christ are the paradigm of all the "good" whose "goodness" is merely a fidelity to ethical prescriptions. But to evade the implications of this we have changed it to read as follows: Christ was crucified by wicked and unbelieving men who loved sin precisely because they were Jews and cursed by God. This overlooks the following facts: the Jews were and remain the people especially chosen and loved by God. The Pharisees were austere and virtuous men who devoted themselves with great energy to doing good as they saw it. They devoutly studied the word of God with deep concern about the coming of the Messiah.

Anti-Semitism conveniently helps the Christian who thinks himself austere, virtuous, concerned with doing good and obeying God, etc., to avoid every occasion of realizing that he may himself be the exact replica of the Pharisee. When will we learn that "being good" may easily mean having the mentality of a "Christ-killer?"

✓  ✓  ✓

One thing above all is important: the "return to the Father."

The Son came into the world and died for us, rose and ascended to the Father; sent us His Spirit, that in Him and with Him we might return to the Father.

That we might pass clean out of the midst of all that is transitory and inconclusive: return to the Immense, the Primordial, the Source, the Unknown, to Him Who loves and knows, to the Silent, to the Merciful, to the Holy, to Him Who is All.

To seek anything, to be concerned with anything but this is only madness and sickness, for this is the whole meaning and heart of all existence, and in this all the affairs of life, all the needs of the world and of men, take on their right significance: all point to this one great return to the Source.

All goals that are not ultimate, all "ends of the line" that we can see and plan as "ends," are simply absurd, because they do not even begin. The "return" is the end beyond all ends, and the beginning of beginnings.

To "return to the Father" is not to "go back" in time, to roll up the scroll of history, or to reverse anything. It is a going forward, a going beyond, for merely to retrace one's steps would be a vanity on top of vanity, a renewal of the same absurdity in reverse.

Our destiny is to go on beyond everything, to leave everything, to press forward to the End and find in the End our Beginning, the ever-new Beginning that has no end.

To obey Him on the way, in order to reach Him in whom I have begun, who is the key and the end—because He is the Beginning.

✓ ✓ ✓

The optimistic radicalism of the thirties is dead and buried and judged. It is most important to realize this, for an attempt to recapture the illusion at the present moment would certainly be disastrous. We cannot forget the mistakes of FDR. Yet at the same time there is a new radicalism and a new optimism which has gone beyond the fears and fanaticisms of the McCarthy era and is breaking through to new areas of dialogue and concern. It is a radicalism that is far less doctrinaire, less concerned with sweeping political programs, more intent on certain immediate practical ends, especially civil rights and disarmament. There is a new generation and a new spirit here, and perhaps it will turn out to have been much more serious and much more effective than anything I can remember from my own youth. I think this new radicalism may be the decisive force and hope of the sixties—or it may simply be the catalyst that will bring on our transformation into something very disagreeable and stupid, a permanently organized warfare state, blind and dedicated to the forceful resolution of imaginary problems.

✓ ✓ ✓

We have been putting off, rather than solving, the problem of the hideous tabernacle in the novitiate chapel by hiding it under a veil (which the Cistercian Ritual frowns on). I also spirited away the square nightclubish candle holders. And I am afraid Frank Kacmarcik is right: our walnut altar does look a bit like a bar. I am afraid the new tabernacle veil is too jazzy, with its Matisse foliage (in brown). But in general the chapel is simple and even austere. I am glad to feel that it now looks *only a little* vulgar. It used to look like an ecclesiastical pawnshop.

✓ ✓ ✓

Father S——, who had to go to the doctor in Louisville, came back with a clipping about a man out in the Kentucky mountains, an old coal miner who, for thirteen years, has lived as a hermit with his dog in a pitiful little shack without even a chimney. He used an old car seat for his bed. When he was asked why he chose to live such a life he replied: "Because of all these wars." A real desert father, perhaps. And probably not too sure how he got there.

✓ ✓ ✓

Reading Chuang Tzu, I wonder seriously if the wisest answer (on the human level, apart from the answer of faith) is not beyond both ethics and politics. It is a hidden answer, it defies analysis and cannot be embodied in a program. Ethics and politics, of course: but only in passing, only as a "night's lodging." There is a time for action, a time for "commitment," but never for total involvement in the intricacies of a movement. There is a moment of innocence and *kairos*, when action makes a great deal of sense. But who can recognize such moments? Not he who is debauched by a series of programs. And when all action has become absurd, shall one continue to act simply because once, a long time ago, it made a great deal of sense? As if one were always getting somewhere? There is a time to listen, in the active life as everywhere else, and the better part of action is waiting, not knowing what next, and not having a glib answer.

✓ ✓ ✓

Brother G——, a postulant who has come to the end of his rope and wants to leave, but who has been dissuaded (not by me), stands in the novitiate library leafing through a book called *Relax and Live*. Sooner or later it comes to that.

✓ ✓ ✓

A basic temptation: the flatly unchristian refusal to love those whom we consider, for some reason or other, unworthy of love. And, on top of that, to consider others unworthy of love for even very trivial reasons. Not that we hate them of course: but we just refuse to accept them in our hearts, to treat them without suspicion and deal with them without inner reservations. In a word, we reject those who do not please us. We are of course "charitable toward them." An interesting use of the word "charity" to cover and to justify a certain coldness, suspicion, and even disdain. But this is punished by another inexorable refusal: we are bound by the logic of this defensive rejection to reject any form of happiness that even implies acceptance of those we have decided to reject. This certainly complicates life, and if one is sufficiently intolerant, it ends by making all happiness impossible.

This means that we have to get along without constantly applying the yardstick of "worthiness" (who is worthy to be loved, and who is not). And it almost means, by implication, that we cease to ask even indirect questions about who is "justified," who is worthy of acceptance, who can be tolerated by the believer! What a preposterous idea that would be! And yet the world is full of "believers" who find themselves entirely surrounded by people they can hardly be expected to "tolerate," such as Jews, Negroes, unbelievers, heretics, Communists, pagans, fanatics, and so on.

God is asking of me, the unworthy, to forget my unworthiness and that of all my brothers, and dare to advance in the love which has redeemed and renewed us all in God's likeness. And to laugh, after all, at all preposterous ideas of "worthiness."

✓ ✓ ✓

The basic sin, for Christianity, is rejecting others in order to choose oneself, deciding *against* others and deciding *for* oneself. Why is this sin so basic? Because the idea that you can choose yourself, approve yourself, and then offer yourself (fully "chosen" and "approved") to God, applies the assertion of yourself over against God. From this root of error comes all the sour leafage and fruitage of a life of self-examination, interminable problems and unending decisions, always making right choices, walking on the razor edge of an impossibly subtle ethic (with an equally subtle psychology to take care of the unconscious). All this implies the frenzied conviction that one can be his own light and his own justification, and that God is there for a purpose: to issue the stamp of confirmation upon my own rightness. In such a religion the Cross becomes meaningless except as the (blasphemous) certification that because you suffer, because you are misunderstood, you are justified twice over—you are a martyr. Martyr means witness. You are then a witness? To what? To your own infallible light and your own justice, which you have *chosen*.

This is the exact opposite of everything Jesus ever did or taught.

✓ ✓ ✓

Hitler regarded the power of his madness as a divine power because he felt inspired. The Communists regard the power of their collective obsession as "divine" (ultimate, or absolute) because it is *not* inspired, but blessed with the infallibility of science. All power politicians proceed on the assumption that *their* power is somehow ultimate, an expression of historic, or cosmic, or divine forces, of eternal laws, ultimate principles. And they say they have no religion? Their very religion is their "absolute corruption" by power.

✓ ✓ ✓

Last evening at Vespers, singing the Magnificat antiphon of the Invention of the Holy Cross, I was happy with the splendor of the Gregorian setting, its rhythm, its verve, its strength and *entrain*. Only when we were singing the last alleluia did I realize that this was probably the last time we would ever have this antiphon. The feast has been done away with. In memory of many sunny May afternoons in which I have sung this, and the hymn, I thought I would make of the antiphon a short English poem:

O Cross, more splendid than all the stars,
Glorious to the world,
Greatly to be loved by men,
More holy than all things that are,
Thou who alone wast worthy to weigh the gold
      of the world's ransom,
Sweet tree, beloved nails,
Bearing the Love-Burden,
Save us who have come together here, this day,
In choirs for Thy Praise!
Alleluia, alleluia, alleluia!

✓   ✓   ✓

It is important to realize when you do not need to know
any more, or do any more. But to know when one acts just
enough, one needs more (or less) than the reflective and
planned knowledge by which one watches one's own acts.
He who acts enough, and no more than enough, is also probably less than aware that he has acted. He does not reflect
that he has acted just enough.

To know about it would add something unnecessary to the
action itself. To stop when there has been enough is, then, to
stop before one knows there was even the question of
"enough, or too much" (Blake). And, of course, "enough" in
this sense is not a limit, but a change of pace. There is nothing but the dynamism, and really one does not stop at all,
one moves in another dimension. To have clear knowledge
of a preconceived and arbitrary limit, and then to impose it,
is to frustrate and falsify vital action. However, sometimes
this has to be done: but we are then in another world, not
that of life itself.

✓   ✓   ✓

Harmony is not bought by parsimony.

To stop in the right way is to go on, to spend more (but
not to buy anything, simply to give more).

To cling to something, to know one has it, to want to use it
more, to squeeze all the enjoyment out of it: to do this consciously is to stop really living. It is to stop, to fix one's atten-

tion and one's hunger on what cannot satisfy it. But life itself "goes on," and as long as there is no "stopping," then it is always content with itself (but does not know that it is so).

To leave things alone at the right time: this is the right way to "stop" and the right way to "go on."

To leave a thing alone before you have had anything to do with it, (supposing that you ought to use it, ought to have something to do with it) this is also stopping before you have begun. Use it to go on.

> To be great is to go on
> To go on is to be far
> To be far is to return.
> —Lao Tzu

✓ ✓ ✓

*A Prayer to God the Father on the Vigil of Pentecost.*

Today, Father, this blue sky lauds you. The delicate green and orange flowers of the tulip poplar tree praise you. The distant blue hills praise you, together with the sweet-smelling air that is full of brilliant light. The bickering flycatchers praise you with the lowing cattle and the quails that whistle over there. I too, Father, praise you, with all these my brothers, and they give voice to my own heart and to my own silence. We are all one silence, and a diversity of voices.

You have made us together, you have made us one and many, you have placed me here in the midst as witness, as awareness, and as joy. Here I am. In me the world is present, and you are present. I am a link in the chain of light and of presence. You have made me a kind of center, but a center that is nowhere. And yet also I am "here," let us say I am "here" under these trees, not others.

For a long time I was in darkness and in sorrow, and I suppose my confusion was my own fault. No doubt my own will has been the root of my sorrow, and I regret it, merciful Father, but I do not regret it merely because this formula is acceptable as an official answer to all problems. I know I have sinned, but the sin is not to be found in any list. Perhaps I have looked too hard at all the lists to find out what my sin

was, and I did not know that it was precisely the sin of looking at all the lists when you were telling me that this was
useless. My "sin" is not on the list, and is perhaps not even a
sin. In any case, I cannot know what it is, and doubtless there
is nothing there anyway.

Whatever may have been my particular stupidity, the
prayers of your friends and my own prayers have somehow
been answered, and I am here, in this solitude, before you,
and I am glad because you see me here. For it is here, I
think, that you want to see me and I am seen by you. My
being here is a response you have asked of me, to something
I have not clearly heard. But I have responded, and I am
content: there is little more to know about it at present.

Here you ask of me nothing else than to be content that I
am your Child and your Friend. Which means simply to
accept your friendship because it is your friendship and your
Fatherhood because I am your son. This friendship is Sonship, and is Spirit. You have called me here to be repeatedly
born in the Spirit as your son. Repeatedly born in light, in
knowledge, in unknowing, in faith, in awareness, in gratitude,
in poverty, in presence, and in praise.

If I have any choice to make, it is to live here and perhaps
die here. But in any case it is not the living or the dying that
matter, but speaking your name with confidence in this light,
in this unvisited place: to speak your name of "Father" just
by being here as "son" in the Spirit and the Light which you
have given, and which are no unearthly light but simply this
plain June day, with its shining fields, its tulip tree, the pines,
the woods, the clouds, and the flowers everywhere.

To be here with the silence of Sonship in my heart is to
be a center in which all things converge upon you. That is
surely enough for the time being.

Therefore, Father, I beg you to keep me in this silence so
that I may learn from it the word of your peace and the word
of your mercy and the word of your gentleness to the world:
and that through me perhaps your word of peace may make
itself heard where it has not been possible for anyone to hear
it for a long time.

To study truth here and learn here to suffer for truth.

The Light itself, and the contentment and the Spirit, these
are enough.

Amen.

✓ ✓ ✓

More and more I appreciate the beauty and the solemnity
of the "way" up through the woods, past the barn, up the
stony rise, into the grove of tall, straight oaks and hickories
around through the pines, swinging to the hilltop and the
clearing that looks out over the valley.

Sunrise: hidden by pines and cedars to the east: I saw the
red flame of the kingly sun glaring through the black trees,
not like dawn but like a forest fire. Then the sun became
distinguished as a person and he shone silently and with
solemn power through the branches, and the whole world
was silent and calm.

It is essential to experience all the times and moods of one
good place. No one will ever be able to say how essential,
how truly part of a genuine life this is: but all this is lost in
the abstract, formal routine of exercises under an official
fluorescent light.

✓ ✓ ✓

Monasticism is often understood as "Christianity for the
few," as an affirmation of sacred life in a sacred realm, the
little, holy, self-contained world-denying world of the monastic enclosure. Is this good? Perhaps. But it is terribly limited.
And the good that is in it is perhaps more "worldly" than we
think. In fact, this institution of a little, perfect world in the
midst of an imperfect world, which is implicitly or explicitly
denied, ends up by being also an affirmation of the world
itself, that is to say, the social institution. Monasticism serves
to give to Christian society (especially in the West from
Charlemagne to the French Revolution) a dash of ambiguity
that seems to spiritualize it more. One can relish this, one
can love it, but one must at the same time frankly see and
admit what it is he loves and relishes: the "Christendom" and
indeed the *Romanitá* of the Medieval and Renaissance Christian *world*.

A monasticism that simply affirms these religious and cultural values, even on the highest "spiritual level," has had its day. But it may yet continue for some time. And it is in fact the monasticism I myself entered, to which I was called, for which my own past had in great measure prepared me. I still love it, but I see I must "renounce" it in the sense of transcending it—for in the face of death it is not yet quite enough. It will "do" of course: but at the risk of evasion from the realities of our present situation, and the abdication of present responsibilities to God's word in the world.

✦  ✦  ✦

The glorification of monasticism as part of the glorification of an essentially medieval culture has been, in fact, disastrous for monks. Medieval monasticism and Christianity in general were inevitably, due to the influence of Germanic converts and Celtic monks, more akin to the Old Testament than to the New. At any rate Celtic penitentials and canonical codices were firmly based on the Old Testament. The New Testament, the Holy Spirit of freedom and Sonship, shine through in the lives of some of the saints, but confused with relics of pagan superstition and with legalist and ascetic rigorism. Note the Celtic affinity for Pelagius. There is much strange beauty in Celtic monasticism, but it is not always the beauty of the Gospel. However, this whole question is very complex. The fact remains that traditional Western monasticism since the Middle Ages has been completely overburdened with cultural and ritual usages and with forms and practices—(vg. interpretations of obedience!)—which have come to stifle the Spirit, though they were useful for keeping monasticism going as an institution.

✦  ✦  ✦

To speak of Christendom, in the sense of Western Christian culture, is to speak of a world of which Paris was the intellectual and spiritual capital. It is to speak of the culture which was inherited from Christian Greece and Rome, transformed by the Franks, Anglo-Saxons, Normans, and perfected by the medieval universities (profoundly influenced by the philosophy and science of Islam).

Paris means in many ways less to me than some other cities, since I never spent more than a few days there at one time. At most a week, perhaps. Yet there is one thing I may say about it: I came into this world because of Paris, since my father and mother met there as art students. Certainly the sign of Paris is on me, indelibly! It is more than the stations through which I came and went. It is more than the cheap ecstatic, Paris propaganda (the songs, *"Mon Paris!,"* the stuff about La Ville Lumière), which you heard all over France when I was a child in school. It is more than the Louvre, the lights in the Seine, the bookstores on the Boulevard Saint Michel, the big cafés, the Odéon, the Luxembourg Gardens, and all that.

What is it? I never went to St. Denis, but Paris is to a great extent the Dionysian legend (Montmartre is where the bishop and mystic is supposed to have been martyred), and Dionysius means the *Divine Names* and the *Mystical Theology,* which (due to the Irishman Scotus Erigena and the Benedictines of St. Denis) set the Middle Ages on its ear. The Left Bank means for me less the Sorbonne of the nineteenth and twentieth centuries than the School of St. Victor and Abelard's school in the twelfth. Dionysius links Paris with Cologne and the Dominican mystics of the Rhineland, with the Cistercians of the Low Countries, the Beguines. St. Thomas was full of Dionysius. Then there is Chartres, and John of Salisbury (more than most names this is one of the key names in the humanism of Christendom).

Paris means also St. Bonaventure, Duns Scotus. But Montmartre brings to mind St. Ignatius of Loyola also (who is not exactly part of my own puzzle, yet he is there too!). Paris means St. Louis, whose name was given me in religion. It means Joan of Arc, whom I have always loved. It means Napoleon, in whom I have never been interested. It means Henry IV, Molière, Racine, La Bruyère (to mention only a few that I felt drawn to). It means Pascal, whom I like, and Descartes, whom I don't.

It means Baudelaire, it means Valéry, Péguy. It means Leon Bloy and the Maritains (not to forget Bergson!). It means Manet and Monet, Renoir, Toulouse-Lautrec, Eric Satie. It means Braque and Picasso and Chagall, Jean Cocteau, Max Jacob and Proust . . . once you start this litany there is no end to it. Through these words, plays, paintings, and poems Paris has kept reaching out and grabbing hold of me in London, in Cambridge, in Rome, in New York, and in this monastery lost in Kentucky.

Hence, though Paris may in a way mean much less to me than cities I have really lived in, every Western city that has a certain kind of dignity and worth has in it something of this archetypal and inescapable Paris. Even Louisville has its own little remnant of character, and certainly this remnant has in it a very minute vestige of the identity of *the* city, which is Paris.

✓ ✓ ✓

Two more names must be mentioned—Paris in the twentieth century means Camus and it means Sartre. For Camus I always had great sympathy. He was one with whom my heart agreed. Sartre I can read, sometimes with excitement, sometimes with a superficial agreement. I can respect his difficulty—the fact that he has to be Sartre, after all!—but he has constructed for himself too much of a personage and a moralizing personage at that. Has Sartre fully transcended the status of a *pion* in a *lycée*? I am not sure. But once that is said (he invites this kind of insult) Sartre must be admitted to be a crucial sign and influence in our time, though he demands to be rapidly outgrown. As for Camus, he was and remains a warmer, more human, more humble prophet. Both Sartre and Camus are inconceivable outside the tradition of Christendom, even though they reject it!

✓ ✓ ✓

The *Theologia Germanica* speaks of the "heaven and hell" that we carry about within us. It is good to experience either one or the other of these, for then one is in God's hands. But when one is aware of neither, one is left to himself in indifference. St. Gregory in today's Office (IV Sunday of August, II Nocturn) speaks of much the same thing: the "contentment" of those whose life is one of total neglect since, thinking that they are happy with what they possess, they are not aware that they have lost everything. Hence they feel no desire and no loss, and "never turn their eyes to the truth for which they were created." It is precisely anguish and inner crisis that compel us to seek truth, because it is these things that make clear to us that we are sunk in the hell of our own untruth.

✑ ✑ ✑

I am deeply moved by Pierre Van der Meer de Walcheren's memoirs, *Rencontres,* which he sent me, having written on the flyleaf that he is a "distant brother who is nevertheless very near" to me. And this is certainly true. This old friend of Bloy and Maritain has now been a Benedictine in Holland for a long time. We have corresponded a little before now. I first met him in his book on the Carthusians, *The White Paradise,* and it was there also that I met another friend, Dom Porion, the unnamed monk in the deeply moving chapter on Carthusian spirituality—one of the best things I have ever read on the monastic and solitary spirit.

Knowing how much I owe to the friendship of the Maritains, how much I owe also to Bloy's books (in those days at Columbia when Raissa Maritain and I were the only people using Bloy's volumes in the library), I feel perhaps part of the same spiritual family of Bloy, one of "his converts," like Pierre Van der Meer and Maritain.

The section on Bloy in *Rencontres* is fine, and even better is that on Raissa. Here for the first time I have found her poem on Chagall, which has direct access to the angelic innocence of the painter. I mean to translate it.

Reading this book in the shadows and cool breezes of the woodshed, I find the place full, once again, of French angels, the way it was a year or two ago when I was reading the *Journals* of Julien Green. Angels of Montauban and Chartres —poor Chartres, where, recently, someone set off a bomb in the doorway of the cathedral!

✓ ✓ ✓

Life is, or should be, nothing but a struggle to seek truth: yet what we seek is really the truth that we already possess. Truth is mine in the reality of life as it is given to me to live: yet to take life thoughtlessly, passively as it comes, is to renounce the struggle and purification which are necessary. One cannot simply open his eyes and *see*. The work of understanding involves not only dialectic, but a long labor of acceptance, obedience, liberty, and love. The temptation of monastic life is to evade this austere responsibility by falling back into passive indifference, thinly veiled resentment disguised as obedience and abandonment. Since in fact one *need not* positively accept what happens, one can be merely resigned and negative. Others make all the important decisions: but the most important decision always falls to me, and if I am in the habit of never deciding, I will evade it. The root decision to accept my own life and to obey its demands may challenge my understanding of those demands, my honesty in their regard. The worst temptation, and that to which many monks succumb early in their lives, and by which they remain defeated, is simply to give up asking and seeking. To leave everything to the superiors in this life and to God in the next—a hope which may in fact be nothing but a veiled despair, a refusal to live. And it is not Christian to despair of the present, merely putting off hope into the future. There is also a very essential hope that belongs in the present, and is based on the nearness of the hidden God, and of His Spirit, in the present. What future can make sense without this *present* hope?

Evil and falsity are unavoidable: but one does not bow down to them passively and without response. Resignation is not enough. God demands of us a creative consent, in our deepest and most hidden self, the self we do not experience every day, and perhaps never experience, though it is always there. This creative consent is the obedience of my whole being to the will of God, here and now. The inner "word" of consent is the coincidence, in the Spirit, the identity of my own obedience and will with the obedience and will of Christ. Such is the depth of our Sonship and of the life of grace.

Gradually, by accepting our place in the world and our tasks as they are, we come to be liberated from the limitations of the world and of a restricted, halfhearted milieu: yet one is content with one's moment of history and one's obscure task in it. One must be detached from systems and collective plans, without rancor toward them, but with insight and compassion. To be truly Catholic is not merely to be correct according to an abstractly universal standard of truth, but also and above all to be able to enter into the problems and the joys of all, to understand all, to be all things to all men. This cannot be done if we do not first completely and honestly accept ourselves, our own problems, our own defeats, with the creative consent and responsibility that unite us to God's will and thus to the dynamism of history in its very source.

*  *  *

Again, the French angels: the tone and value of my own interior world! This, I know, is not "Christianity": yet there is a Christian element in it, a Christian resonance which will sound in me as long as I am on earth, and perhaps in heaven, and in the new creation, in the world to come. It is the tone of fourteenth-century mysticism, of the Latin Fathers, of twelfth-century monasticism, but it is open also to China, to Confucianism and to Zen, to the great Taoists. All this is not purely supernatural, doubtless: and yet it is precisely in this quasi-sacramental way, by means of this cultural matter with a mysterious Christian form, that God works in our lives, since we are creatures of history, and tradition is vitally important to us.

It is therefore of great importance to me that I have known the narrow streets of Cordes (they are discovering there, now, places where the Albigensians hid in catacombs). It is important to me that I have walked the dusty road under the plane trees from St. Antonin to Caylus and from Caylus to Puylagarde: to have passed through the nondescript, dusty subprefecture of Caussade, and to have stood by the tower

of the hanged men or on the fortified bridge of Cahors. Or
lifted my eyes in the thin rain of a Sunday evening to look
at the brick tower of Saint Jacques, by the Tarn bridge, in
Montauban (hurrying back to the *lycée*). It is important for
me forever to have stood in the ruined castles of Penne and
Najac, or waited for a long time in the train by the rows of
winebarrels below the bluff of Beziers, with the cathedral
up on top. (How was such a citadel ever stormed, how did
the Albigensians lose it?) It is important to have seen the
jagged outline of the towers of Carcassonne against the evening sky. To have smelled the sun and the dust in the streets
of Toulouse or Narbonne. There are times when I am mortally homesick for the South of France, where I was born.

English angels also: The quarterboys of Rye never cease to
ring in my ears. I have known the silence of the marsh between Rye and Winchelsea, and the silence of the little roads
that led back into the downs. Silence of the Rother's cool
stream below the hill of Wittersham, on the way to Bodiam
Castle. Silence of the fens at Ely. Silence out toward Norwich
and Lady Julian. (Silence of Little Gidding, which I have
heard only in Eliot, but I am part of the same silence.) Angels of the English west: of Exeter, where the cathedral was
smaller than I thought, that gray afternoon, coming from
Plymouth along the green-brown river. Of Bristol, the completely dark and empty church at St. Mary Redcliffe. The
small cathedral. Angels of Oxford: Oriel, where I did not go.
Lincoln, with the wide court, which I liked. Angels of Cambridge the backs of Clare and Kings . . . the bell in the
tower of St. John's, striking by night, heard in my digs in
Bridge Street. And all the little roads and hills and villages
and fields and hedges and corners of woods around Oakham.
The tower of Oakham Church and the broad vale.

The sunny North Downs in Surrey, the ruins of Waverley
and Miss Maud's house near the village, the name of which I
have forgotten. And Ripley—the tall elms. The frosty mornings. The broad cricket field. The road to Horsley, pitch dark
on a winter night, and the wagging, feeble lamp of my bicycle. . . . The long wall of Lord Onslow's place, no end
to it.

The high roofs of Strasbourg, Tauler's city. Streets known to Eckhart. The Maison Oliver, good coffee and whipped cream. The Cercle Evangelique and Professor Héring, with his red beard, his phenomenology, and Plato's Apology. . . .

(Eckhart, in a sermon on the divine birth, says that, when a person is about to be struck by a thunderbolt, he turns unconsciously toward it. When a tree is about to be struck, all the leaves turn toward the blow. And one in whom the divine birth is to take place turns, without realizing, completely toward it.)

✓ ✓ ✓

Continuing with the angels: I think of the village church at West Horsley and the church at Ripley (with all the little boys from school dressed in Eton jackets and I in the middle of them, most jacketed of all because the jacket was brand new!). Newark Priory, an Augustinian ruin, was near Ripley, across the river. Christopher Pearce, brother of the head-mistress, knew all about the drains. I helped him measure them. My first intimate contact with monastic life! (I must get back that book of David Knowles, the first volume on the *Religious Orders in England,* and get on with it.)

High Street Guildford, a steep climb. I think I had to walk it with my bicycle. The long Abbey Church at St. Albans: I used to see it from the LMS on the way to Oakham.

All this was in some way sacramental, and all of it had me turning somewhere, I did not know where.

Now I live in a world which is to some extent (though at least I am in a monastery) bare of all such meanings and such signs. The place I am in does, nevertheless, have something of this climate. However, it is trying to lose the climate and substitute another. What other? I cannot say, I do not know. For my own part, I know I must keep alive in myself what I have once known and grown into: and if anyone else wants a part of it, I can try to pass it on.

✓ ✓ ✓

Both Newman and Fénelon loved Clement of Alexandria, which is not surprising. To Newman, Clement was "like music." This meant much, for Newman was a profoundly musical person and all that was best expressed itself, for him, in terms of music, harmony, oneness, sound. There are people one meets in books or in life whom one does not merely observe, meet, or know. A deep resonance of one's entire being is immediately set up with the entire being of the other (*Cor ad cor loquitur*—heart speaks to heart in the wholeness of the language of music; true friendship is a kind of singing).

Yet for a long time I had no "resonance" with Newman (because I did not bother to listen for any; I think pictures of him scared me). I was suspicious of letting him in. Clement the same. But now I want all the music of Clement, and am with difficulty restrained from taking too many books of Newman out of the library when I have more books than I need all ready.

Resonances: here is a good choir: Maritain, Van der Meer de Walcheren, Bloy, Green, Chagall, Satie . . . variety and unity.

Another, earlier music, most deep with me: Blake, Tauler, Eckhart, Ruysbroeck (Maritain gets in here, too, with Raïssa doing most of the singing). Coomaraswamy sings with any of them. They sang me into the Church, these voices. And Dante's voice.

Music: the marvelous opening of Clement's *Protreptikos*, the "New Song," the splendid image of the cricket to replace by his song the broken string in the lyre of Eunomos at Delphi. While repudiating the myth he uses it splendidly and in its full spirit: man is a musical instrument for God. Our singing together is perhaps the best and most evident manifestation of God in His world: by His music in us. This is a deep reason for monastic psalmody: this, and the morning that our music is, after all, out of tune.

✓  ✓  ✓

I dreamt I was lost in a great city and was walking "toward the center" without quite knowing where I was going. Suddenly I came to a dead end, but on a height, looking at a great bay, an arm of the harbor. I saw a whole section of the city spread out before me on hills covered with light snow, and realized that, though I had far to go, I knew where I was: because in this city there are two arms of the harbor and they help you to find your way, as you are always encountering them.

Then, in this city, I speak with a stranger in the library (being still on my way). I realize that there is a charterhouse here, and that I have been meaning to go there, to speak to the prior about my vocation. I ask "where is the charterhouse?" He says: "I am just going to drive that way, and I go right by it. I will take you." I accept his offer, realizing that it is providential.

✦ ✦ ✦

I think sometimes that I may soon die, though I am not yet old (forty-seven). I don't know exactly what kind of conviction this thought carries with it or what I mean by it. Death is always a possibility for everyone. We live in the presence of this possibility. So I have a habitual awareness that I may die, and that, if this is God's will, then I am glad. "Go ye forth to meet Him." And in the light of this I realize the futility of my cares and preoccupations, particularly my chief care, which is central to me, my work as a writer. I do not feel very guilty about it, but it remains a "care," a focus that keeps my "self" in view, and I feel a little hampered. Though I know by experience that without this care and salutary work I would be much more in my own way, much more obstructed by my own inertia and confusion. If I am not fully free, then the love of God, I hope, will free me. The important thing is simply turning to Him daily and often, preferring His will and His mystery to everything that is evidently and tangibly "mine."

✦ ✦ ✦

A horrible book is being read in the refectory, a novel about convent life. All the cells are austere, all the nuns are severe, and sanctity consists in discovering the faults of others and mercilessly causing them to be punished and corrected. Some seem to love the book for its opportunities for coy laughs at postulants who trip up over their new habits and land on their faces, or whose veils fall off in church. It is an immoral book, but everyone can listen to it with a perfectly good conscience, unaware that sado-masochism is a form of sexual expression (in this case mildly pathological). In any case, the book is not supposed to be "serious": it is for "relaxation" and "enjoyment." Another nun is caught smiling. Another one is morally flayed for looking in a mirror. Another postulant trips up and nearly breaks her neck. Religious life is sheer delight, for at every moment the Lord is always playing practical jokes on His brides. I can barely eat my dinner.

*  *  *

I translated a bit from Clement of Alexandria (the *Protreptikos*—with much help from the new French version) about Zeus being dead as swan, dead as eagle, dead as dragon, dead as a lustful old man.

*  *  *

Man is most human, and most proves his humanity (I did not say his virility) by the quality of his relationship with woman. This obsession with virility and conquest makes a true and deep relationship impossible. Men today think that there is no difference between the capacity to make conquests and the capacity to love. Women respond accordingly, with the elaborate deceit and thinly veiled harlotry—the role assigned to woman by fashion—and there is a permanent battle between the sexes, sometimes covered over with the most atrocious and phony play acting. In all this everyone completely forgets the need for love. A desperate need: not the need to receive it only, but the need to *give love*.

In the monastery, with our vows of chastity, we are ideally supposed to go beyond married love into something more pure, more perfect, more totally oblative. This should then make us the most *human* of all people. But that is the trouble: how can one go "further" than something to which one has not yet attained? This does not mean that one cannot validly embrace a life of virginity until he has first been married: a nice contradiction to put a person in! But it does mean that we cannot love *perfectly* if we have not in some way loved maturely and truly. Family life should ordinarily provide the climate in which this is possible: but if the family is simply a place where the sexes fight for supremacy . . .

✙ ✙ ✙

What happened to the gray cat with the white spot on her chest? The gray cat that got thinner and thinner, and rubbed more and more desperately against your ankles, at evening, in the novitiate garden?

✙ ✙ ✙

It is beautifully cool and, above all, quiet in the novitiate conference room. One of the novices, Frater B——, laughed and laughed more and more week after week until he finally laughed all day long and had to go home. I am told that once, before one of the singing classes, he laughed so much he rolled on the floor. Life here is funnier than we think. And now, it is once again, quiet.

✙ ✙ ✙

Supposing, for a moment, that our society is headed for cataclysm. One is supposed not to think that it is, yet at the moment everyone is talking about fallout shelters. (Build one in your backyard, come out after two weeks and resume the American Way of Life amid the ashes.)

What kind of attitude should one take personally, quite apart from the question of protest, or of testimony against the folly and brutality of certain policies: is it enough to hope that the fallout will find me "doing my duty" and conforming to a great, prosperous, inane, and self-destructive system?

Or should one try to stand above the water level in which all minds drown: to escape the deluge of falsehood, to build a moral ark? Is this only a worse temptation?

It implies perhaps that one can easily decide between true and false, right and wrong. But that is precisely what constitutes the "deluge." We are flooded, carried away with tidal waves of judgment, opinion, analysis. If at every instant one feels bound to grasp the entire and absolute truth supposedly underlying a concrete and contingent series of acts, and if his political life is nothing but a series of absolute judgments of right and wrong, determined, from moment to moment, for all eternity: this is an insane way to exist.

The first thing one must learn to accept, indeed to choose, is the evident impossibility of giving everything a clear, definitive meaning. Should one even force himself to believe that these contingent events *have* a special relevance? Is it not possible that the whole works may go up in smoke, a perfect waste, and yet thus serve some other final purpose, some other meaning we have not grasped and foreseen?

One must accept the fact that one's own life may, from a human and historic point of view, be rendered absolutely meaningless by the course of events in which, while trying to participate reasonably, one has only added to the general confusion—if he has added anything at all. The point is, most people seem to think that this implies despair. That it implies renunciation of all hope and all reason. I don't see that. I don't consider that my life has to make perfect sense to me at every moment. I certainly do not think it is at all possible for our society to make sense in the way it thinks it can.

The history of the world during my own lifetime seems to me to be marked by a monumental, almost comic senselessness, the comedy being provided not by the horror of some of the most characteristic events, but by the pompous futility of the men who have stood up and tried to tell us what it was all about. Churchill. Roosevelt. De Gaulle. Stalin. Khrushchev. Eisenhower. But we believe them, forgetting how much their "wisdom" has been conditioned by an attempted dialogue with the insanity of people like Hitler.

Personally, I am willing to give them top marks for effort. They have certainly tried to make it all seem reasonable, and at moments they have appeared to succeed. Until the flow of events has washed away their contribution, their sand structure, and somebody else comes along—Kennedy for instance—and tries to give it a meaning. I like Kennedy. I am all for him. He is better than most. But I cannot say he has me fully convinced.

Meanwhile, we all think that we can understand history by stopping the movie and looking fixedly, for a moment, at one of the frames. The motion is continuous, and one moves with it, inevitably. But one must think in and with the movement, not pretend he is looking at it all, like God, from the outside. (I am not so sure it makes sense either to say that God "looks at it from the outside." Where?)

✓ ✓ ✓

The flow of events: our youngest postulant, from Canada, is busy today with a wrecking bar, smashing up the partitions of the room in the old guesthouse, on the third floor, where, twenty years ago, I first came on retreat, that silent, moonlit night at the end of Lent. I remember the spiritual awe of that night! And now, in the clear light of a summer day, the plaster crashes to the floor and sunlit clouds of dust float out the window where I wrote that poem about the abbey and Matins. This kid was not even born then. He is the son of an airman who married an English girl, as my brother did, during the war. He was born in the Blitz, in England. And now he is tearing down that room and my own history—a fact which I gladly accept, but with this sense of loss nevertheless!

Eighteen years since the three survivors in John Paul's crew dropped his body off the lifeboat into the North Sea. His back was broken when the plane hit the surface.

✓ ✓ ✓

Apparently there has been another "Berlin Crisis." This is the favorite sport of the Russians (and indeed of the Americans). It is good business for the newspapers, one has to grant that.

Symbolic problems, with symbolic solutions! This is an elaborate, quasi-ritual game.

After weeks of ranting and stamping by Khrushchev, a symbolic task force of American troops rides down the road to Berlin, treated with utmost courtesy by Russian troops. Vice President Johnson lands in West Berlin, steps off the plane hitching up his pants and looking around like the sheriff in a TV western (I didn't see this, I was told), and goes around making speeches and giving out ball-point pens.

Berlin Crisis? It is all in the head. It is a sacred rite, an esoteric and purifying mystery. It is all an elaborate TV production, including the wall: fun for everybody except the wretched people for whom it is not a game, for whom it is life and death, and who get shot trying to get over the wall. But that, too, is good for business.

Good not only for the newspaper business, but for *all* business. Everything, they say, is booming. Meanwhile a man in Chicago has built himself a fallout shelter in his cellar, and declares that he and his family will occupy it, keeping out all intruders with a machine gun. This is the final exaltation of our culture: individualism, comfort, security, and to hell with everybody else. (As if other people might be interested in getting in there, being baked slowly to death by the fire storm, in warm togetherness.)

✦ ✦ ✦

Meanwhile I am just finishing Dawson's *Understanding Europe.* As against Barth, he contends that, if you simply discard or ignore the value of Christian culture, you do nothing but hasten the total secularization of the society that *needs* whatever it can still keep of its Christian heritage. It is certainly true that few people can maintain themselves in a world like ours with the austere faith of a Barth, and not simply submit in complete unreason to the forces of destruction. For myself, I am more and more convinced that my job is to clarify something of the tradition that lives in me, and in which I live: the tradition of wisdom and spirit that is found not only in Western Christendom but in Orthodoxy, and also, at least analogously, in Asia and in Islam. Man's sanity and balance and peace depend, I think, on his keeping alive a continuous sense of what has been valid in his past.

But it is not simply a question of the individual. It is a matter of crucial importance both for the Church and for the world. And at this point the witness of Bonhoeffer becomes very significant. He agrees completely with Dawson and indeed goes further. Speaking of the Nazi persecution of Christianity and the Nazi attack on civilized values, he notes that suddenly "reason, culture, humanity, tolerance and self-determination, all these concepts which had . . . served as battle slogans against the Church" all found themselves allied with the Church against the Nazis. This was no pragmatic and temporary political alliance, nor was the Church simply taking refuge in and with the "civilized world." On the contrary, says Bonhoeffer, "These concepts had become homeless and now sought refuge in the Church" (*Ethics*). They were returning to their origin. (This shows, by the way, how close Bonhoeffer is to the theology of St. Irenaeus, and this gives him a great advantage over Barth.)

Here we have the real theological principle that must govern all discussion of the Church in the modern world. A turning to the world that merely seeks an arbitrary accommodation that will make the Church respected and popular in the world of science is shameful to the Church and to Christ. A demand that science and culture bow down to curial authority is shameful to civilization and to man. What is needed is the recapitulation of culture and civilization in Christ. And this means also the renewal of Christian culture.

✓ ✓ ✓

A great deal of virtue and piety is simply the easy price we pay in order to justify a life that is essentially trifling. Nothing is so cheap as the evasion purchased by just enough good conduct to make one pass as a "serious person."

A great deal of libertinism, vice, and rebellion is in the end much the same thing. It does not "justify" trifling, but nevertheless expresses impotence and refusal to do anything else. The fact that the rebellion is an implicit criticism of the shallow and the respectable proves absolutely nothing.

And when you come to look more deeply into man's present condition you find that many forms of "seriousness" and "achievement" come to this in the end. In our society, a society of business rooted in puritanism, based on a pseudo-ethic of industriousness and thrift, to be rewarded by comfort, pleasure, and a good bank account, the myth of work is thought to justify an existence that is essentially meaningless and futile. There is, then, a great deal of busy-ness as people

invent things to do when in fact there is very little to be done.
Yet we are overwhelmed with jobs, duties, tasks, assignments,
"missions" of every kind. At every moment we are sent north,
south, east, and west by the angels of business and art, poetry
and politics, science and war, to the four corners of the universe to decide something, to sign something, to buy and sell.
We fly in all directions to sell ourselves, thus justifying the
absolute nothingness of our lives. The more we seem to accomplish, the harder it becomes to really dissimulate our
trifling, and the only thing that saves us is the common conspiracy not to advert to what is really going on.

Some men make it their business to cover their own emptiness by pointing out the fraudulency of others, but always
the emphasis is on the fact that others have nevertheless *done
something*, even though it was a matter of perpetrating a
fraud. They have perpetrated *something*. And so the general
myth prospers. No matter how empty our lives become, we
are always at least convinced that something is happening
because, indeed, as we so often complain, *too much is happening*. There is so much to be done that we do not have
time to live. . . . Such is the cliché.

But it is precisely this idea that a serious life demands "time
to live" that is the root of our trifling.

In reality, what we want is time in which to trifle and
vegetate without feeling guilty about it. But because we do
not dare try it, we precipitate ourselves into another kind of
trifling: that which is not idle, but dissimulated as *action*.

*    *    *

Though I have some sympathy with the existentialist, or
pseudo-existentialist, swing toward "situation ethics" (in reaction to an exaggeratedly formal and legalist emphasis on
the objective demands of authority), I am very much afraid
that in practice this leads also to another and worse form of
trifling.

In the name of "love" and "the person" one removes the
"real" from the objective world and puts it entirely in the
realm of interpersonal and subjective choice. It is true that,
when one is fully a person, when one can love without any

suspicion of trifling, this realm of subjective choice becomes extremely creative and fertile. But it seems to me that the very ones who make the most fuss about what they call "love" are simply trifling with their own lives and those of others. What do they mean by fidelity and authenticity? Is "authentic" decision that which arises out of the feelings of the moment, *as opposed to* the "objective" demand of a law in which we do not happen to be interested? To think this, to "decide" in this way, is to trifle with the very idea of the person and of decision.

To remove everything into this area of total indetermination is not to "liberate" the person but to reduce him to passivity and inertia. "Freedom" then becomes merely another name for infantile regression. Then there is no other truth and reality than the arbitrariness of feeling. Feeling itself, without discipline or culture, loses all its tone. Fidelity is impossible.

The logical end of this deterioration comes when conscious fidelity is replaced by an addiction—drugs, alcohol, sex, or just plain business.

✓  ✓  ✓

One of our monks, a former student of mine (Father S——), is planning to join Dom Jacques Winandy, a retired Benedictine abbot who is living as a hermit in Martinique. Dom Winandy writes that the poor share their vegetables with him, and fruit is easily had. He says: "If you are in a financial predicament just come as you are with your Bible and Breviary, and trust in Providence." One of the other hermits is off to Holland to study and Father S—— will apparently have his hermitage. Dom Winandy also advises: "Bring plenty of books. To make a principle of anti-intellectualism [in the solitary life] would be crazy. It has no place in true monastic tradition. But the ideal is to make all studies center on the Bible." And he adds: "I have been here three years and I am each day happier than I came. You cannot believe how truly sanctifying is genuine departure from one's own country, from one's family, and all that one has known and loved."

I am also reading the three wonderful chapters in the *Cloud of Unknowing* on Martha and Mary. They end with this, which to my mind, sums it all up.

Therefore you who set out to be a contemplative as Mary was, choose rather to be humbled by the unimaginable greatness and the incomparable perfection of God than by your own wretchedness and imperfection. In other words, look more to God's worthiness than to your own worthlessness. In the perfectly humble, there is nothing lacking, spiritual or physical. For they have God in whom is all abundance, and whoever has Him needs nothing else in this life.

—Chapter 23

✓ ✓ ✓

Confucius said: "The higher type of man is not like a vessel which is designed for special use." He was wiser than we monks are: we are very much concerned with our "special function." But that is precisely what the monk does not have.

✓ ✓ ✓

There is a story of a tiger cub that was brought up among goats. One day he got lost in the jungle and ran into a big strong tiger who took one look at him, saw him acting like a goat, and with one cuff of his paw knocked him halfway across the jungle.

I meet a tiger in myself who is not familiar, who says "Choose!" and knocks me halfway across the jungle.

✓ ✓ ✓

Aidan Nally, who has worked for fifty years on the monastery farm, came up to me today and said, with great solemnity and sorrow: "Father, they're all mobilizing out in No Man's Land."

I wonder if this is not perhaps the most intelligent piece of political comment I have heard in years. But in any case Aidan, like everyone else, is caught in the great symbolic game. Being a simple man, he plays it with great seriousness, not realizing that he is in a different world and therefore in a different game. He was probably referring to remarks made by Kennedy about the possibilities of "war in outer space."

✓ ✓ ✓

Zen story:

A monk said to Joshu: "What is the way?"

Joshu replied: "Outside the fence."

The monk insisted: "I mean the Great Way? What is the Great Way?"

Joshu replied: "The Great Way is that which leads to the Capital."

The Great Way is right in the middle of this story, and I should remember it when I get excited about war and peace. I sometimes think I have an urgent duty to make all kinds of protest and clarification: but, above all, the important thing is to be on the Great Way and stay on it, whether one speaks or not. It is not necessary to run all over the countryside shouting "peace, peace." But it is *essential* to stay on the Great Way which leads to the Capital, for only on the Great Way is there peace. If no one follows the way, there will be no peace in the world, no matter how much men may preach it.

It is easy to know that "there is a way somewhere," and even perhaps to know that others are not on it (by analogy with one's own lostness, wandering far from the way). But this knowledge is useless unless it helps one find the way. If it merely becomes a standard of judgment, a means of showing up others and judging them for having lost their way, it is no use to anyone. It helps neither me nor them to find the way—(it inspires them to find *arguments* to justify their own wandering. Etymologically, "error" means wandering off the way). If I am on the way myself I judge no one—though I may try to help him find the way, knowing, however, that it does not look the same to him and that he may be on it too without that being evident to me (another good reason for not judging).

✓  ✓  ✓

Perhaps peace is not, after all, something you work for, or "fight for." It is indeed "fighting for peace" that starts all the wars. What, after all, are the pretexts of all these Cold War crises, but "fighting for peace?" Peace is something you have or do not have. If you are yourself at peace, then there is at least *some* peace in the world. Then share your peace with everyone, and everyone will be at peace. Of course I realize that arguments like this can be used as a pretext for passivity, for indifferent acceptance of every iniquity. Quietism leads to war as surely as anything does. But I am not speaking of quietism, because quietism is not peace, nor is it the way to peace.

✓  ✓  ✓

My Aunt Kit from New Zealand is here, and this is the first time in forty years that I have seen her. She is on her way home to Christchurch after spending the summer at Horsley in England. She is delighted to have hopped over New York in a helicopter and she says she saw all she wanted to see of it that way. It rained yesterday so we sat in the gatehouse drinking tea and talking about the family. The Mertons went out to New Zealand from Suffolk in 1856. My great-great-grandfather James Merton was bailiff of a family called Torless. His family and theirs went out together to New Zealand. His son Charles, my great-grandfather, was born in New Zealand and taught music at Christ College, Christchurch, where my father, Owen, went to school. My grandmother, Gertrude Grierson, was the best of the lot (she died at a hundred and two). She is one of the people of whom I retain the strongest impression in my childhood. She taught me the Lord's Prayer. She was born in Wales of a Scotch father. But the best that is in us seems to come from her Welsh mother, whose family name was Bird. This is where our faces come from, the face Father had, that I have, that Aunt Kit has: the look, the grin, the brow. It is the Welsh in me that counts: that is what does the strange things, and writes the books, and drives me into the woods. Thank God for the

Welsh in me, and for all those Birds, those Celts, including the one who was a lieutenant in the navy and whose face, in a miniature which Aunt Maud had, is said to prove all this. Aunt Maud, too, had the Bird face, and the humor, and the silences.

As for Granny, that Bird of all the Birds, when she wanted to meet anyone in London she would always arrange to meet them "by the Elgin Marbles in the British Museum."

There we go again with that old Hellenic-European-Christendom!

✓   ✓   ✓

A close study of Bonhoeffer's *Ethics* shows that in his reaction against Barthian radicalism he emphasizes the rights and dignity of nature in a very Catholic, humanistic way, always in view of "the ultimate" and the coming of Christ. (What he lacks, from the Catholic viewpoint, is a firm metaphysical basis such as we find in St. Thomas. But his ethic has something of Thomist balance and reasonableness.) I quote from Bonhoeffer:

The homes of men are not, like the shelters of animals, merely the means of protection against bad weather . . . they are places in which man may relish the joys of his personal life in the intimacy and security of his family and of his property. Eating and drinking do not merely serve the purpose of keeping the body in good health but they afford natural joy in bodily living. Clothing is not intended merely as a means for covering the body but also as an adornment for the body. Recreation is not designed solely to increase repose and enjoyment. Play is by its nature remote from all subordination to purpose. . . . Sex is not only the means of reproduction, but independently of this, it brings its own joy, in married life, in the love of two human beings for one another. From all this it emerges that the meaning of bodily life never lies solely in its subordination to its final purpose. *The life of the body assumes its full significance only with the fulfilment of its inherent claim to joy.*                          —*Ethics*

This is genuine Christian humanism, and Catholic, too, when understood in its context (his doctrine of the earthly life as "penultimate," deriving its dignity, seriousness, and meaning from its ordination to the ultimate coming of Christ). This is a "Christian worldliness" with which I thoroughly agree. It is also the voice of all that is best in the cultural tradition of Western Christendom, and contradicts especially Nazi and Fascist "vitalism" (idolization of the life force while subordinating the individual entirely to collective power), Marxist "humanism" as interpreted by Stalin and Co., and even the baseless pragmatic and behavioristic optimism that treats man merely as a mechanism to be kept in good order.

Note, he bases this on quotes from *Ecclesiastes* (2:24, 3:12, 9:7 ff, 11:9, 2:25), often thought to be pessimistic. *Ecclesiastes* is critical of enthusiasms and facile idealisms, not of true wisdom based in the realities of life as God has made it.

*  *  *

"Vitalism," the enthusiastic exaltation of life in neopagan and totalist forms of mass-society is, as Bonhoeffer saw, in reality a masked hatred of life, and a radical unfitness for its common and simple joys, the natural joys implanted in nature by God, and which prepare us, by gratitude and hope, to enter into His Kingdom.

Where the animal "joy of living" is expressed brutally with ferocity, and with many violent images, what we have is no longer a superabundance of life but a failure and a deficiency of life. Perhaps the mixture of satiety, boredom, violence, and despair which characterizes our mass-society comes from the impotence of well-fed bodies with empty and lost minds. The obsession with lust and violent, erratic forms of sex is not a sign of great passion but of the *absence* of passion. On the contrary, Western society is characterized above all by its abstraction, its confusion, its pseudo-passion (passion fabricated in the imagination and centered on fantasies). There seems to be excitement—but there is only the superficial agitation of a nervous daydream. So much for our lusty apes with cowboy hats—they are not even comic any more!

But collect them together, put uniforms on them, give them a leader that fits into the pattern of their fantasies and knots their dream images all together into a psychosis—then the whole thing comes alive in *destruction*. The total incapacity for love is let loose, with extreme and efficient effect, in hate that smashes cities and ravages whole countries. *Yet even this hate is impotent.* It can burn buildings and ruin crops, it can smash and mutilate bodies, it can torture and degrade: but life comes back all the stronger and derides it.

⚹ ⚹ ⚹

There is a certain amount of historical irony in the effort to make of St. Thomas a unique and supreme authoritative teacher of Catholic theology who must have the last word in everything. When St. Thomas himself studied Aristotle at Naples, Aristotle was under the Church's ban and was not supposed to be read or taught. He was being taught at Naples, however, by an *Irishman!*

Not only that, but St. Thomas was himself quoting Aristotle in his lectures in the University of Paris while Aristotle was still banned. St. Thomas' Master, St. Albert the Great, even wrote a commentary on Aristotle during the time of the ban on "the Philosopher." Finally, St. Thomas' own commentaries on Aristotle broke down the official resistance, though Thomas himself was condemned for a time.

Pieper* makes no bones about saying that Aristotle as taught at Naples and as studied and followed by St. Thomas (in Latin translations from Arabic translations from Syriac translations of Aristotle's Greek) was presented *"not in a moderate but in an extreme and altogether dangerous form,"* and furthermore, St. Thomas (still in his teens) knew this— yet he calmly proceeded to devour Aristotle, danger and all, and completely assimilate him, showing that he was compatible with the Biblical and evangelical movement of the men-

* References to Pieper in this section should urge the reader to consult his excellent *Guide to Thomas Aquinas,* New York, 1962, which in turn owes much to M.-D. Chenu's *Guide to Understanding St. Thomas,* Chicago, 1964.

dicants, of whom St. Thomas was one. What St. Thomas found in Aristotle was not merely the interesting and satisfying system devised by a great intelligence—what he found was the *one* truth in which he was interested. Not a "Greek truth" that harmonized with a "Judaeo-Christian truth." St. Thomas was not simply an "Aristotelian." His claim to fame is not just that he had the acumen to get on a bandwagon that had not yet been generally recognized for what it was. He took what he needed from Aristotle (his realism, his respect for the concrete, his metaphysic of being), but he never made a cult of Aristotle as some of his contemporaries did. When St. Thomas quoted Aristotle he was not simply affirming that a proposition was true merely because it could be found in Aristotle. Still less did he mean that a proposition was *Christian* merely because it was found in Aristotle. When St. Thomas himself was put on an official pedestal ("a statement is proved true if it is shown to have been made by St. Thomas") the people who put him there proved, by that fact, that they were alien from his true spirit. I do not say that the Church proposed him as an authority: the real sense of the Church's approval of St. Thomas was simply that he was designated as a model and guide for philosophers and theologians. But certain textbooks made him purely and simply an authority—and nothing could be better calculated to undermine his teaching. St. Thomas had scant respect for the "argument from authority" in philosophical matters.

What Aristotle gave to Christian thought in the thirteenth century was its *"turning to the world,"* its respect for nature, for the physical, for the concrete reality of the universe. The theology of St. Thomas is a reaction against a theology that denatures nature by engrossing itself in allegorical and symbolic systems. St. Thomas returned to the realities that the symbols were intended to signify.

Pieper sums up St. Thomas' attitude to Aristotle: "In Aristotle's fundamental attitude toward the universe, in his affirmation of the concrete and sensuous reality of the world, *Thomas recognized something entirely his own, belonging to himself as a Christian* because it had been present from the very beginnings of Christianity. This element was the same as the Christian affirmation of creation." But as Pieper shows, and he is quite right, this was the result of the action of theology as aware of itself *in the world,* not out of it or above it. The theology of St. Thomas was fully rooted in the Christian culture of his time, but also in the culture that was resulting from the encounter between Christianity and Islam, which did so much to create the modern Western world.

✓ ✓ ✓

The current popular reaction against St. Thomas is not due to anything in Thomas himself, or even the "scholastic method." No one who takes the trouble to read St. Thomas and understand him will be surprised to find that the values people now seek elsewhere have from the first been present in him and can always be made accessible without too much difficulty. There is first of all that "turning to the world"— that awareness of the modern world, the world of poor people, of cities, of politically minded burghers and artisans, of men more interested in the authority of reason than of ecclesiastics. But there is also the Bible. And there is the turning to the non-Christian world—to Aristotle and to Islam.

The spirit and perspectives of St. Thomas are "modern" in the soundest sense of the word, although admittedly his Aristotelian physics, cosmology, biology, etc., are hardly up to date. The point is that they do not affect the worth of his thought as a whole, and where it needs to be transposed into slightly different terms, the transposition is not difficult.

The whole difficulty of St. Thomas today arises, not from Thomas himself, but (as has been said so often) from Thomists. Where Thomas was open to the world, they have closed him in upon himself in a little triumphalist universe of airtight correctness. They have unconsciously sealed off his thought in such a way that in order to embrace Thomism one has to renounce everything else. One has to undergo a full-scale conversion, thereafter becoming a militant for the cause, a militant serenely exempt from even listening to a non-Thomist argument, let alone understanding it.

Regrettable that, all of a sudden, it has become fashionable to discredit St. Thomas, to set him aside and run madly to catch up with the new philosophies (which, by the time we have caught up with them, will be themselves discredited). This unseemly haste to get off one bandwagon and find another is the most embarrassing aspect of the whole event. But it had to happen, and it is a clear judgment upon the complacency of those who thought they had "their side" forever enshrined in Canon Law, forever in a citadel of indisputable supremacy.

Now the windows are open in the *Summa* too, and there is a little peace and some fresh air!

✓   ✓   ✓

The great originality of St. Thomas lies in his vocation: the realization that he was called by God to evangelical perfection and to the study of Aristotle. This combination had momentous implications, because it meant being a theologian, not of the return to paradise through sacrament and symbol, in the monastery or sanctuary, but a theologian in the city, aware that truth is not excluded from any realm where there is being, and that it can also be confronted directly without the medium of symbol. Hence the theology of St. Thomas is a theology of intellectual reconciliation, which, instead of maintaining itself in existence by the insistence on those opposites which create problems, justifies itself by uniting opposites and looking beyond the stereotyped solution of problems.

This archetypal reconciliation was present in his own vocation which, as he lived it, told him daily that the confrontation of apparently irreconcilable opposites presented no problem at all. One could love and serve God in the city, teaching Christian clerks from the book of a pagan philosopher.

✓   ✓   ✓

In the usual structure of his articles, St. Thomas first lines up the arguments he finds not fully satisfactory, then gives his own view, and finally discusses the arguments he first set forth. Note the way I have expressed this—one is usually inclined (by the bad habit acquired in seminaries) to say that "he first lines up *the wrong opinions,* then gives *the right*

*answer,* then *demolishes the wrong answers."* Pieper shows
how the *articulus* is really a sympathetic but disciplined dialogue—even a kind of Platonic dialogue—reduced to the
briefest and most practical form. Each article could be considered as a note for a Platonic dialogue. Very often St.
Thomas has better insight into the *videtur* (the "it seems"
opinion, which he does not fully accept) than the ones who
themselves hold it. Very often, too, his answer is not a refuta-
tion but a placing in perspective, or a qualified acceptance,
fitting the seemingly adverse opinion into the broader context
of his own view.

There is in St. Thomas more than the dry light of the
classroom and the businesslike proving of theses. His understanding, which is clear as day, owes much also to the "night
spirit" which communes with what he did not know—witness
his fondness for pseudo-Dionysius. He is not all talk, not a
scholastic machine for grinding out answers. Though he was
a prodigious teacher and writer, the force of his words comes
from his silence and his respect in the presence of what could
never be said.        (See Pieper, *The Silence of St. Thomas*)

✦ ✦ ✦

It is curious that both the opponents of the mendicants
(William of St. Amour) and their strongest supporters
(Joachim of Flora) were convinced that the appearance of
friars in the Church meant the end of the world—simply because it meant the destruction of habits of thought they were
used to. Those who could not bear to see the old removed or
changed were bitter and hostile. Those who were sick of the
old and wanted something entirely new were carried away
with an apocalyptic enthusiasm which, in the end, could
have completely nullified the really creative work of the
mendicants. Joachim of Flora's idea of a new theocracy of
Mendicant Friars in the Reign of the Holy Spirit would in
fact have sterilized the real fruitfulness of the new theology
in the world by imposing it, with the unquestionable authority of charism, upon the world. St. Thomas did not seek
to be imposed on the world. He asked only to be understood
in the world, as revealing the possibilities the world had in

itself. In a time of drastic change one can be too preoccupied with what is ending or too obsessed with what seems to be beginning. In either case one loses touch with the present and with its obscure but dynamic possibilities. What really matters is openness, readiness, attention, courage to face risk. You do not need to know precisely what is happening, or exactly where it is all going. What you need is to recognize the possibilities and challenges offered by the present moment, and to embrace them with courage, faith, and hope. In such an event, courage is the authentic form taken by love.

*✔ ✔ ✔*

St. Thomas speaks of the anguish, the *angustia* (the pain and frustration caused by confinement within limitations), which he sensed in the *praeclara ingenia* (brilliant minds) of Averroes and Aristotle, in their not being able to see all the way to the end in their aspiration to truth and happiness. This is remarkably borne out by the story of Averroes' contact with and interest in the young Sufi mystic, Ibn al' Arabi, and his *angustia* at not being able to grasp what Arabi had seen clearly through a divine gift. It is a poignant story and I made a poem of it.

(See "Song for the Death of Averroes" in *Emblems of a Season of Fury*)

*✔ ✔ ✔*

The psychology of crisis and change:

The fear of change is the fear of disruption, disintegration of one's own inner unity and the unity of one's accustomed world. (These two are inseparable.)

A personal crisis occurs when one becomes aware of apparently irreconcilable opposites in oneself. If the tension between them is strong enough, one can no longer "keep himself together." His personal unity is fractured. There are various pathological ways of trying to handle the fracture. For instance, reconstructing a unity built on one half of the opposition and projecting the unacceptable half upon the world and upon other people. Then the half of oneself that is still acceptable becomes "right" and the rest of the world becomes wrong. If the conflict is intense, then the outer world, other people, other societies are regarded as heretical, malicious, subversive, demonic, etc.

A personal crisis is creative and salutary if one can accept the conflict and restore unity on a higher level, incorporating the opposed elements in a higher unity. One thus becomes a more complete, a more developed person, capable of wider understanding, empathy, and love for others, etc. All this is familiar.

What is less familiar is the fact that crisis becomes constant and permanent when a man allows himself to be preoccupied, before all else, with "holding himself together"—with his own inner unity. This is one of the great dangers of the enclosed contemplative life for weak and introspective minds —precisely the ones who seem most drawn to it.

Basically, one who is obsessed with his own inner unity is failing to face his disunion with God and with other men. For it is in union with others that our own inner unity is naturally and easily established. To be preoccupied with achieving inner unity *first* and then going on to love others is to follow a logic of disruption which is contrary to life.

So, too, in times of rapid change. He who is disconcerted by the fear of change, who anticipates more and more threatening upheavals in society and in life, guards himself against the future by condemning it in advance—and preparing himself for the worst. In preparing for the worst he comes, in a way, to *accept* it, and in accepting it he desires it. Thus in the end he reconstitutes a fictitious unity for his disrupted psyche by imagining that he is able to contemplate the worst without fear and even with courageous acceptance.

This is the way the "nuclear realist," for example, is able to be quite cool and deliberate in his games with his computer and his ladders of escalation. This is his way of holding himself in one piece. And if he can get others to play the same games with him they will all go on into the future, real cool, in a perfectly calm dementia, quite willing to destroy themselves and everybody else—as long as their inner unity is no longer threatened.

Underlying this is a sin of solipsism, an intellectual and moral blindness that comes from basing all truth and all love upon one's inner relation to oneself, and not upon one's relation to others. Individualism makes this sin completely endemic in our society.

But now that we are beginning to see this, a greater temptation logically follows: the temptation to give up the whole struggle and find another kind of unity in the compact pseudorelatedness of mass-society and totalism.

✓ ✓ ✓

The disastrous misunderstanding: When a Christian imagines that "saving his soul" consists simply in getting himself together, avoiding those sins which disrupt his inner unity by shame, and keeping himself in one piece by self-approval. As if saving my soul were nothing more than learning how to live with myself in peace! Why is this disastrous? Because the worst evils may well have no disruptive effect on one's psyche. One may be able to commit them and live in perfect peace. Society can offer plenty of help, in quieting one's conscience, in providing full protection against interior disruption! A great deal of psychotherapy consists precisely in this, and nothing more.

✓ ✓ ✓

Ibn al' Arabi has God saying these words to the Sufi:

"I am known by no one but thee, just as thou existest only by Me. He who knows thee, knows Me—although no one knows Me. And thus thou also art known to no one."

This is the nonlogical logic of mysticism and of direct experience, expressed in statements which do not agree and which nevertheless finally explode into a meaning that can be seized if one has some experience of what is being said. Otherwise, it remains totally unintelligible.

Another Sufi, Al' Hujwiri, says:

"It is glorious for man to bear the burden of trouble laid upon him by his Beloved."

This is not cryptic at all: it has all the directness and clarity of the greatest mystics. But once again, it is not self-evident without a certain logic of its own, learned in prayer and perhaps in years of seeking.

"Sufism is essence without form."

This is challenging, but one has to know something of the subtle metaphysical background of their thought. Hence it is merely esoteric. Much better, much more direct, and unequivocal is this:

"The Sufi is he whose thought keeps pace with his foot."

✓ ✓ ✓

A holy day in December.

It rained at first, but now the day has turned softly bright, in the afternoon. There is a little cutting wind, but the sun is out. Most of the monks are in the scriptorium writing their Christmas letters, but I saw Brother D—— bobbing off down the back road in his white hood, and Brother R—— taking off into the pine woods with a mysterious sack, while Brother M—— walked off with sober joy, dressed in coveralls.

I pray much to have a wise heart, and perhaps the rediscovery of Lady Julian of Norwich will help me. I took her book with me on a quiet walk among the cedars. She is a true theologian with greater clarity, depth, and order than St. Theresa: she really elaborates, theologically, the content of her revelations. She first experienced, then thought, and the thoughtful deepening of experience worked it back into her life, deeper and deeper, until her whole life as a recluse at Norwich was simply a matter of getting completely saturated in the light she had received all at once, in the "shewings," when she thought she was about to die.

One of her most telling and central convictions is her orientation to what one might call *an eschatological secret,* the hidden dynamism which is at work already and by which "all manner of thing shall be well." This "secret," this act which the Lord keeps hidden, is really the full fruit of the Parousia. It is not just that "He comes," but He comes with this secret to reveal, He comes with this final answer to all the world's anguish, this answer which is already decided, but which we cannot discover (and which, since we think we have reasoned it all out anyway) we have stopped trying to discover. Actually, her life was lived in the belief in this "secret," the "great deed" that the Lord will do on the Last Day, not a deed of destruction and revenge, but of mercy and of life, all partial expectations will be exploded and *everything* will be made right. It is the great deed of "the end," which is still secret, but already fully at work in the world, in spite of all its sorrow, the great deed "ordained by Our Lord from without beginning."

She must indeed believe and accept the fact that there is a hell, yet also at the same time, impossibly one would think, she believes even more firmly that "the word of Christ shall be saved in all things" and "all manner of thing shall be well." This is, for her, the heart of theology: not solving the contradiction, but remaining in the midst of it, in peace, knowing that it is fully solved, but that the solution is secret, and will never be guessed until it is revealed.

To have a "wise heart," it seems to me, is to live centered on this dynamism and this secret hope—this hoped-for secret. It is the key to our life, but as long as we are alive we must see that we do not have this key: it is not at our disposal. Christ has it, in us, for us. We have the key in so far as we believe in Him, and are one with Him. So this is it: the "wise heart" remains in hope and in contradiction, in sorrow and in joy, fixed on the secret and the "great deed" which alone gives Christian life its true scope and dimensions!

The wise heart lives in Christ.

*   *   *

Night watch.

Even though I am Novice Master and am in the novitiate all the time, the novitiate takes on a great air of mystery and revelation when I pass through it on the night watch. The rooms which I hardly notice during the day seem, when they are empty, to have something very urgent to say, so that I want to linger in them and listen.

The novitiate no longer speaks to me of my own past (see "Firewatch" in *Sign of Jonas*). To begin with, it was re-modeled six years ago, and now it speaks more of the present generation of novices.

As I was going through absent-mindedly on my round, I pushed open the door of the novices' scriptorium and flashed the light over the desks, and the empty room spoke again. I stood there for a long time before going up to the chapel. Four long rows of desks. Their desks are all they have that is more or less "theirs." It is there that they sit reading, writing, thinking whatever is most personal, most truly their own. They keep their letters, their own few books, their own notes there.

Looking at the dark empty room, with everyone gone, it seemed that, because all that they loved was there, "they" in a spiritual way were most truly there, though in fact they were all upstairs in the dormitory, asleep.

It was as if their love and their goodness had transformed the room and filled it with a presence curiously real, comforting, perfect: one might say, with Christ. Indeed, it seemed to me momentarily that He was as truly present here, in a certain way, as upstairs in the Chapel. The loveliness of the humanity which God has taken to Himself in love is, after all, to be seen in the humanity of our friends, our children, our brothers, the people we love and who love us. Now that God has become Incarnate, why do we go to such lengths, all the time, to "disincarnate" Him again, to unweave the garment of flesh and reduce Him once again to spirit? As if the Body of the Lord had not become "Life-giving Spirit."

You can see the beauty of Christ in each individual person, in that which is most his, most human, most personal to him, in things which an ascetic might advise you sternly to get rid of. But these attachments, too, are relevant to your life in Christ, and I have noticed that novices who try to be too grimly detached from parents and friends, and from other people in general, often lack a most important spiritual dimension in their lives, and frequently fail altogether as monks. Those who are more "human" make better monks, precisely because they are more human and because they simply do not believe the injunctions of those who try to tell them that they must be less human.

In any case, I felt there was something quite final and eternal in looking at this empty room: that though they themselves might not understand what they are going through, and though many of them may fail, may leave, or may have to look elsewhere to get the real meaning of their lives, yet the sign of love is on these novices and they are precious forever in God's eyes. Certainly, it has been a great gift of His Love to me, that I am their Novice Master. It is very good to have loved these people and been loved by them with such simplicity and sincerity, within our ordinary limitation, without nonsense, without flattery, without sentimentality, and without getting too involved in one anothers' business.

From this basic experience one can, after all, recover hope for the other dimension of man's life: the political. Even though we have the power to destroy the whole world, life is stronger than the death instinct and love is stronger than hate. It does not make logical sense to be too hopeful, but once again this is not a question of logic and one does not look for signs of hope in the newspapers or the pronouncements of world leaders (in these there is seldom anything really hopeful, and that which is supposed to be most encouraging is usually so transparently hopeless that it moves one closer to despair). Because there is love in the world, and because Christ has taken our nature to Himself, there remains always the hope that man will finally, after many mistakes and even disasters, learn to disarm and to make peace, recognizing that he *must* live at peace with his brother. Yet never have we been less disposed to do this.

The fact remains, this is the one great lesson we have to learn. Everything else is trivial compared with his supreme and urgent need of man.

# PART FOUR

## The Fork in the Road

*Life comes without warning.*
*—Lieh Tzu*

*A man of massive meditation*
*Is like a man looking at death,*
*Looking at death as at a bull's-eye.*
*He watches before he crosses the tracks.*
*—Richard Eberhart*

Father Tavard, taking a different position from that of C. Dawson, says in an article, "Christian culture today is a problem rather than a fact." In other words, when "Christendom" is dead can we guarantee that "Christian culture" will survive? Christendom is not the Church, of course. The Church is now in a world that is culturally "post-Christian." (Theologically one cannot really speak of a "post-Christian era." The "Christian era" is the time of the end, the last era. Nevertheless, that does not mean that the "Christian era" must necessarily continue in the shape of Christian culture.)

Tavard's idea is that, by turning to the world and working with those who are not explicitly Christian, we can perhaps in our convergence with them bring about a resurrection of basically Christian values in secular culture. Christianity can embrace the whole world without fear precisely because it is greater than the world.

This is the spirit with which John XXIII is speaking: the spirit of openness and dialogue. Certainly in John XXIII I can see not only the greatness and simplicity of a truly Christian view of man, but also the living reality of the Christian and European tradition in culture. A true sense of Christian civilization. He at least does not seem to doubt that it can survive, even as culture. However, that is not precisely what all the progressives are saying. There are many who call for a frank "secularization" of Christianity on the ground that Christian values have persisted in the secular milieu and do not necessarily have to have an explicitly "religious" orientation.

One of the admirable things about Pope John is his simple fidelity to the *Socratic* principle which is essential to our

Western cultural tradition. This is a very profound element in Pope John's thought, and he has shown in fact that true Christian renewal implies an understanding of and a commitment to Christian Socratism. This means respect for *persons,* to the point where the person of the adversary demands a hearing even when the authority of one's own ecclesial institution might appear to be temporarily questioned. Actually, this Socratic confidence in dialogue implies a deeper faith in the Church than you find in a merely rigid, defensive, and negative attitude which refuses all dialogue. The negative view really suggests that the Church has *something to lose* by engaging in dialogue with her adversaries. This in turn is a rejection of the Christian Socratism which sees that truth develops in conversation. And, after all, that is the spirit of the Gospel also. We see it everywhere in the New Testament. Those who were *open* to Christ and the Apostles, received the truth. Those who refused dialogue, or who engaged in it only with political intentions, with pragmatic reservations and tactical subtlety, ended by crucifying Christ and slaying the Apostles.

The Socratic principle, as Pope John definitely sees, means not only the willingness to discuss, but the readiness to meet one's adversary *as an equal and as a brother.* The moment one does this, he ceases to be an adversary.

Some seem to fear that in such encounters, meeting the adversary on his own ground, we leave the protection of the Church and Catholic truth. They forget that if we meet the non-Christian *as a brother* we meet him on ground that is *Christian.* If we fear to meet him on what is really our own ground, is this not perhaps because we ourselves are not sufficiently Christian?

✓  ✓  ✓

An H-bomb, I am told, costs only two hundred and fifty thousand dollars to make. Was there ever such a bargain? I ask you, who can give you more destruction for your dollar? Is it believable that we can resist getting all that we have paid for?

*✓  ✓  ✓*

From a purely human estimate, one would be tempted to think that at the rate we are going we can hardly avoid a major war between now (1962) and 1967.

Without serious reason, without anybody really "wanting it," without anyone being able to prevent it, war can overwhelm the tactics of adroit politicians. The powerful do not rule by their power, it rules them. It rules us through them, it is not *their* power. Whose is it then? It is certainly not "ours." Whose power is it? Is there still a message for us in St. Paul's statement that our combat is not against flesh and blood?                                   (Ephesians 6:12)

Whether or not a major war—a nuclear war—should finally break, we have to live in a way that daily takes this possibility seriously into account.

This implies certain important choices, certain preferences. Even though one may not be able to halt the race toward death, one must nevertheless *choose life,* and the things that favor life. This means respect for every living thing, but especially for every man, made in the image of God. Respect for man even in his blindness and in his confusion, even when he may do evil. For we must see that the meaning of man has been totally changed by the Crucifixion: every man is Christ on the Cross, whether he realizes it or not. But we, if we are Christians, must learn to realize it. That is what it means to be a Christian: not simply one who believes certain reports about Christ, but one who lives in *a conscious confrontation with Christ* in himself and in other men.

This means, therefore, the choice to become empty of one's self, the illusory self fabricated by our desires and fears, the self that is here now and will cease being here if this or that happens.

It means finally preferring silent action and interior sacrifice, because words have become too cheap, and programs grow on every tree. Better than any program is the decision to accept suffering, knowing why, and for what, without justifying oneself. People today are learning once again to *fast* for peace.

✓ ✓ ✓

Winter, Shakertown.

Marvelous, vast, silent, white open spaces around the old buildings put up by the Shakers at Pleasant Hill a hundred or a hundred and fifty years ago. (Already a hundred years ago, about the time of the Civil War, the Shakers reached their peak and began to decline.) Cold, pure light. Some great old trees. I took some photographs but it was so cold my finger could no longer feel the shutter release. Marvelous subjects. I have no way of explaining how the bare, blank side of an old frame house with some broken windows can be so indescribably beautiful. The Shaker builders—like all their craftsmen—had the gift of achieving perfert forms. There is nothing so good anywhere in Kentucky. Those few moments of eloquent silence in the snow stay with me, follow me home, do not go away.

✓ ✓ ✓

All being is from God.

This is not simply an arbitrary and tendentious "religious" affirmation which in some way or other robs being of autonomy and dignity. On the contrary, the doctrine of creation is, when properly understood, that which implies the deepest respect for reality and for the being of everything that is.

The doctrine of creation is rooted not in a desperate religious attempt to account for the fact that the world exists. It is not merely an answer to the question of how things got to be what they are by pointing to God as a cause. On the contrary, the doctrine of creation as we have it in the Bible and as it has been developed in Christian theology (particularly in St. Thomas) starts not from a *question about being* but from a *direct intuition of the act of being*. Nothing could be further from a merely mechanistic and causal explanation of existence. "Creation" is then not merely a pat official answer to a religious query about our origin.

One who apprehends being as such apprehends it as an act which is utterly beyond a complete scientific explanation. To apprehend being is an act of contemplation and philosophical wisdom rather than the fruit of scientific analysis. It is in fact a gift given to few. Anyone can say: "This is a tree; that is a man." But how few are ever struck by the realization of the real import of what is really meant by *"is?"*

Sometimes it is given to children and to simple people (and the "intellectual" may indeed be an essentially simple person, contrary to all the myths about him—for only the stupid are disqualified from true simplicity) to experience a direct intuition of being. Such an intuition is simply an immediate grasp of one's own inexplicable personal reality in one's own incommunicable act of existing!

One who has experienced the baffling, humbling, and liberating clarity of this immediate sense of what it means to *be* has in that very act experienced something of the presence of God. For God is present to me in the act of my own being, an act which proceeds directly from His will and is His gift. My act of being is a direct participation in the Being of God. God is pure Being, this is to say He is the pure and infinite Act of total Reality. All other realities are simply reflections of His pure Act of Being, and participations in it granted by His free gift.

Now my existence differs from that of a stone or a vegetable—or even from that of an irrational animal.

The being that is given to me is given with certain possibilities which are not open to other beings. And the chief of these possibilities is that I am capable of increasing the intensity and the quality of my act of existence by the free response I make to life.

And here we come to the root problem of life. My being is given me not simply as an arbitrary and inscrutable affliction, but as a source of joy, growth, life, creativity, and fulfillment. But the decision to take existence only as an affliction is left to me.

The real root-sin of modern man is that, in ignoring and contemning *being*, and especially his own being, he has made his *existence* a disease and an affliction. And, strangely, he has done this with all kinds of vitalistic excuses, proclaiming at every turn that he stands on frontiers of new abundance and permanent bliss.

This ambiguity and arbitrariness appear most clearly in technology. There is nothing wrong with technology in itself. It could indeed serve to deepen and perfect the quality of men's existence and in some ways it *has* done this. As Lewis Mumford said: "Too many thought not only that mechanical progress would be a positive aid to human improvement, which is true, *but that mechanical progress is the equivalent of human improvement,* which turns out to be sheer nonsense."

We have not even begun to plumb the depths of nonsense into which this absurd error has plunged us.

It is precisely this illusion, that mechanical progress means human improvement, that alienates us from our own being and our own reality. It is precisely because we are convinced that our life, as such, is better if we have a better car, a better TV set, better toothpaste, etc., that we contemn and destroy our own reality and the reality of our natural resources. Technology was made for man, not man for technology. In losing touch with being and thus with God, we have fallen into a senseless idolatry of production and consumption for their own sakes. We have renounced the act of being and plunged ourself into *process* for its own sake. We no longer know how to live, and because we cannot accept life in its reality life ceases to be a joy and becomes an affliction. And we even go so far as to blame God for it! The evil in the world is all our own making, and it proceeds entirely from our ruthless, senseless, wasteful, destructive, and suicidal neglect of our own being. This moral and spiritual disease is manifesting itself daily in symptoms that are more and more critical. We can do nothing about it, apparently. Sometimes it seems that we don't even want to. And the most pitiful thing of all is that, in the name of God, Christians who ought to know better are busy blessing and praising the disease on the ground that this is a matter of "openness to the world" and "adjustment to modern times."

A respect for "the world" that does not rest on a real intuition of the act of being and a grateful, contemplative, and Christian sense of being will end only in the further destruction and debasement of the world in the name of a false humanism which has no other fruit than to make man hate himself, hate life, and hate the world he lives in.

✦   ✦   ✦

True Christian "openness to the world" proceeds from a genuine respect for being and for man, and for man's natural and historical setting in the world. But to "respect" man in his historical situation today without taking account of his need, his anguish, his limitations, and his peril, above all without consenting to share in his guilt, ends only in a cruel mockery of man. What is the good of exalting the "greatness of man" simply because the concerted efforts of technicians, soldiers, and politicians manage to put a man on the moon while four fifths of the human race remain in abject misery, not properly clothed or fed, in lives subject to arbitrary and senseless manipulation by politicians or violence at the hands of police, hoodlums, or revolutionaries? Certainly the possibilities and the inherent nobility of man are stupendous: but it is small help to crow about it when the celebration of his theoretic greatness does nothing to help him find himself as an ordinary human being.

Instead of an idolatrous cult of technology and power, and the senseless magnification of man's greatness (in reality the self-magnification of police chiefs and entrepreneurs) let us "turn to the world" in the sense of regaining command over our vast powers and using them to fulfill man's needs.

✦   ✦   ✦

We fear the thought of suicide, and yet we need to think rationally about it, if we can, because one of the characteristics of our time is precisely that it is a suicidal age.

One might go on imagining that suicide is something that incidentally happens in any age, and happens more frequently now simply because there are more people to be defeated, and life is perhaps more ruthless. Yet let us face the fact that life is in many ways less ruthless than it has ever been. For the well-to-do—and they are the ones who are most suicidal—there is comfort, security, no end of distraction, life should be livable and even happy. They are able to have

almost anything they want. Almost. For there remain a few
things that cannot be had on demand, no matter how much
you may be willing to pay for them: for example, self-respect,
love, faith, peace, fulfillment.

Here is precisely where the trouble begins:

Man, thinking of himself secretly as a completely free autonomous self, with unlimited possibilities (after all he is
taught by his society that this is what he is), finds himself in
an impossible predicament. He is "as a god" and therefore
everything is within reach. But it turns out that all that he
can successfully reach by his own volition is not quite worth
having. What he *really* seeks and needs—love, an authentic
identity, a life that has meaning—cannot be had merely by
*willing* and by taking steps to procure them. No amount of
ingenuity can "buy" these—no psychological or sociological
manipulation can encompass them, no inspirational religious
self-help, no ascetic technique, no drug can do the trick!

The things we really need come to us only as gifts, and in
order to receive them as gifts we have to be open. In order to
be open we have to renounce ourselves, in a sense we have to
*die* to our image of ourselves, our autonomy, our fixation
upon our self-willed identity. We have to be able to relax
the psychic and spiritual cramp which knots us in the painful,
vulnerable, helpless "I" that is all we know as ourselves.

The chronic inability to relax this cramp begets despair. In
the end, as we realize more and more that we are knotted
upon *nothing*, that the cramp is a meaningless, senseless,
pointless affirmation of nonentity, and that we must nevertheless continue to affirm our nothingness *over against* everything else—our frustration becomes absolute. We become incapable of existing except as a "no," which we fling in the
face of everything. This "no" to everything serves as our
pitiful "yes" to ourselves—a makeshift identity which is
nothing.

There are certain refusals which are noble, which are affirmations of higher truth, epiphanies of reality, witnesses to
God. The man-in-a-cramp of freedom, knotted up in frustration, may obscurely *mean* his cramp to be a noble refusal.
In a sense he may seem to be right in his protest. He may

seem to be protesting against the iniquity of a situation that impoverishes and destroys him. With this as his justification he hardens himself in total refusal. He builds himself a final identity out of cramp, resentment, and negation.

It is at this point that the logic of the cramp begins to demand one final solution. Since the cramp itself is intolerable, and since he cannot relax it, he can only destroy it. And since he has reduced himself, narrowed himself down to the point where he is nothing but his miserable cramp clutched on to itself, when the cramp destroys itself it destroys him.

The important thing, then, is to be able to stop refusing and "cramping" before it is too late. One must learn to say "no" to the cramp, and "yes" to everything else.

I see no other way than the clear recognition of the nature of this "cramp." This "refusal" is fundamentally a refusal of faith. Not necessarily of theological and Christian faith in the full sense of the word, but at least a refusal of the natural readiness, the openness, the humility, the self-forgetfulness that *renounce absolute demands,* give up the intransigeant claim to perfect autonomy, and *believe in life.* Belief here means also trust, the ability to take risks, to advance into the unknown trusting that life itself can and will take care of us if we let it. Yet to my mind a mere "faith in life" is precarious and misleading. Today there are too many errors and confusions about "life." The mentality of suicide is built into our technological society—the mass media, focused always on violence and crisis, destroy sane hope, keep everybody in a cramp of fear and suspicion.

There is only one remedy—the surrender that seeks faith in God as a gift that is not our due, and that is willing to suffer great indigence and peril while waiting to receive it.

This means in fact recognizing that one is not absolutely alone, and that one cannot live and die for himself alone. My life and my death are not purely and simply my own business. I live by and for others, and my death involves others. "No one of us lives for himself, no one dies for himself, but whether we live or die, we are the Lord's."     Romans 14:8

The temptation to despair is something we can hardly avoid, but there is a fruitfulness and a possibility of new life in the very threat of despair. It forces us to choose. And we will *always* have the strength to choose life, unless we are so ill and so destroyed that we are no longer ourselves at all. The real pity and sin of suicide is the *needless* and arbitrary refusal of this last gift and possibility: the chance to prefer life even in defeat—a refusal of this *hope precisely because* the chance and the hope come to us *not from ourselves*. Thus it happens that the man on the edge of suicide may in fact also be on the edge of a miracle of hope that saves him in spite of himself, pulls him out of the cramp. If he can understand what has happened, he may completely revise his idea of what constitutes "defeat" and what bestows freedom and fulfillment. And he may begin to live as another person—as one who has the humility to accept gifts which come to him on conditions he cannot foresee or determine, which come to him from an unknown source, and which are in no way subject to his own imperious demand.

Yet this is no strange supernatural state: it is simply the ordinary way of human existence!

If our time is in fact marked with the sign of suicide, the reason is that this ordinary human mode of life is consistently forgotten—so consistently that the mentality of our world may lay upon many people a burden of despair so great that they cannot meet even the ordinary exigencies of human existence, or muster up the common courage which is an essential component of life. But I think there remain creative possibilities for those who can recognize some other source of hope and understanding than that which is offered by society speaking through the mass media. One who can exchange the refusal to live for an intelligent and creative social dissent may perhaps discover ways of his own out of the general confusion. But in any case these ways will open themselves to him only as providential gifts.

*1  1  1*

Comparing the tracts on patience by Tertullian and by St. Cyprian, I much prefer Tertullian—whom Cyprian in any case imitated. There is great vigor in Tertullian's thought, greater still in his style. He could write better about patience because he was obviously a less patient man. His struggle was greater, and so his understanding was deeper. Here, in fact, was a violent man who realized that he had to take, with total seriousness, Christ's command to renounce violence! And he saw that for him this was, naturally speaking, impossible. So when Tertullian reduces all sin to a root of impatience with God, he is not being arbitrary. A mild man can mildly and innocently ignore the will of God, and think he is doing right. A violent man, if he pays attention to the will of God, realizes that he himself refuses to wait for the slow working out of what he does not immediately see and understand. And when something does happen, he immediately sees consequences that drive him to extremes: but the consequences perhaps come out quite differently.

Like Nietzsche, Tertullian is worth reading even when he is completely wrong. Like Calvin, he has a bitterness, a pessimism that are nevertheless salutary—if you do not become engulfed in them. He is always bringing out internal contradictions and ironies. For instance the irony of "torture" and "confession" in the case of a Christian. You torture a criminal, he says, in order to make him confess his crime. But confessing Christianity is the crime for which you torture the martyrs. And when they stop confessing, you stop torturing them. You torture them to make them *deny* their crime. Hence there is a basic ambiguity in torture itself and in the processes of law as practiced in the late empire: and this ambiguity should warn all men of law that there is perhaps a secret force at work in their law itself that makes legal judgment perhaps the ruin of judgment: in a word, when they apply the law in this equivocal fashion, they are destroying themselves by it.

This discovery is valid for all cases in which law is misused to persecute a minority: the purpose of law becomes the evasion of justice and of truth. Law is used so that they *may not know* right and wrong.

Where custom and law systematically conceal rights and truth, then the Holy Spirit inspires men to carry out actions that violate custom and law in order to bear witness to truth. Even in their unjust judgment, truth and right become clear.

✓  ✓  ✓

Lanza del Vasto noted a deep connection between *play* and *war*, even before the games theory and nuclear war strategy became practically identified. In our society, everything, in fact, is a game. But if everything is a game, then everything leads to war. Play is aimless and yet multiplies obstacles so that the "aim," which in fact does not exist, cannot be attained by the opponent. For instance, getting a ball in a hole. War is caused by similar aimless aims. Not by hunger, not by real need. War is a game of the powerful, or of whole collectivities devoted to self-assertion. It is "the great public vice that consists in playing with the lives of men." War plays with life and death, and does so magnificently. Everybody becomes involved. Everybody has to live or die—so that the other side may not get a ball in a hole. But the real excitement of the game comes from the suspension of conscience. In all play, one has to prescind from real conditions. One has to assume that such and such a thing is real and everything else unreal. In war, one assumes that it is not only right, but necessary, to kill. The great sacrifice in war is not so much the sacrifice of life as the suspension of conscience (a sacrifice which, however, most people find easy and delightful as long as everybody makes it at the same time). If there is any "need" at all that drives men to war it is this. The need for a massive suspension of conscience, a total irresponsibility, in which everyone can *let go* and devote himself to one task: destroying the enemy. Reasonable? Obviously not. If war were only reasonable, it would not be the menace that it is. The great danger of war is precisely this universal need for *mass immorality*, which the game of war so completely satisfies. The satisfaction is all the greater when the suspension of conscience can be seen as a charismatic response to a higher, more mystical summons: to destroy the devil by a delicious recourse to the devil's own methods.

✓ ✓ ✓

I never thought I would find myself enjoying something like Cassiodorus' routine chapters on the teaching of grammar and rhetoric. And yet I do, because of the clarity with which he handles his subject. He is a bit of a pedant, and yet he obviously loves the values he is trying to preserve. (As he grows older he becomes more and more desperately committed to saving the most elementary things: in the end he is fighting for correct spelling.) Vivarium was, in a way, an ideal monastery: but it never survived. Yet the spirit of Vivarium had an extraordinary influence on Anglo-Saxon monasticism (Bede) and on the Celtic monks, at least those on the continent. (The library of Vivarium was moved to the Celtic monastery of Bobbio.)

✓ ✓ ✓

Cassiodorus on the knowledge of God: he is not original, but beautifully expresses the teaching of the (Platonising) Fathers: The soul knows the divine Light obscurely in so far as it is itself light from that Light.

That unspeakable mystery which we worship
and which is everywhere whole and invisibly present
Father, Son and Holy Spirit
One essence, undivided Majesty
Splendor beyond all radiances and glory beyond all praise
This the perfectly pure mind wholly surrendered to God may
    in some manner perceive, but not adequately explain:
For how should it be possible to speak comprehensively of
    Him who cannot be grasped by the mind of a creature?
                                                —De Anima

The prose of Cassiodorus looks back to antiquity. There is another style, that of St. Gregory the Great, which tuned all the prose harmonies of the medieval commentators on the Bible. The ear of the Middle Ages was trained not only by the music of Gregorian chant but also by the slow swing of the *cursus* and the simple, balanced, reflective sentences of Gregory's *Moralia*. I am very happy that in the novitiate I spent about a year on the *Moralia* and loved it from the beginning. Once you get used to the rhythm of these monastic conferences (Gregory delivered them to monks who accompanied him on an embassy to Constantinople) you recognize their influence without fail in monastic writers of the eleventh and twelfth centuries. To know Gregory is to know the language and the mentality of medieval Benedictinism.

St. Odo of Cluny even saw St. Gregory in a dream. The Pope gave Odo a pen (which he took from behind his ear) and told him to start writing!

✓ ✓ ✓

Gloom and murk of drizzling rain across the valley, more like a cloud than falling rain. I wonder what is in it? Both we and the Russians are testing (bombs) again. In the dim light, daylilies flare discretely, and poplar leaves turn up in a wind that does not move the fog anywhere. The valley remains dark and drenched in it. I had long talks with two novices who will eventually leave. Then read a little of a new book, a collection of essays on monastic theology (its title is *Theologie Monastique*), which seldom reaches the level of theology. One might rather call them historical background notes for monastic theology. And I suppose this is the purpose: to assert that there is such a thing as monastic theology, so that if people become convinced of it, they will not leave the monastery.

✓ ✓ ✓

The King of Death, says a Buddhist poem, does not see you if you do not see any self in yourself. "Where there is no thing, where naught is grasped, there is the Isle of No-Beyond."

✓ ✓ ✓

Each year the new tractors get bigger and bigger, louder and louder. The one in the valley now sounds like a tank or a big bulldozer. Round and round the alfalfa field in fury. What thoughts it represents: what fury of man; what restlessness; what avidity; what desperation.

It is desperation, not love, that makes the world go round.
Around and around it goes, clacking its despair.

✓ ✓ ✓

After the great Chilean earthquake, after bigger and bigger bombs, after a plague of sharks along the California beaches, it is finally reported that near San Francisco a whale was washed ashore dead—of ulcers!

✓ ✓ ✓

John Wu is a man of profound and Zen-like humor, a humor which adds to the depth of his Christianity—and to his Christian *parrhesia*. He does not mind what he says. He got into an argument with Pope Pius XII, who told him that it was because of "his merits" that he had such a lovely family. John protested, and I think very rightly.

When Sister Pauline (Prioress of the Lisieux Carmel and sister of St. Therese) tried to get him to do something in Rome (where he was ambassador) about the book of Maxence Van der Meersch, he told her that she was "not Theresian." Another friend of the saint's family was complaining that the "new pictures" (which are simply photographs showing St. Therese as she actually was) were implicitly discrediting the idealized paintings made by another of Therese's sisters. "Well," said John, "Celine is in heaven in spite of her paintings."

He spoke to us in the monastery and said blandly: "You monks can be happy and you can laugh, in this monastery, since you know that nothing worse can happen to you." I wish some of us had the sense to see it that way.

When one of the monks asked him what he thought was most "dangerous" to American monasticism he did not reply "love of comfort" or anything like that, but "a spirit of pragmatism." Bull's-eye!

✓ ✓ ✓

Businesses are, in reality, quasi-religious sects. When you go to work in one you embrace *a new faith*. And if they are really big businesses, you progress from faith to a kind of mystique. Belief in the product, preaching the product, in the end the product becomes the focus of a transcendental experience. Through "the product" one communes with the vast forces of life, nature, and history that are expressed in business. Why not face it? Advertising treats all products with the reverence and the seriousness due to sacraments.

Harrington says (*Life in the Crystal Palace*): "The new evangelism whether expressed in soft or hard selling, is a quasi-religious approach to business, wrapped in a hoax—a hoax voluntarily entered into by producers and consumers together. Its credo is that of belief-to-order. It is the truth-to-order as delivered by advertising and public relations men, believed in by them and voluntarily believed by the public."

Once again, it is the question of a game. Life is aimless, but one invents a thousand aimless aims and then mobilizes a whole economy around them, finally declaring them to be transcendental, mystical, and absolute.

Compare our monastery and the General Electric plant in Louisville. Which one is the more serious and more "religious" institution? One might be tempted to say "the monastery," out of sheer habit. But, in fact, the religious seriousness of the monastery is like sandlot baseball compared with the big-league seriousness of General Electric. It may in fact occur to many, including the monks, to *doubt* the monastery and what it represents.

Who doubts G.E.?

✓ ✓ ✓

"Only when death is grasped in its ontological character are we justified in asking what is after death."    —Heidegger

The "ontological" grasp of death is implicit in the Christian doctrine of original sin. It is characteristic of a "fallen" existence that death is built into it. To exist as "fallen" or as "lost" is to exist with an existence one has not chosen, which may well prove meaningless, destined for a death one cannot evade. But another characteristic of the fallen existence is that it seeks to forget death by immersing itself in "the world." Man, as Heidegger says, flees from himself and "desires to fall into the world." That is to say, he seeks to forget his inner dread of death by concern with objects, by aimless immersion in public opinion and action. Such a temptation could not be serious if he were not able to persuade himself of the great importance of his concerns, his opinions, and his acts. But certain forms of social life—particularly the routines of mass society—are so patently artificial and fictitious that it is difficult even for those who are not very intelligent to be completely taken in by them. Hence a general sense of uneasiness, a sense that one has been "had," and a consequent resurgence of anxiety and dread. Yet man seeks to justify his inauthentic existence by the illusion that he remains master of his own destiny and of the world, and by the further illusion that he has almost reached the point where he will have conquered sickness, despair, and even, perhaps, death itself. Thus he goes on frivolously and dishonestly, without thinking of death and without making any decision that would orient his life in the face of death.

To live inauthentically in the world, to spend one's whole life evading the reality of death, and then, on top of all that, to tell oneself that one has the answer to the question of what happens after death: this can be a further depth of self-deception. One can perhaps succeed in this by a naïve and stubborn insistence on believing that after death everything will continue to be just as it is now: except that care and pain will not be problems any longer. Such an attitude is not Christian, it is simply a regression to a crass form of paganism. The Christian faith does not give us detailed and precise answers as to what happens after death: but it does urge us to face death, and take it into account, and overcome our fear of it, and conquer it in Christ. That is quite another matter.

More Christians ought to realize this, instead of making their pious considerations of heaven and hell (if any) simply a way of evading the need to face death in its reality. But, once again, the Christian faith does not seek merely to answer the question "What comes after death?" Rather it answers the question we ask about death itself: what is death? What does death mean, in my own existence now? For death is not merely the inevitable *end* of life, an end that must come

whether one likes it or not. It is not merely a painful necessity, like paying income tax. The fact of death is not merely
the closing of all possibilities, the negation of choice and
hope. I am not free not to die, but I remain free to make
what I like out of a life that must end in death. But an
authentic use of this freedom demands that I take death into
account. To pretend to live as if I could not be touched by
death is not a rational and human use of freedom. Such
"freedom" is actually without any meaning at all. It is a
delusion.

At the heart of the Christian faith is the conviction that,
when death is accepted in a spirit of faith, and when one's
whole life is oriented to self-giving so that at its end one
gladly and freely surrenders it back into the hands of God
the Creator and Redeemer, then death is transformed into a
fulfillment. One conquers death by love—not by one's own
heroic virtuousness, but by sharing in that love with which
Christ accepted death on the Cross. This is not apparent to
reason: it is, precisely, a matter of faith. But the Christian
is one who believes that when he has united his life and his
death with Christ's gift of Himself on the Cross, he has not
merely found a dogmatic answer to a human problem and
a set of ritual gestures which comfort and allay anxiety: he
has gained access to the grace of the Holy Spirit. Therefore
he lives no longer by his own forfeited and fallen existence,
but by the eternal and immortal life that is given him, in
the Spirit, by Christ. He lives "in Christ."

What then "comes after death" is still not made clear in
terms of a "place of rest" (a celestial cemetery?) or a paradise of reward. The Christian is not concerned really with a
life divided between this world and the next. He is concerned
with one life, the new life of man (Adam—all men) in Christ
and in the Spirit, both now and after death. He does not ask
for a blueprint of his heavenly mansion. He seeks the Face of
God, and the vision of Him Who is eternal life. (John 17:3)

✓ ✓ ✓

The Persian Sufi poet Rumi (thirteenth century) writes
this about death, showing that our attitude toward death is

in reality a reflection of our attitude toward ourself and toward our life. He who truly loves life and lives it, is able to accept death without sorrow.

Rumi's poem is on "The Beauty of Death." It reads in part:

He who deems death to be lovely, as Joseph, gives up his soul in ransom for it; he who deems it to be like the wolf, turns back from the path of salvation.
Everyone's death is of the same quality as himself, my son: to the enemy of God an enemy, to the friend of God a friend . . .
Your fear of death is really fear of yourself: see what it is from which you are fleeing!
'Tis your own ugly face, not the visage of death: your spirit is like the tree, death like the leaf.

Yet this "friendship" with death is not the same as a pathological death wish. The death wish is merely a refusal of life, an abdication from the difficulties and sorrows of living, a resentment of its joys. The death wish is an incapacity for life. True acceptance of death in freedom and faith demands a mature and fruitful acceptance of life. He who fears death or he who longs for it—both are in the same condition: they admit they have not lived.

✓ ✓ ✓

We imagine that propaganda is always something patently false, or at least in great part fictitious: a malicious and systematic misrepresentation of truth. And of course this is sometimes true. But propaganda need not be blatantly false. On the contrary, the more effective propaganda contains in it a large measure of truth, and it is effective precisely because the facts on which it is based can be verified. Men who think themselves intelligent enough not to be taken in by "mere propaganda" and who assume that all propaganda is easily detected by the evident falsity of the facts let themselves be completely taken in by the mere subtle variety which, today, is much more common than the other. After all, we are making progress in this area too!

Propaganda is an ostensible appeal to reason and to action which is in fact essentially *irrational*. But it is not necessarily *untrue*. Yet how many men are capable of telling the difference between a statement that is simply untrue, and one which, though containing true facts, joins them together in a way that is irrational and therefore makes no real sense? For instance one can say that there are Communists in a certain neighborhood and say that Senator X has been seen in that neighborhood, and both statements may be perfectly correct. But when one joins the two together in such a way as to suggest the conclusion that therefore Senator X is a Communist, and that he was in that neighborhood precisely in order to attend a Communist meeting, then the statement is irrational. It does not prove what it appears to prove. Propaganda exploits just such suggestions and insinuations, and we are all the more susceptible to its irrational appeal since we are constantly subjected to the same systematic irrationality in advertising.

The most effective propaganda is, then, that which makes use of strictly true facts, but facts which do not mean what the propagandist claims they mean and which, in reality mean nothing whatever. They only lend a spurious air of authority and even "scientific objectivity" to the conclusion, which is addressed not to reason but to the emotions.

Jacques Ellul shows that a mass of factual and correct information can, even if not illogically presented, have the same effect as completely false and irrational propaganda. Even supposing that the information itself may be rational, when the reader or the listener is deluged with facts and arguments that he cannot possibly assimilate, he ends up with nothing but a global impression, which is something quite different from a firm rational judgment. One reads or hears lists of statistics, editorial opinions, the results of opinion polls, the decisions of statesmen. This mass of information from various sources has been hastily read and not assimilated. You do not have time to think about it, or weigh the meaning of it. You are simply left with a general sense that such and such a policy is wise, that because those who *know all this* have come to certain conclusions, their conclusions are probably the right ones. Hence, instead of making a reasoned judgment one makes an act of faith in his government or his political party and leaves it at that!

It is these impressions and "acts of faith," rather than rational and well-informed judgments, that guide the decisions not only of ordinary citizens but even of experts and "authorities." Because they have *scanned* the information and have perhaps discussed it with others who have gone through the same summary process, they think they are informed. Because they have *formed an impression*—and are satisfied that others have formed the same impression—they feel as if they had reached a fully rational conclusion. On such impressions wars are built. And because the original facts were perhaps perfectly correct, one takes it for granted that all the other steps were reasonable too, whereas they were not. How much worse it is when the facts themselves are doctored or suspect: or when one does not even know the relevant facts at all?

✦ ✦ ✦

There is such a thing as a labyrinth of information: the information is truly abundant and complex, and yet one does not really have a choice. Other vital information is withheld or unavailable. One enters the labyrinth of available facts, and there is no rational way out. On the contrary, every path eventually leads to the same center, an inescapable conclusion which may even be quite logical: but it has been predetermined by the selection of certain facts and the willful exclusion of others. "Thus rational propaganda gives birth to an irrational situation and remains before all else propaganda, that is to say an interior possession of the individual by a social power, which corresponds to his surrender of self-possession."

—Ellul

The real violence exerted by propaganda is this: by means of apparent truth and apparent reason, it induces us to surrender our freedom and self-possession. It predetermines us to certain conclusions, and does so in such a way that we imagine that we are fully free in reaching them by our own judgment and our own thought. Propaganda *makes up our mind* for us, but in such a way that it leaves us the sense of pride and satisfaction of men who have made up their own minds. And, in the last analysis, propaganda achieves this effect *because we want it to*. This is one of the few real pleasures left to modern man: this illusion that he is thinking for himself when, in fact, someone else is doing his thinking for him. And this someone else is not a personal authority, the great mind of a genial thinker, it is the mass mind, the general "they," the anonymous whole. One is left, therefore, not only with the sense that one has thought things out for himself, but that he has also reached the correct answer without difficulty—the answer which is shown to be correct because it is the answer of everybody. Since it is at once my answer and the answer of everybody, how should I resist it?

✓ ✓ ✓

This very special and tempting force of propaganda—that it helps sustain the individual's illusion of identity and freedom—is due to the isolation of the individual in mass society, in which he is in fact a zero in the crowd in which he is absorbed. It is this simple act of apparently thinking out what is thought out for him by propaganda that saves the individual from totally vanishing into the mass. It makes him imagine he is real. Moreover it gives him the sense of being not only real, but right. It *justifies* him. To think that there are many people in mass society who consider themselves Christians, and who, psychologically at least, seek their justification not from faith in Christ or from the works of Christ's love, but from propaganda, which enables them to think out "for themselves" a few simple political opinions that add up to a crusade "in the name of Christ." One would think that modern man was so sophisticated that he would not be tempted by the idea of devils and of Antichrist. On the contrary, there is nothing easier. Today men are looking for Antichrists: for if the enemy is Antichrist that makes everything much simpler. There is no need to make any further reservations or ask any more questions. One can hate with a good conscience.

✟ ✟ ✟

The hardest people to propagandize are those who are ignorant of the news, either because they are not interested in it at all, or because they are not reached by it, or because they feel themselves so excluded from society (for instance in a ghetto) that they are able to treat the news of that society as if it could not concern them. It becomes meaningless to them. They acquire other sources of information. The fabulous grapevine that exists and functions, for example, in Harlem! You set foot in a store at one end of the block, and before you are out of the store everybody on the block knows you are there, who you are, what you are doing. In such a milieu it is true that very simple and primitive forms of "propaganda" exert a tremendous force. But they are not really propaganda. They are spontaneous myths formed by the social milieu itself, out of its own spontaneity. They are not transmitted to it from above. Thus there comes a moment when a Negro youth is hit by a cop, or shot by him, and the news travels like wildfire all over the area: instantly there is a riot. Perhaps the story is exaggerated or untrue: it is not yet propaganda. But it corresponds to the mental tensions and frustrations of the people. Anyone who had seriously read any Communist propaganda will find it hard to imagine that this turgid, complicated, and obscure stuff could start a riot among American Negroes. But still, that is what "agitation propaganda" is for, and if the situation ever becomes desperate enough, it is quite likely that such propaganda will circulate in the Negro ghettoes and will stimulate the emotions that are needed to start a revolution. It is a great mistake to act as if that point had been reached already. But as the situation becomes more critical and the Negroes are more and more alienated from white society, they will be more and more tempted by Communist propaganda—the Chinese variety.

✟ ✟ ✟

In primitive societies, where men are just beginning to read and having nothing to read but propaganda, we can say that they are its innocent victims. But in an evolved society there are no innocent victims of propaganda. Propaganda succeeds because men want it to succeed. It works on minds because those minds want to be worked on. Its conclusions bring apparent light and satisfaction because that is the kind of satisfaction that people are longing for. It leads them to actions for which they are already half prepared: all they ask is that these actions be justified. If war propaganda succeeds it is because people want war, and only need a few good reasons to justify their own desire.

✓ ✓ ✓

The mentality of propaganda.

On January 30, 1939, seven months before invading Poland and setting in motion the events that led to catastrophe for his own Thousand Year Reich, Hitler had this to say in a Reichstag speech: "If the international Jewish financiers should again succeed in plunging the nations into a world war, the result will be the annihilation of the Jewish race throughout Europe." This "prophecy" was repeated five times at various intervals. On the face of it, the statement means that the Jews are striving to plunge the world into war, and that Hitler and his peace-loving Nazis are trying to prevent this. But he foresees that he will fail to preserve peace, alas!—the world will be plunged into war, and the Jews will have to pay for it. Translated into the language of truth, the statement meant simply that Hitler was planning to plunge the world into a war and found it expedient to blame the war in advance on the Jews. Thus he was in fact announcing two plans he had in mind: one to plunge the world into war, and the other to exterminate the Jews. He succeeded in the first and nearly succeeded in the second. He was simply proposing his future actions in a form in which he knew they would be acceptable to self-righteous people. But Hitler had no monopoly on this kind of utterance. We hear the same thing every day and on all sides, the only difference being that the myths are somewhat more modest and the threats a little more restrained.

✓ ✓ ✓

Technology and death.

Excerpt from a letter of I. A. Topf and Sons, manufacturers of heating equipment, to the commandant of Auschwitz, concerning a new "heating system." "We acknowledge the receipt of your order for five triple furnaces including two electric elevators for raising the corpses and one emergency elevator."*

Excerpt from a letter of Didier and Co., Berlin, to the same: "For putting the bodies into the furnace we suggest simply a metal fork moving on cylinders. . . . For transporting the corpses we suggest using light carts on wheels." Business is business!

Excerpt from a letter of another firm: "We are submitting plans for our perfected cremation ovens which operate with coal and have hitherto given full satisfaction. . . . We guarantee their effectiveness, as well as their durability, the use of the best material and our faultless workmanship."

For the product: straight *A. B*-plus for salesmanship.

The camp commandant of Auschwitz was of course eager to surpass the other camps in efficiency and good results. Even when he was being tried in court he wanted to make clear that he had done a very commendable job. For instance, he declared: "Another improvement we made over Treblinka was that we built our gas chambers to accommodate 2000 people at a time, whereas at Treblinka their gas chambers only accommodated 200 people each."

Food for thought: "how to accommodate people." The word "accommodate" implies to "make comfortable."

The double-talk of totalism and propaganda is probably not intentionally ironic. But it is so systematically dedicated to an ambiguous concept of reality that no parody could equal the macabre horror of its humor. There is nothing left but to quote the actual words of these men.

Himmler, in a speech to the SS generals, October 4, 1943, praised them for the dedicated and self-sacrificing zeal with

* Facts and quotations from W. L. Shirer, *The Rise and Fall of the Third Reich*, New York, 1960.

which they had applied themselves to the task of extermination.

"Most of you must know what it means when 100 corpses are lying side by side, or 500, or 1000. To have stuck it out and at the same time—apart from exceptions due to human weakness—to have remained decent fellows, that it is what has made us hard. This is a page of glory in our history which has never been written and is never to be written."

Pardon, Herr General, I cannot refrain from writing it.

*  *  *

A simple straightforward exegesis of the commonplaces of propaganda and of public opinion would doubtless suffice as basis for a philosophy of our history. For instance, where Himmler said "most of you must know what it means when 100 corpses are lying side by side . . ." it is curious to notice that he is completely by-passing the most obvious meaning of this singular fact. What it means is not merely that there are 100, or 500, or 1000 smashed and repugnant human bodies, but that 100, 500, or 1000 people *have just been murdered. By whom?* But the question of their murder and its circumstances is not considered worthy of discussion: the "meaning" of these corpses, for the SS men, is simply that they are corpses, whose presence implies a call to courage, heroism, sacrifice. After having caused the noble SS the tiresome bother of putting them to death in the first place, these thoughtless corpses are now prolonging the test of patience by being so repugnant! But the SS, as Himmler well knows, will "stick it out." They will no doubt be decent fellows to the end, though somewhat hardened by their sacrifice. There will be a few deplorable cases, due to pardonable weakness, in which even the standards of decency current in the SS could not quite be met. One is tempted to shudder a little, in thinking of these cases of pardonable weakness. But no, let us always look at the positive side: it was a page of glory, and this, too, had its little sting. The page of glory could not be written. Others would barely know of the glory which the SS had earned by sticking it out in the presence of 100, 500, or 1000 corpses.

There were many other such cases of hidden sacrifice, many other unwritten pages of heroism. For instance the heroic sacrifice of those who unloaded the gas vans in which men, women, and children were asphyxiated by the exhaust of the motor. The brave and sensitive SS men suffered much from their disagreeable work. They got severe headaches after each unloading. Imagine them, as the truck pulls up beside the ditch, taking aspirins, reminding themselves it was all for *Volk und Führer*, and going to work!

Not all policemen are to be compared to the SS. Nevertheless this tendency to self-pity and self-congratulation on the part of men who do a ruthless and brutal job of work on other people is not confined to Nazi Germany and Communist Russia. A race riot occurs. Between thirty and forty people are killed. Hundreds are injured. There are in some quarters expressions of compassion and congratulation to the brave police. But it turns out that most of the dead were killed not by the rioters but by the police, and most of the injured were beaten by the police.

Obviously order must be kept and violence calls for forceful repression. But there is some danger in this syndrome of being sorry for oneself because he has to kill other people and still remain a "decent fellow."

✓ ✓ ✓

"If the Church allowed the word of God to be sharper than a two-edged sword . . . it might help white people to see that the very hysteria of their attack on the Negro is the evidence of an uneasy conscience."  —Reinhold Niebuhr

✓ ✓ ✓

The Yin kings said their ancestor was divine because his mother conceived him after eating a swallow's egg.

The Chou kings said that their ancestor was divine because his mother conceived him after having walked in some giant footsteps that could only have been those of God.

Neither of these statements is more inordinate than those which are made everywhere by present-day propaganda.

✓ ✓ ✓

Maritain on the practical atheism of many Christians:

They keep in their minds the settings of religion for the sake of appearances or outward show . . . but they deny the Gospel and despise the poor, pass through the tragedy of their time only with resentment against anything that endangers their interests and fear for their own prestige and possessions, contemplate without flinching every kind of injustice if it does not threaten their own way of life. Only concerned with power and success, they are either anxious to have means of external coercion enforce what they term the "moral order" or else they turn with the wind and are ready to comply with any requirement of so-called historical necessity. They await the deceivers. They are famished for deception because first they themselves are trying to deceive God.                                    —*The Range of Reason*

These are terrible and prophetic words, and their light picks out with relentless truth and detail the true face of what passes for "Christianity," and too often tries to justify itself by an appeal to the "Christian past."

✓ ✓ ✓

Rose MacCauley's *Personal Pleasures* is a book which both fascinates and baffles me. Here is the complete world I believed in and lived in at Cambridge thirty years ago. (She speaks of swimming in the Cam when I swam in the Cam.) What fascinates me is the presence of that world as a living reality, and what baffles me is its absence: the definitive absence of something that is completely finished. Yet thirty years ago that was the only world I dreamed was possible. The world of civilization and books, of ease and humor, of good conversation, art and music, of good restaurants, at least in London—and of course on the Continent. The world of Cambridge colleges, and rowing, and rugger, and concerts, and audit ale in Hall, and tea at my Italian tutor's. Certainly there was a lot of nonsense in it, a lot of falsity, but one did not take all that seriously.

Since that day absurdity has won.

But, you will say, there are still good books, good restaurants, Cambridge colleges. . . .

I especially like her lovely piece on "Bird in a Box." Now I can see that the bird has become a symbol of the world that has disappeared, and she seems to have sensed it even then. The box no longer works, the bird no longer sings. There are of course other toys. But not that one.

✟ ✟ ✟

The Red Cross came for blood, and Brother C——, one of the novices, was very happy because he was the one to give the first pint. I was happy because he was happy. I don't know what pint I gave, but I felt lighter after it. On the way in they told me, for the first time, that I had high blood pressure and called the doctor (one of the monks) to check it. I forget the adverb he used for how high it was and was not. Anyway, not *that* high. And my pulse was fast, but not *that* fast. You know how high *that* is, and how fast *that* is.

✟ ✟ ✟

Everything I see and experience in Kentucky is to some extent colored and shaped by the thoughts and emotions I had when I first came to the monastery. It cannot be otherwise. All these are possibilities that were latent in that experience and in the decision which followed. So this brilliant day, too, is another link in the chain that was begun then, and began in fact long before then. Yet it is slowly, through these possibilities and realizations, that I work my life into another dimension in which these things count less and less, and there is a growing liberty from the succession of events and experiences. It seems to me that they become less and less *my* experiences. They are more and more woven into the great pattern of the whole experience of man, and even something quite beyond all experience. I am less and less aware of myself simply as this individual who is a monk and a writer, and who, as monk and writer, sees this, or writes that. It is my task to see and speak for many, even when I seem to be speaking only for myself.

✓ ✓ ✓

Hawk. First the shadow flying downward along the wall of sunlit foliage. Then the bird itself, trim, compact substance, in the sky overhead, quite distinct from woods and trees, flying in freedom. Barred tail, speckled wings, with sunlight shining through them. He cut a half circle in emptiness over the elm. Then he seemed to put his hands in his pockets and sped, without a wing beat, like a bullet, to plunge into the grove across the open field.

✓ ✓ ✓

The old Zen writer Suzuki, when asked to speak in a scientific symposium on "New Knowledge in Human Values," handled it with all the wisdom and the innocent, latent irony of Zen: the humble, serious, matter-of-fact humor of emptiness. His contribution to this scientific inquiry was: "If anything new can come out of human values it is from the cup of tea taken by two monks."

✓ ✓ ✓

A great full-throated cry of hounds is heard in the wood, echoing hell-cries, conjuring up a hallucinated pursuit of an escaped criminal from a chain gang, with bloodhounds, through the cypress swamps . . . but this is real! One pities any animal they may be after. They sound like the hounds of hell itself. They come closer and closer.

A movement in the bushes and I see them: they are a bunch of the most absurd, idiotic, nondescript mongrels, tails of setters and legs of terriers, ears of bloodhounds and bodies of shepherds, fussing without real excitement over the traces of something that obviously vanished three hours ago. Yet the blood freezing bay continues! The parliament of hounds is in session. The self-important noise of a body politic fully aware of its own urgent and final responsibility, the momentousness of pronouncements, the terrible full-throated utterance of decision.

And we *act!*

(They scuffle importantly in the bushes, while all the rabbits for miles around seek safety.)

✦    ✦    ✦

Yesterday I offered Mass for the new generation, the new poets, the fighters for peace and for civil rights, and for my own novices. There is in many of them a peculiar quality of truth that older squares have rinsed out of themselves in hours of secure right-thinking and noncommitment. May God prevent us from becoming "right-thinking men"—that is to say men who agree perfectly with their own police.

✦    ✦    ✦

Lament of Ezechiel over Tyre:

Who is like unto Tyre that has fallen silent in the midst of the sea?
Now the sea has smashed you: now your wealth is in the depths of the waters.
And your men of war fall into the heart of the sea in the day of your ruin.                                    —Ezechiel 27

✦    ✦    ✦

I like the antique and stoical tropes of St. Eucher (the best writer of the Lerins school in the fifth century) in his *De Contemptu Mundi*. The splendor of that prose is the splendor of stoicism rather than of Christianity perhaps, and so too is the splendor of his "contempt." But it is a gentle and noble contempt for the world, not spiteful, not bitter: in a sense, it celebrates the world which it seems to contemn. It praises the beauty of the world, but with sadness: for it is perishing beauty.

The Latin of Eucher is very moving in the light of today's rising sun: indescribable magnificence. Cirrus clouds on the east horizon, first glowing with an angry, subtle, purple fire, then gradually burning higher into a great, mottled curtain of iridescent flame, of a color I cannot name or describe. To the south of this, light high clouds were piled together in dappled gray with all kinds of pink underlights, delicate as Oriental porcelain. And Eucher says:

"What if we reflect what great splendor of light will hereafter meet our eyes, when already He suggests Himself in such splendor: what magnificent form will blaze in things perpetual when even now it is so lovely in things perishing?" This does not sound much like "contempt" to me.

There is no real need for me to specialize, but I intend to keep to the writers of Christian Antiquity and those of the Middle Ages for a while, to defend myself against the levity of what happens at the moment to seem urgent just because it is popular. I can resist the general madness (not that the issues are not serious, but the madness about them is absurd), and I have done this lately by sticking to Migne's Latin Fathers. For instance today I found much to interest me in the *Life of St. Honoratus*, by St. Hilary of Arles. The classical commonplaces might seem corny, but they are not. There is a firm and deliberate structure of conventional images, with no self-conscious need to appear "original" or profound. The writer simply says that Honoratus had all that one would expect in a saint: and he constructs his statements solidly with a rhetoric that represents a very real culture, and a very different culture from the medieval Latin of Peter of Celles, whom I have also been reading. There is a totally different temperament in the twelfth-century French writers, a nerve, a fluidity, a grace, a dynamism that would perhaps have surprised the men who wrote before the final fall of Rome.

*   *   *

I am averse to slogans, to the pressure people, to any unseemly eagerness to affirm that Christianity is great for boys of the twenty-first century.

Why? Perhaps because I feel that they are trying, implicitly, to get others to serve their purposes, to inflate their egos for them? Is not this suspicion itself a sin against charity? After all, I think I can be dispensed from sharing their jamborees without judging them for it, and then needing to be pardoned. If I get myself too deeply involved in this need for pardon, I will find myself jumping higher than all the others and shouting louder, just to prove I meant no harm.

I think the Church is generous enough to tolerate me even though I am not leading a movement—or even following one.

✦ ✦ ✦

No one so far has included Erasmus in a symposium on monastic theology. Of course he was not a monk, and got very tired of his little religious community where they were fonder of drinking beer than of intellectual conversation. (After all, Erasmus did a lot better with his secular friends. Thomas More was a saint. I do not recall that any of Erasmus' brethren in the cloister ever got canonized.) In any case, this word of Erasmus is not too wide of the mark:

"True piety, which flourishes only when the spirit spontaneously strives to grow in charity, withers when the spirit sluggishly reposes in external ceremonies chosen for it by others."

✦ ✦ ✦

Emerson said of Thoreau: "His senses were acute and he remarked that by night every dwelling house gave out bad air like a slaughter house. He liked the pure fragrance of melilot."

Thoreau's idleness (as "inspector of snowstorms") was an incomparable gift and its fruits were blessings that America has never really learned to appreciate. (Industrious and affluent America, busy making more money than ever, has little time for him. At best he was a beatnik who came a hundred years early!) Yet Thoreau proffered his gift nevertheless, though it was not asked for, and he knew it would be neglected. Then he went his way, without following the advice of his neighbors. He took the fork in the road.

✦ ✦ ✦

Dark dawn. Streaks of pale red, under a few high clouds. A pattern of clothes lines, clothes pins, shadowy saplings. Abstraction. There is no way to capture it. Let it be.

✓ ✓ ✓

When you grow to be a big boy you are tempted about the Church. Shall you measure the temptation? Is it bigger than you think? Is it only imagination?

Certainly I find in myself not the slightest inclination to "be" anything but "Catholic." Any further question of other institutions, other organizations, appears to me to be totally ludicrous. I believe in the Church. I am in the place where Christ has put me. Amen.

On the other hand, I wish I had more charity. Perhaps I should say I wish I had at least a little charity. I wish I were less resentful of dead immobilism: the ponderous, inert, inhuman pressure of power bearing down on everyone to keep every beak from opening and every wing from moving. Authority sitting in its office, with all the windows open, trying to hold down, with both hands, all the important papers and briefs, all the bits of red tape, all the documents on all the members of the Body of Christ. I wish I could stop hoping the whole mess would blow away. I wish we were less a Church of paper. But what can you do in the twentieth century? We are becoming not only a Church of baroque seals and Renaissance chanceries, but of IBM machines!

The Spirit is stifled in paper. People and energies are used up in triumphal projects that move nowhere, and only glorify the pompous ones who manage them. But this glory is no glory. No one pays any attention to it—except for those who, like me, murmur and complain.

Complaining gives the triumphalists at least a *little* glory. It is at least a reaction. Sometimes I think they will settle for that. But, as I say, it does me no particular good either to complain or to think about it.

Thank God, it is the highest authority of all, Pope John, that opened the windows. And he did so knowing exactly what it meant. He knew that at least some of the paper would fly out across the square and across the river and across the forum and not stop until it landed in the sea.

And then this, from Jung (In Selections from the Eranos Yearbooks, on *Spiritual Disciplines*).

"People will do anything no matter how absurd to avoid facing their own psyches. They will practice Indian Yoga and all its exercises, observe a strict regimen of diet, learn theosophy by heart, or mechanically repeat mystic texts from the literature of the whole world—all because they cannot get on with themselves and have not the slightest faith that anything useful could ever come out of the psyche."

Father Dan Berrigan was here: an altogether winning and warm intelligence and a man who, I think, has more than anyone I have ever met the true wide-ranging and simple heart of the Jesuit: zeal, compassion, understanding, and uninhibited religious freedom. Just seeing him restores one's hope in the Church.

The real dimensions of living charity came out clearly in his talks to the novices. They exorcised my weariness, my suspiciousness, my dark thoughts. The community was delighted with him. But I know too that he is not an acceptable man everywhere.

✦ ✦ ✦

Up to now (August 1962) there have been 106 nuclear tests since testing began again (almost a year). Thirty-one of these by the USSR, seventy-four by the USA, and one by Britain, in the USA (Nevada). The USA has made twenty-nine atmospheric tests, twenty-six in the South Pacific and three in Nevada. The USA has also made forty-four underground tests and one in the stratosphere. Total of all nuclear tests since the beginning: USA 229, USSR 86, UK 22, France 5.

Grand total: 342 nuclear tests, of which 282 were in the atmosphere.

Nice going, boys!

✦ ✦ ✦

There has recently been a death from bubonic plague, of an incurable form, in England. It was that of an English doctor, an expert in microbiological warfare.

There had been no cases of plague recorded in England since 1910.

There were barely three hundred cases in the whole world in 1960.

But, at Parton Downs, Wiltshire, where science is exploring the possibilities of the use of pathogenic microorganisms in warfare, having discovered a virus that resists every known cure, one of the scientists caught the plague and died of it.

It was announced in the press that, having found this virus, they were trying to find a defense against it. Actually, according to the logic of Tertullian, what they were trying to do was *not* to find a defense against it, and they proved to everybody's satisfaction, including that of Dr. Brown, that they had succeeded.

Contradiction is an essential element in the new logic of the atomic age.

The U. S. Deputy Secretary of Defense, a very articulate proponent of the new logic, has declared that: "To pursue at the same time policies of armament and disarmament is not contradictory." What he means of course by this interesting contradiction is that it *is* contradictory but this contradiction is considered perfectly logical, since the policy of disarmament is not to be taken seriously and is, in reality only an aspect of the policy of armament.

✓ ✓ ✓

The high-altitude H-bomb explosion set off by the USA on July 9 of this year (1962) has permanently knocked out communication with several satellites sent up by us, and has also created a new radiation belt, "a phenomenon that is not fully understood," so we are told. Another fruitful contradiction emerging from the recesses of the military and scientific mind.

✓ ✓ ✓

Lines from the Japanese poetess Komachi, quoted by Laurence Binyon in the *Flight of the Dragon:* "It is because we are in paradise that all things in the world wrong us

When we go out from paradise, nothing hurts us, for nothing matters."

✓ ✓ ✓

Technology can elevate and improve man's life only on one condition: that it remains subservient to his *real* interests; that it respects his true being; that it remembers that the origin and goal of all being is in God. But when technology merely takes over all being for its own purposes, merely exploits and uses up all things in the pursuit of its own ends, and makes everything, including man himself, subservient to its processes, then it degrades man, despoils the world, ravages life, and leads to ruin.

✓ ✓ ✓

Bonhoeffer, who is certainly acclaimed as the apostle of "Christian worldliness," says that when human livelihoods are destroyed in the interest of the necessities of business, and when violence is accepted as a normal rational standard instead of an extraordinary and irrational solution sought in a "limit-situation," then man's worldly activity is no longer pertinent and ordered. It is headed only for chaos. A world which in fact is thus "impertinent" cannot be regarded as other than guilty, and Bonhoeffer's famous worldliness does not consist, like that of some of his disciples, in absolving the world from all guilt. It begins, on the contrary, with a very clear recognition of the modern world as guilty and fallen— but also, therefore, as having the greatest claim on Christian mercy, all the more so as Christians themselves are deeply implicated in the same guilt. Thus Bonhoeffer's worldliness is no denial of guilt, but "entering into the fellowship of guilt for the sake of other men." This is surely quite a different optimism from the free-wheeling and breezy propensity of some Christians to accept the torn and anguished world of the twentieth century as the flowering of Christian humanism and happiness! This other "optimism" shows not only the most pitiable lack of imagination and understanding, but is also a cruel and scandalous failure of Christian compassion. It is a humanism which, appealing to man and to Christ, actually derides both—but more out of stupidity than out of malice.

✓ ✓ ✓

Here was yesterday's boredom in the world: in a resort town on the West Coast, a thousand youths with nothing to do started rioting and tearing the place apart. This is now becoming a rather popular form of recreation. These zestful beings were apparently great jumpers, for the report I read* on them declared: "Some persons jumped atop buildings and began pelting police with beer bottles and rocks." They could have had a better headline, in that case: BORED HUMAN GRASSHOPPERS RIOT MAIM THREE.

There is also boredom in Africa (besides the usual boredom in Algeria and in the Congo, where it is not so easy to "jump atop buildings" as the buildings are scarce). Colonists, leaving the newly freed nation of Kenya, have left pets behind with houseboys, giving the houseboys sums of money with instructions to mercifully exterminate the pets. But, due to boredom or something else, the houseboys have neglected to exterminate the pets. Ok, when this has been made clear, I am all keyed up for the story. But no, this is the story. The pets are not exterminated, and it constitutes a problem. What kind of a problem? Is Kenya being suddenly populated with millions of Scotch terriers? Is frolicsome nature perhaps developing, without aid from science, a new breed of Pekingese ten feet long? Or is it just that the pets hang around and howl? I am left in an ambiguity which is beyond bearing. O, the boredom of the world. But I am open to it, I turn to it.

✓ ✓ ✓

After a few days of newspapers and reflection on their contents, I am convinced that what we need above all, and seem to have lost, are the following:

First, we need to recover the belief that order is possible, and that it rests with us to preserve it. Then we need the desire to do this.

* These entries were written in the hospital, when by exception, I was able to read the papers.

In order to resurrect this dead belief in the possibility of a genuine and living order, we have to try to believe that the good potentialities of men can be revived, though they have been cruelly wasted and misused. But the crucial point is this: an order imposed on people purely from outside themselves, and with no apparent relation to their real inner needs as persons, destroys all faith in the possibility of true order, which is rooted within the person and is in accord with his own intelligence and freedom. If, today, genuine order has become incredible it is because people are not fully capable of experiencing themselves as persons with sufficient dignity and responsibility to contribute to an order in which all are fully and personally concerned. So it turns into a vicious circle. Society alienates people while at the same time summoning them to cooperate in the work of their own alienation. They rebel. The machinery of alienation is then tightened up, and social control becomes more and more arbitrary. The result is a more widespread and more furious rebellion. The end of it all is a revolution and the establishment of a totalist "order" more rigid than any other, but one in which people are now systematically indoctrinated so that they seem to have at least some motive for cooperation.

If we are going to be personally free and productive human beings we need to recover some kind of interest in the possibility of attaining a relatively human and civilized condition, in which we ourselves can find ourselves and help others do the same. And that we might even be able to communicate something of what it means to attain these goals.

Finally, all this requires the hope that independent and personal initiative will not be entirely useless: we need to recover the belief that it is worthwhile and possible to break through the state of massive inertia and delusion created by the repetition of statements and slogans without meaning and without any effect in concrete action. In a word, the arbitrary, fictitious, and absurd mentality of our society—reflected in its advertising and entertainment particularly—must be recognized as an affront to man's personal dignity.

✓ ✓ ✓

In how many ways our old Western outlook is bankrupt. After centuries of "observation," "objectivity," "comment," and "investigation" (not to mention polls of public opinion) we have lost our way in a desert of meaningless and uninterpretable facts, and finally, not only of facts but of completely *fictitious events*, news that never happened or, if it happened, was never news. We are surrounded with fake objects which we continue, out of sheer boredom and inertia, to "inspect," to "study," to "evaluate," thus perpetuating the mystification. Fictitious experiences, fraudulent conclusions: nothing is real, and the least real thing of all is life, which still struggles to survive in this strait jacket of conceptual fabrications. Life is poisoned with falsity and unreality, because everything becomes a fake object. And we have no way of recovering our authentic subjectivity. But we try to do so by "jumping atop buildings" and throwing beer bottles. The future of the human grasshopper, an object jumping impulsively over and at other objects, is, to say the least, hazardous.

My point is not that one has said what needs to be said when one has deplored the state of affairs: but that this state of affairs need not exist, since we are not grasshoppers or ants, either. We are human, and the only thing stopping us from living humanly is our own deeply ingrained habit of delusion, a habit which some of us stubbornly continue to associate with original sin.

✓ ✓ ✓

In the hospital, life is covered over with a kind of organized ugliness for which no one is responsible: it is in large part the ugliness of sickness and suffering which the hospital attempts to alleviate. But under this drab and routine front, there is a great deal of human goodness and beauty, a deep fund of richness and generosity in the nurses, the doctors, the nuns, and all the people who work here. I think the question of "turning to the world" is in fact a question of being patient with the unprepossessing surface of it, in order to break through to the deep goodness that is underneath. But to my way of thinking, "the world" is precisely the dehumanized surface. What is under the surface, and often stifled and destroyed, is *more* than "the world": it is the spirit and likeness of God in men. Much of the ambiguity in talk about the world—especially mine—is that everyone tends to be quite selective about the elements he admits into his concept of "the world." My particular concept focuses on the sham, the unreality, the alienation, the forced systematization of life, and not on the human reality that is alienated and suppressed. This has to be made clear.

✦ ✦ ✦

Returning to the monastery from the hospital: cool evening, gray sky, the dark hills. Once again I get the strange sense that one has when he comes back to a place that has been chosen for him by Providence. I belong to this parcel of land with rocky rills around it, with pine trees on it. These are the woods and fields that I have worked in, and walked in, and in which I have encountered the deepest mystery of my own life. And in a sense I never chose this place for myself, it was chosen for me (though of course one must ratify the choice by a personal decision).

Cities, even Louisville (which, being the city nearest to home is in some sense my city), leave me with a sense of placelessness and exile. There is an immense movement spread all over everything: the ceaseless motion of hot traffic, tired and angry people, in a complex swirl of frustration. While one could easily have all that one needs within easy reach, the purpose of a city seems to be to guarantee that everybody has to travel about eighteen to fifty miles a day just in the performance of the routine duties of everyday life. One must move through noise, stink, and general anger, through blocks of dilapidation, in order to get somewhere where anger and bewilderment are concentrated in a neon-lit air-conditioned enclave, glittering with "products," humming with piped-in music, and reeking of the nondescript, sterile, and sweet smell of the technologically functioning world. Then back again into the heat, through the devastated areas, blocks and blocks razed by the bulldozer, empty fields of ragweed, with an occasional gutted building standing in the void: a wreck in which the winos come to howl, or where the bums sleep, or sinners sin, vast areas for the grasshoppers of the apocalypse. (There are of course more polite and more intricate sins in the bright new buildings.)

Even where war has not yet touched, cities are in devastation and nonentity: and yet, once again, under the surface of glitter and trash, in the midst of all the mess of traffic, there are the people, sick and distraught, drunk, mad, melancholy, anguished or simply bored to extinction. It is the people that I love, not the roles in the city and not the glitter of business and of progress.

Can't we do something more than give them air-conditioning?

*  *  *

When I got back to the monastery and went to supper there was a surreptitious note tucked under my napkin from Father Gerald, saying he had left to join the hermits in the West Indies and wanted me to write to him—which of course will never be permitted. Meanwhile Father Bruno James is in New York and wants to come down, but he writes to ask if I am here. For, he says, he has heard at Downside that I have joined the Carthusians and wants to make sure I have not done so before he starts for Kentucky.

*  *  *

(Fall, 1962.) How long can the menace of war grow and grow, and still not end in war? We seem to be close: closer than last year, anyway. Things seem deeper and more sinister than they were then (with the fuss about shelters and the absurd debate as to whether it was "Christian" to propose that anyone who tried to invade your shelter would be shot). We are victims of a monstrous irrationality—which we call "means of communication," but which in actual fact obstruct real communication—a vast machine which processes "events" and reduces them to gibberish in which reality is a total loss. No clarity, no perspective. It is precisely with this nonmeaning and nonperspective that the leaders have to deal in the elaborate system of double-think in which they confront one another and parry one another's thrusts: each thrust being a new, fabricated crisis of one sort or another. How long can we go on provoking and needling each other in this climate of total ambiguity without something breaking down? Or do computers make it possible to carry on such nonsense indefinitely without ever tripping up and dropping all the explosives we are weighed down with?

Meanwhile, of course, the purpose of every war, cold or hot, is *total* victory, the unconditional surrender and annihilation of all opposition. As long as this continues to be regarded as a sane objective, we can have nothing but struggle and tension. What else is there? This is paranoia.

On top of this, a letter arrives from some woman in France, a total stranger, evidently an ardent Catholic, of the *intégriste* variety. She seriously asks me for the prayers of the monks of Gethsemani that America may at last start a nuclear crusade against Russia and draw all the fearful, pusillanimous Western nations with her into it. All this in the name of religion, Christ, Christian heroism, etc., etc. And *serious*. "We cannot stand it any longer," she said. I wonder that God can stand it.

✓ ✓ ✓

"To resign oneself to doing or letting others do what one is not profoundly convinced of, and not to seek coherence at the highest level of one's carefully examined conscience, is to fail to lead a true life," says Danilo Dolci, and from his own life one might assume he meant it.

✓ ✓ ✓

In John of Salisbury I ran into a familiar quotation from Vergil's *Georgics,* lines which are not only familiar but have entered deep into my being since I learned them thirty years ago at Oakham. It was the year I took the Higher Certificate exams, and we had all worked hard on the *Georgics.* One June morning before the exams I got up very early and walked out into the hills, taking Vergil along, and wandered with the *Georgics* along the ridge of Brook Hill and the rather imaginary golf course that was up there among the old pre-Roman British forts, marked by grassy mounds and dikes. Then I came down across the Uppingham Road, by the little village of Egleton, and ended up sitting on a fallen tree trunk over a brook behind Catmose House. There I read (for the fifteenth time) these lines:

> *Felix qui potuit rerum cognoscere causas*
> *Atque metus omnes, et inexorabile fatum*
> *Subjecit pedibus, strepitumque Acherontis avari.*

The Stoic ideal of knowledge, seeing into the root of things and thus conquering fear and fate, and even "the roar of hungry Acheron," the river of hell! For me the lines retain an inexhaustible beauty. Though it is not a Christian beauty, yet its classic purity has something in it that Christianity was wise to assimilate, and John of Salisbury rightly sees that to have gained something of this Classic temper leaves one ready for faith and for the highest truth because, he says: "It is not possible for one who with his whole heart seeks and embraces truth, to love and cultivate what is merely empty." To have learned such lines as these and many others is to have entered into a kind of communion with the inner strength of the civilization to which I belong, and whatever may be the roar of Acheron (which these days seems much more definitive than the quiet voice of Classicism) this inner strength is, in itself, indestructible. But one can abandon it, and get carried off by the rising of the dark winds, not remembering to hold fast to the root of things.

✓ ✓ ✓

Yesterday there was a little comedy and exaltation in my own heart, at Vespers of the Sunday, and at the Magnificat antiphon. Thinking of Chartres, and of the fact that what the School of Chartres had was something permanent, that cannot be taken away. The antiphon: "Friend, go up higher" made me think of entering into the banquet of heaven where all this subsists forever. A nice, pious thought. But just imagination. One can get too much of that!

Meanwhile autumn is setting in, and wind is swinging the long branches of the weeping willow behind the chapel, on the way down to the woodshed. As the branches swing, curtains open on to the fall woods and the sheep barn. Everything is rusty, woods and barn together!

So I, too, come to a turning point of some sort, not knowing yet what it is. More than the nice thought about Chartres and the eternal banquet. More serious. But still a matter of coming up out of Egypt into my own country. I am nearly forty-eight. I have work to do: to get free within myself, to work my way out of the cords and habits of thought, the garments of skins (as if I could do that by myself). But one must want to begin. Even if the thought of it comes clothed in a good coat of nonsense and imagination.

Meanwhile there is work to be done in the Church: and we are beginning a novena before the first session of the Second Vatican Council.

✓ ✓ ✓

We are all going around telling ourselves how important the Council is, and trying to get adjusted to the fact that we are *having* one at all. Trying, also, to distinguish between the window dressing, the "image of the Church," and the supernatural event of the Council itself. I have no patience with those who simply view it as a chance to show the world that the Church is united, coherent, articulate—though there is in fact talk about conflict, and it would not be a bad thing to see some real debate and some real disagreement, against the background of common agreement. This Council will certainly not be a display of monolithic and prearranged agreement, a congress of bishops with big mitres on their heads and rubber stamps in their hands!

To my mind, the mere fact that the Council has been called and is actually convening (though as everyone knows, there has been a lot of opposition and foot dragging in Rome) is already a thing of great importance because it draws attention to the *bishops*, and to the diversity-in-unity of the universal Church, which is not simply a corporation with a head office in Rome.

✓ ✓ ✓

The change in my own inner climate: the coming of autumn. I am still too young to be thinking about "old age." Really, these years when you approach fifty and get ready to turn the corner are supposed to be the best in your life. And I think that is true. I do not say that for me they have been the *easiest*. The change that is working itself out in me comes to the surface of my psyche in the form of deep upheavals of impatience, resentment, disgust. And yet I am a joyful person, I like life, and I have really nothing to complain of. Then suddenly a tide of this unexpected chill comes up out of the depths: and I breathe the cold air of darkness, the sense of void! I recognize it all right, it does not bother me. And I say to my body: "Oh, all right, then *die*, you idiot." But that is not what it is trying to do. It is my impatience that thinks of this in terms of death. My impatience of degrees, and of gradualness, and of time. My body is not sending up signals of emergency and of death, it is only saying: "Let's go a little slower for a change."

Nor is it just "the body" that is talking. Where does this naked and cold darkness come from? Is it *from* myself, or is it a momentary unmasking of my self? Who is it that experiences this sudden chill? What does it mean? When I turn to it, I sense that this chill and this fear has a friendly and perhaps important message. If I stand back from it and say "it is nothing," then it returns more forcefully the next time. But if I do not evade it, if I accept it for what it is, I find it is, after all, nothing. What is this nothing which, when you run away from it, becomes a giant? And when you accept it, is nothing?

I think one must say it is a positive nothing, an unfulfilled possibility—almost an infinite possibility. A frightening one, in the sense that it is a possibility which includes the postulate that I myself cease to exist.

Thus, putting it in the form of a question, it comes out like "Who are you when you do not exist?"

Is this question an absurd one? On the contrary, it is I think a most attractive and fascinating one because of the obscure promises that it contains and because the answer to it can never be grasped by the mind. It is a question into which one must plunge himself entirely before it can make any sense—and that means, in a way, plunging entirely into nothingness, not just struggling with the *idea* of nothingness.

When the question presents itself as an alien chill, it is saying something important: it is an accusation. It is telling me that I am too concerned with trivialities. That life is losing itself in trifles which cannot bear inspection in the face of death. That I am evading my chief responsibility. That I must begin to face the deepest of all decisions—the "answer of death"—*the acceptance of the death sentence*—and with joy, because of the victory of Christ.

✓ ✓ ✓

The constant menace of war, the constant untrustworthy assurance that there will not be war, then another political crisis that may or may not be real: this makes the job of growing old a rather bitter business. And again, one refuses to be patient, to go on quietly not demanding to know how it will all come out: as if the Cold War and all that goes with it were in fact one's only reality. Certainly the danger is real, and there is no doubt about our society hanging over the edge of an abyss. But the precise critical issues seem to me to be more and more fictitious. And I suppose that makes it worse: that we should be so near, at all times, to such enormous folly and tragedy, and all for the fictions and delusions manufactured by our own greed and our own fear! There is a huge sense of desperation running through this whole society, with its bombs and its money and its death wish! We are caught in the ambiguities of a colossal sense of failure in the very moment of the most phenomenal success. We have everything we ever claim to have wanted, and yet we are more dissatisfied than we have ever been. People are eating their hearts out with fury and self-hate, just when they have all the money and all the leisure and all the opportunity, apparently, to really live. They find that the kind of life everyone dreams of is in fact impossible. They cannot face leisure. They cannot handle prosperity. I think we would be happier in a real crisis, instead of in a constant series of imaginary ones that we cannot possibly live with. Perhaps this unconscious sense of unreality will finally drive us all into a real cataclysm, just to have the relief of getting away from fictions and imaginations!

As for me, I am to some extent out of it. I am not prosperous, my life is not easy, I have real difficulties, and that, surely, ought to keep me amused. It does. Also I have a lot of work to do, and I like it, and apparently it succeeds. That is good too. I thank God for it.

Well, then, what is the matter? Why are you making your will as a writer already? Impatience. Go on, fool! Forget it! You may well write another twenty books, who knows? But what does it matter? It is not the writing that matters, or the books either, or who reads them.

That is just the point. This idea of a "writing career" which begins somewhere and ends somewhere is also a beautifully stupid fiction. Yet I can comfort myself with the idea that St. Thomas occupied his mind with it for a while, when he was my age. He told his secretary and biographer Reginald that if his days as a writer and teacher were over, then he wanted to die fast. I don't feel that way about it. And I don't feel that my days as a writer are over. I don't care where they are. The point for me is that I must stop trying to adjust myself to the fact that night will come and the work will end. So night comes. Then what? You sit in the dark. What is wrong with that? Meanwhile, it is time to give to others whatever I have to give and not reflect on it. I wish I had learned the knack of doing this without question or care. Perhaps I can begin. It is not a matter of adjustment or of peace. It is a matter of truth, and patience, and humility. Stop trying to "adjust."

Adjust to what? To the general fiction?

✓    ✓    ✓

"Trying to adjust" involves a whole galaxy of illusions.

First of all you take yourself very seriously as an individual, autonomous self, a little isolated world of reality, something quite definitive, something established in its own right: the thinking subject. (When you try to find out just *what* the reality of this subject is you get no answer. But you think it is proved real. It has been established by Descartes: "I think therefore I am.")

This thinking reality sets itself to consider what is all around it, to get everything in focus. Clear ideas. Clear ideas of *what?* Don't ask too many embarrassing questions, please! What is important is to establish that A is A, and that ten minutes from now it will still be A and a hundred years from now . . . already one has to start adjusting. A hundred years from now A will have vanished forever but the *statement* A is A will be true, adjusted of course to read A *was* A. Then you might have to adjust it to read that at least you thought A was A. However, since you yourself are no longer around, and nobody cares what you thought anyway . . .

To start with one's ego-identity and to try to bring that identity to terms with external reality by thinking, and then, having worked out practical principles, to act on reality from one privileged autonomous position—in order to bring it into line with an absolute good we have arrived at by thought: this is the way we become irresponsible. If reality is something we interpret and act on to suit our own concept of ourselves, we "respond" to nothing. We simply dictate our own terms, and "realism" consists in keeping the terms somewhat plausible. But this implies no real respect for reality, for other persons, for their needs, and in the end it implies no real respect for ourselves, since, without bothering to question the deep mystery of our own identity, we fabricate a trifling and impertinent identity for ourselves with the bare scraps of experience that we find lying within immediate reach.

To assume that my superficial ego—this cramp of the imagination—is my real self is to begin by dishonoring myself and reality. Then I am left with a choice between a servile adjustment that submits to facts and manipulates my ego-concept to defend it against subversion by the facts, or else a rebellious attitude which denies the facts and tries to flout them, again in the interests of the ego-image.

"Adjustment" becomes a constant play of "yes" and "no," an organized system of ambivalences, circling around one central ambivalence—a relative and contingent ego-image trying to constitute itself as an absolute. Here what we first intend as an absolute "yes" becomes inexorably an absolute "no." But our life continues as a more and more desperate struggle to keep ourself in focus as an *affirmation* not as a *negation*.

Such a project is simply and utterly futile.

We must go back to the beginning. What beginning? The beginning of our thought? Or the real beginning which we cannot reach, which is too close to ourselves to be seen? How can we ever "go back" to it? Back where? The beginning is *now*.

If we take a more living and more Christian perspective we find in ourselves a simple affirmation which is not of ourselves. It simply *is*. In our being there is a primordial *yes* that is not our own; it is not at our own disposal; it is not accessible to our inspection and understanding; we do not even fully experience it as real (except in rare and unique circumstances). And we have to admit that for most people this primordial "yes" is something they never advert to at all. It is in fact absolutely unconscious, totally forgotten.

Basically, however, my being is not an affirmation of a limited self, but the "yes" of Being itself, irrespective of my own choices. Where do "I" come in? Simply in uniting the "yes" of my own freedom with the "yes" of Being that already *is* before I have a chance to choose. This is not "adjustment." There is nothing to adjust. There is reality, and there is free consent. There is the actuality of one "yes." In this actuality no question of "adjustment" remains and the ego vanishes.

The "adjustment" of "yes" and "no" presupposes that the primordial *yes* of being is called into question or ignored completely. No longer do we attend to what *is*. Rather we set ourselves the task of making a selection from an indefinite number of unrealized and often unrealizable possibilities. This calls for a constant adjustment of "yes" and "no" as we try to walk on a tightrope over an abyss of nothingness.

The "adjustment" is a fiction and so is the tightrope. The abyss of nothingness is, in fact, the abyss of Being.

✓ ✓ ✓

Unfortunately we cannot attain by philosophy or psychology to this awareness that what we experience as void (if we experience it at all) is the fullness of a being that is not at our own disposal. The "realization" that our "nothingness" is in fact our being, understood as pure gift, pure affirmation, without any admixture of "yes" and "no," can be arrived at only, in Christian terms, "in Christ." I will not attempt to discuss here the way in which Buddhism, for instance, tackles the same question (by not making a question out of it!).

The Christian does not struggle to "make an adjustment." He does not try to make "yes" and "no" fit together comfortably. He accepts "yes" with complete joy, docility, and abandon because he believes that the "yes" of being and the "no" of man's refusal and evasion of being have been completely reconciled in Christ. The Christian choice is therefore not a perilous guess that seeks to make an exactly right division at the point where "no" ends and "yes" begins. It is simply a complete, trusting, and abandoned consent to the "yes" of God in Christ.

This means not an adjustment of right and wrong, of faith and unbelief, of truth and falsity, reality and unreality. It does not mean cleverly walking the tightrope so that one gets across the abyss without falling into it either on the side of "yes" or the side of "no." It means realizing that the whole conception of the abyss has been revealed as a fiction and delusion. In Christ there is no abyss: all is being and fullness.

But "outside" Christ (i.e. in the fiction we create by refusal of consent) all becomes an abyss and there is not even a tightrope with which to cross it. There is no adjustment possible.

Practical conclusion: one must learn to live and act not merely on the basis of ideological principles which seem to suit one's own sense of identity and which enable one to make plausible adjustments between "yes" and "no." One must live as a Christian, act as a Christian, with a life and an activity which spring from the unconditional "yes" of Christ to the Father's will, incarnated in our own unconditional

"yes" to the reality, truth, and love which are made fully
accessible to us in the Person and in the Cross of Christ.
This means that my life and my actions are seen as "justified" by the love of Christ for the world and for the
Father. My life and action seek their meaning in a world
which has been reconciled with its own truth and its origin
by Christ's love for it and for His Father. My acts are meaningful, not merely when I do what I consider right (still less
when I do what I imagine will let me be at peace with
myself) but when my acts accord with the goodness and
blessedness which are in man and in the world by reason of
Christ's love.

This is the great flaw in my writing and in my life. I, too,
rarely act in the full awareness of what it means that I am a
Christian. But, on the other hand, my fidelity to Christ demands that I avoid too facile a recourse to Christian unction
and pious phrases. I will continue to do what I can with the
little faith I have, because to pretend I had more would do
no honor to the truth. It would, in fact, be only a fraudulent
"adjustment."

✝   ✝   ✝

I wish religious life were less of a perpetual cold war, on a
very amiable level of course, between subjects and superiors—usually over nothing but niceties of observance:
whether the hoods should be up or down when we listen to
reading in the refectory, and other little proprieties that mean
nothing! But we can argue about them interminably and
there are even people playing politics over such issues. Who
is to have the last word? And who is boss? In the end this
kind of nonsense produces Luthers, or would do so if we had
anyone around capable of becoming a Luther. Fortunately
we are all too stupid, or too lazy.

Meanwhile I have developed a great sympathy for Abelard, and a profound admiration for the human greatness of
Héloïse, which Gilson brings out so well in his book about
them. Abelard in the end suffered far more than St. Bernard
ever did (if one can estimate such things: and what would
be the point of running up a score?). Abelard's weaknesses

were great, his character had enormous flaws, he was vain and impulsive, he never learned to control himself as Bernard did (and Bouyer has rightly shown that Bernard's character had its flaws too). Bernard had vanity but overcame it, or controlled it. Abelard could never control his. It ruined him.

And now it is a hot fall day, and I am sure everybody in the world is very kind and nice. Kind, concerned people, soft-spoken men with big bombs. The Bernards and Abelards of the twentieth century will not be content, I think, with words and excommunications. But the Bernards and Abelards of our time will be, perhaps, not people but machines: great, brilliant, temperamental computers. One of these days the most brilliant computer will take offense. Then watch!

We have an instrument flying very fast toward Venus. In December it will pass Venus in thirty seconds, taking pictures. Then it will go on endlessly nowhere, and we will have an eye out nowhere, with no way of knowing or caring what it may see.

Meanwhile, closer to home, a machine is making war on the soybeans.

ィ ィ ィ

When John XXIII was first elected Pope he would wake up in the night thinking of a problem and tell himself dreamily: "I must ask the Pope about this," and then, as his mind cleared, he would say: "But I am the Pope!" It is like the Zen koan: "Where do you go from the top of a twenty-foot pole?"

Well, he is on top of the pole, and he has his Council up there with him. The opening was great. John's opening speech was that of a very great, charismatic Pope. Also he received the diplomats in the Sistine Chapel, pointed up to Michelangelo's Last Judgment and said: "Well, gentlemen, what will it be?"

He said what needed to be said, and said it forcefully and directly. He said the people of the world want peace. That God will severely judge the rulers who fail in their responsibility to their people. Meanwhile the United States is spending more each year on armaments than was spent in any

year before 1942 for the *entire national budget*. Yet, as far
as I can see, Kennedy sincerely wants peace. Most Americans also want peace—if they think about it at all. If they
had to give a yes or no answer they would all say "yes" they
wanted peace. But it is not a matter of yes or no answers, because there are also a lot of people who think that this country is just about to be destroyed by "the enemy" and that
it is almost our last chance to destroy him. With such a mentality—and it is found in positions of power—peace is not
possible.

✓  ✓  ✓

It has been said that in its first session the Second Vatican
Council has *already ended the era of the Counterreformation*. That is a great claim, and I think it is a true one. On
every side there are new attitudes, especially in ecumenism.
There is a whole new understanding of the Christian task in
our time. A note came today from Father Daniélou and he
is very pleased at the way things are going.

✓  ✓  ✓

Mass before sunrise, without lights, in the novitiate chapel.
At such a time there is a beautiful "spirituality" in the pre-
dawn light on the altar. Silence in the chapel, and this pearl-
gray light on the white altar cloth. Two candles burning with
silent life. What more beautiful liturgical sign than to have
this light as witness to the greatest Mystery?

✓  ✓  ✓

Jacques Maritain has had Raissa's *Journal* printed pri-
vately, and sent me a copy. A most moving, humble, lucid,
cleansing book. It is not the kind of thing that is popular
today, as if that had anything to do with it: but it is a pity
that this record of a true, hidden, and crucified contemplative life will not be read by more who would profit by it.
Perhaps Jacques will allow a commercial edition later. One
need only add that those who will benefit by this book are
not necessarily the ones who follow all the latest fashions.

That does not mean that it is merely "dated" as some might be tempted to think, a record of the Catholicism of World War I and the twenties in France, the Thomist revival, and Garrigou-Lagrange's synthesis of Thomism with St. John of the Cross. It is a record of a life that could have been lived anywhere, and I am sure that, if the book reaches them, it will appeal to as many Protestants as Catholics.

⚹   ⚹   ⚹

Evening, rain, silence, joy. I believe that, where the Lord sees the small point of poverty, extenuation, helplessness which is the heart of a monk after very long and very dry celebrations in choir, when He sees the point of indigence to which this one is reduced, He Himself cannot refuse to enter this anguish, to take flesh in it so to speak, making it instantly a small seed of infinite joy and peace and solitude in the world. There is for me no sense, no truth in anything that elaborately contrives to hide this precious poverty, this seed of tears which is also the seed of true joy. Demonstrations and distractions that try to take one away from this are futile. They can become infidelities if they are eagerly sought. I may speak to others only in so far as I address myself to this same small spark of truth and sorrow in them, to help resolve their doubts, to assuage their anguish, to lighten their grief by helping them to be strong in this same small spark of exhaustion in which the Lord becomes their wisdom and their life forever.

What else do the Psalms talk about but this?

It is the very nature of our monastic office to bring us to this simplicity and sobriety of heart. But there are ways of approaching the office that rob it of all sobriety, self-conscious ways, with emphasis on the office as a kind of production. This does harm.

⚹   ⚹   ⚹

I saw two fine pictures of Brother Antoninus, one especially good, in his black and white Dominican habit, standing among some birch trees. I know he often feels as I do. Perhaps I ought to write him again, just a note, and say: "Courage! We are honest men!" But are we? At least we try to be.

✓   ✓   ✓

A brilliant, cold autumn night, alive with stars. After the night office one of the novices called me aside and, standing in the dark doorway, whispered that there was some news about a crisis over Cuba. A big speech had been made to the nation the evening before by Kennedy. There were Russian missile sites in Cuba. There are Russian boats going to Cuba with missiles on them. The Navy is blockading Cuba. The situation is very tense.

✓   ✓   ✓

The crisis over Cuba lasted about a week, when Khrushchev capitulated, promised to dismantle all the missile sites, etc. All this was a surprise and a great relief to everyone. The thing that I ask myself is this: why did Khrushchev not try to *hide* the missiles and the missile sites? Why did he, evidently, want them to be seen? Why were the missiles on the freighters quite obviously displayed? Evidently he wanted to find out how we would react. We reacted and he found out. Within the framework of power politics, I think Kennedy did what was expected of him. Not what was precisely in accord with international law, but what was demanded by the big political game. There is a difference.

This one decisive "win" seems to have cleared the air and had quite a definite effect, but I am only just beginning to realize that we were very close indeed to nuclear war: never so close! The very undignified way Khrushchev backed down makes this very clear indeed. The bombers were all ready to go, and he had no doubts on that score. Thank God it is over.

✓   ✓   ✓

A letter from a university professor about the Cuba crisis: "Three of our graduate students came to me during the week and in various shy ways contrived to say that they were about to remove their wives and kids to Mexico. . . . Another added that that day he had gone out to buy an Enfield 303 rifle to protect his wife and kids. Two faculty members were on the point of decamping to Mexico Friday. . . . Eavesdropping on CD rehearsals disclosed what the press is censoring, namely that there were heavy runs on gasoline and food supplies all over the country last week as people bought and hoarded these commodities."

I am told that the members of the Oxford Union decided to drink up all their best wine during the crisis. That leaves only the second best for the next one. Though I must admit tensions seem relaxed.

✓ ✓ ✓

Kennedy has announced that the United States will discontinue nuclear testing in the atmosphere. Old Aidan Nally came slowly toward me down by the woodshed and I knew he was preparing one of his usual oracular pronouncements. It was a propitious one: "Father," he said, "it appears that the wars have ceased."

## PART FIVE

## The Madman Runs to the East

> The madman runs to the East
> and his keeper runs to the East:
> Both are running to the East,
> Their purposes differ.
> —Zen Proverb

> He is the Truth.
> Seek Him in the Kingdom of Anxiety,
> You will come to a great city
>    that has expected your return for years.
> —W. H. Auden

Everyone agrees that after the Cuba crisis we had an extraordinarily peaceful New Year. Nuclear war came close but was avoided, and the general atmosphere is one of relaxation, as if we would not have to worry again for a long time. There is no logic in this, but one feels that the relaxation is a "fact." In any case the Russians are not acting so tough, in fact they seem disposed to get along with us as best they can, and it looks as though their belligerency is going to be turned eastward. They are not getting along too well with China.

Optimism? Why this sudden conviction that "everything will come out all right?" Perhaps it is based on a feeling of satisfaction at having pushed things to a showdown and won, instead of the usual inconclusive and frustrated state of never quite knowing where one stood. But this is no basis for genuine hope. It is merely a matter of transient feeling. If our "optimism" were a matter of real trust in God, it would be a different matter. It is one thing to trust in God because one depends on Him in reality, and quite another to assume that He will bless our bombs because the Russians are atheists and He cannot possibly approve of atheism.

✓ ✓ ✓

Many of the problems and sufferings of the spiritual life today are either fictitious or they should not have to be put up with. But because of our mentality we block the "total response" that is needed for a fully healthy and fruitful spirituality. In fact the very idea of "spirituality" tends to be unhealthy in so far as it is divisive and itself makes total response impossible. The "spiritual" life thus becomes something lived "interiorly" and in "the spirit" (or worse still in the "mind"—indeed in the "imagination"). The body is left out of it, because the body is "bad" or at best "unspiritual." But the "body" gets into the act anyway, sometimes in rather disconcerting ways, especially when it has been excluded on general principles.

So we create problems that should never arise, simply because we "believe" with our mind, but heart and body do not follow. Or else the heart and the emotions drive on in some direction of their own, with the mind in total confusion. The damnable abstractness of the "spiritual life" in this sense is ruining people, and it is also one of the chief reasons why many modern men and women cannot endure a lifetime in a monastery or convent. All is reduced to "intentions" and "interior acts," and one is instructed to "purify one's intention" and bear the Cross mentally, while physically and psychologically one is more and more deeply involved in an overworked, unbalanced, irrational, even inhuman existence. I do not speak for myself now, my life is all right. But I think of the lives led by thousands of nuns.

The peculiar suffering of some deeply spiritual people—and it is very acute suffering indeed—is due to the fact that their mind and will reach out to God but this is not yet a total love. One's whole being has to obey God, and there is no way of it doing so when in fact one's life is involved in the exhausting and stupid external routines of academic and social life (in one case I am thinking of) or of the convent. Merely working out the spiritual equation that says "this must be God's will" is no satisfactory answer. These people remain paralyzed, inarticulate, incapable of helping themselves. I am sure that in spite of everything they can gain something from this experience, and it can indeed be "purifying." But the glib doctrine that makes this out to be the "best way" to union with God is an affront to God as well as to man. One may have to put up with the situation out of necessity, but I refuse to believe that the spiritual life, as willed by God, is nothing better than organized masochism.

Perhaps we ought to be a little more critical of this whole concept: "the spiritual life."

As long as thought and prayer are not fully incarnated in an activity which supports and expresses them validly, the heart will be filled with a smothered rage, frustration, and a sense of dishonesty. When one is not able to experience this consciously, then it comes out in masochistic tribulations and even in sickness.

*   *   *

The two novitiates, choir and brothers, have merged into one, and I think it has been an excellent move. To begin with, they get along very well together. Then it is another step toward a deeper unity of spirit in the house, though I shall have to take great care to see that the proper grace of the brothers' vocation is respected. There is a rather irresponsible tendency on the part of some to simply sweep the brothers into the confined and artificial life of the choir on the pretext of giving them something "better." To begin with, I am not sure it makes sense to call the life of the choir monk "better" than that of the brothers, and in any case those who have come with a well-defined brothers' vocation have little taste for standing in choir and would rather be out working, since in this way they get more time out in the open and are also left more to themselves. There is no question that there is a special grace in their life of work, which keeps the brothers from getting too obsessed with themselves. (Some of the choir stand there struggling with emotional problems or ideological debates instead of losing themselves in prayer.) There is much less bother about "spirituality" in the brothers and consequently much more real and simple union with God. I notice, too, that the brother novices can tackle anything and get it done without any of the hesitations that seem to afflict the choir. The brothers just pitch in and *do* it. They do not have to be told each new move.

At the same time there is no question that the brothers are in many ways "poorer," simpler, and more vulnerable. One of them, for instance, speaks about "faults" he has which in reality are simply the wounds that come from being *poor* and living a hard life without privileges or respect in the

world. He comes from a really poor environment. The rest
of us (who were by no means rich, but we "belonged") have
no idea what it means to be one of the truly poor, pushed
around by the police, always having the worst of everything,
always hounded by debt, having to work extremely hard to
get very little, and then going for long periods without work.
. . . I cannot say how deeply moved I am when Brother
S——, a Mexican from Texas, speaks in all simplicity and without any resentment about his life in the world, his work,
traveling for days in open trucks to go and pick fruit in another part of the country, living in barracks, kicked around,
cheated. He does not complain of any of these things, just
speaks of them as if that were the way everybody had to
live.

Dealing with these brothers my attitude toward the monastery changes. I see they have need of me, and I have need
of them, and I am glad to do what I can for them. This is
a source of peace, and makes much more sense than aiming
at something less attainable and then being dissatisfied because one has not "attained" it.

✓    ✓    ✓

We are on retreat. Very cold morning, about 8° above. I
left for the woods before dawn, after a conference on sin.
Pure dark sky, with only the crescent moon and planets shining: the moon and Venus over the barns, and Mars over in
the west over the hills and the fire tower.

Sunrise is an event that calls forth solemn music in the
very depths of man's nature, as if one's whole being had to
attune itself to the cosmos and praise God for the new day,
praise Him in the name of all the creatures that ever were
or ever will be. I look at the rising sun and feel that now
upon me falls the responsibility of seeing what all my ancestors have seen, in the Stone Age and even before it, praising
God before me. Whether or not they praised Him then, for
themselves, they must praise Him now in me. When the sun
rises each one of us is summoned by the living and the dead
to praise God.

✓  ✓  ✓

False humility and the illusory ideal of self-annihilation. I distinguish this quite clearly from the real annihilation of the mystics, which is another matter. But a contrived "annihilation" simply sets up one figment against another and has them cancel each other out. The "self" sits by, smugly watching the operation and indeed directing it, and is not annihilated at all. On the contrary, this is a sure way of avoiding annihilation. Such "humility" becomes a last refuge in which the self remains impregnable.

✓  ✓  ✓

It suddenly dawned on me that the anti-Americanism in the world today is a hatred as deep and as lasting and as all-inclusive as anti-Semitism. And just about as rational. I see now that I must understand myself in the light of this hatred. To identify myself completely with this country is like accepting the fact of a hidden Jewish grandfather in Nazi Germany. My European background gives me a protective coloring, no doubt. I am, as it were, a Jew with blond hair and blue eyes. But no, I remain a citizen of a hated nation, and no excuses will serve. I know for a fact that this does have some influence on the way my books are received in some places in Europe.

✓  ✓  ✓

Ash Wednesday. The ashes smelled of kerosene.

Bored with Counterreformation Italian saints in the refectory.

✓  ✓  ✓

The hills are almost black, with a thin transparent line of woods along the hogback ridge, like bristles on an animal. Down there, somewhere, is Oak Ridge. It must be a couple of hundred miles away, but I would not want to be looking at this view should Oak Ridge be hit by an H-bomb.

✓ ✓ ✓

I must admit that Fénelon is sometimes quite dull. Whoever got the idea that he was *dangerous*? Yet he is an attractive person and one loves him for the injustices he suffered with such great patience, for his loyalty to that unoriginal and rather neurotic Guyon woman, so sick and so discredited. Everyone is still afraid of poor Fénelon, and I think some are disturbed that I should now be writing a sympathetic preface to his letters. The man is just not *approved*. And Bossuet, a great loud bull, he had his way and he is still fully approved by everybody. He was a friend of King Louis, he was powerful, and Fénelon was in disgrace. There is a lot of pragmatism in our evaluation of figures in the history of spirituality. We gladly fall into step with Bossuet and march off with the band blaring, even though the band turns out to be Gallican. Poor Fénelon made no noise at all, and is not followed. So much the better for him.

✓ ✓ ✓

In a Zen koan someone said that an enlightened man is not one who seeks Buddha or finds Buddha, but simply an ordinary man *who has nothing left to do*. Yet mere stopping is not arriving. To stop is to stay a million miles from it and to do nothing is to miss it by the whole width of the universe. As for arriving, when you arrive you are ruined. Yet how close the solution is: how simple it would be to have nothing more to do if only—one had really nothing more to do. The man who is unripe cannot get there, no matter what he does or does not do. But the ripe fruit falls out of the tree without even thinking about it. Why? The man who is ripe discovers that there was never anything to be done from the very beginning.

✓ ✓ ✓

Looking to the future of the arts in a more and more collectivist, cybernated mass culture, Sir Herbert Read conjectures that the massively subsidized state of art twenty years from now is not promising:

"It is not a cheerful prospect for the arts, though there will be more and more artists in the sense of the word used by the entertainment industry. It will be a gay world. There will be lights everywhere except in the mind of man and the fall of the last civilization will not be heard above the incessant din."

I cannot help agreeing with this, even though I can see that, as others argue, this pessimistic outlook does nothing to change the future. Can the future of civilization not be somehow directed away from mechanical formalization and spiritual disruption? Or should we bravely regard ourselves as called to abandon light and renounce spirit as a superfluous luxury, a remnant of feudalism?

Sir Herbert Read is simply saying what he sees to be obvious and he is a competent judge. For my part I think that such things have to be repeated over and over, and they *may* conceivably be of some help, where a naïve optimism will only accelerate decay. It is not a matter of resisting change, change is inevitable. But one must also at the same time be ready to point out in what respects change is not an improvement.

On the other hand I think I know enough of art and of artists to be optimistic to some extent. Artists will continue to be independent enough—or some will—to do what they know they must do, paint and write and create outside and against the officially subsidized culture. One can count on the arts, I believe, to carry on a disreputable, insolent, and prophetic diatribe against art with a capital "A" and with official approval.

✓ ✓ ✓

There is an obvious analogy between pop art as a cult and "religionless religion" as a religion. In either case the total acceptance of mass secular culture as the one significant reality, and the consequent rejection of "spirituality," "interiority," and "contemplation" is taken as the only form of honesty. Art without art—the abandonment of the artist's "special experience"; religion without mention of God and of religion, but simple openness to "the world" as it is, in its massive confusion, *accepted as the only thing that makes sense*: this, strangely, I understand. I can sympathize with it as a gesture of compunction and purification. The sins of art and of religion in our Western culture have been so great! Someone has to acknowledge them.

However, for my own part, I have no interest either in pop art or in religionless religion and I think neither has any real significance for man. They are facts and I can accept them as such, but I have better things to do than be involved in them—and I see no reason why they have to be resisted or condemned. In ten years the whole scene will have changed and they will be forgotten.

This suggests a clarification of my (monastic) idea of "worldliness" in the present age. For me the "worldly" attitude which I think is nefarious is not simply the "turning to the world" or even the total and would-be uncompromising secularism of the "honest to God" set. Still less is it the noble concern for social justice and for the right use of technology to serve the real needs of modern man in his indigence and his despair. What I mean by "worldliness" is the involvement in the massive and absurd mythology of technological culture and in all the contrived and obsessive gyrations of its empty mind. One of the symptoms of this is precisely the anguished concern to keep up with an ever-changing, complex, and fictitious orthodoxy in taste, in politics, in cult, in belief, in theology and what not, cultivation of the ability to redefine one's identity day by day in concert with the self-definition of society. "Worldliness" in my mind is typified by this kind of servitude to care and to illusion, this agitation about thinking the right thoughts and wearing the right hats, this crude and shameful concern not with truth but only with vogue. To my mind, the concern of Christians to be in fashion lest they "lose the world" is only another pitiable admission that they have lost it.

✓ ✓ ✓

Evening light. Purple caves and holes of shadow in the bosom of the hills. The little white gable of Newton's house smiles so peacefully amid the bare trees in the middle of the valley! This is the peace and luminosity Blake loved.

✓ ✓ ✓

The taste for Zen in the West is in part a healthy reaction of people exasperated with the heritage of four centuries of Cartesianism: the reification of concepts, idolization of the reflexive consciousness, flight from being into verbalism, mathematics, and rationalization. Descartes made a fetish out of the mirror in which the self finds itself. Zen shatters it.

✓ ✓ ✓

Heavy snowflakes fall, flying in all directions. But when there is no wind they descend so slowly that they seem determined not to land on the ground. When in fact they do touch the ground they vanish completely. Then the pale sun comes out for a moment, shines uncertainly on the grass, the wheel, the pale pine logs, the rusty field, the fence, the valley. It is St. Benedict's, the first day of spring.

✓ ✓ ✓

A Zen line in Job: "Is it by your wisdom that the hawk soars?" (39:26)

✓ ✓ ✓

"Sinners always want what is lacking to them," says Fénelon, "and souls full of God want only what they have."

✓ ✓ ✓

I turn to Nicholas of Cusa and find in him a comfort which perhaps I need inordinately after reading Hannah Arendt on the Eichmann case. Her study is incredible and shattering. Not just an indictment of one man and one system, but a sordid examination of conscience of *the entire West*. It has proved singularly inconclusive because no one seems to grasp anything definite about it (if they have even tried to grasp anything). All that remains is a general, all-pervading sense of moral failure, horror, disorientation, sickness. But even the horror itself is diffuse and seemingly superficial. Where does one begin to respond to the multiple indictment of our world? The stereotyped answers all fall to pieces. No new ones are to be found. There is no faith and no honor left to sustain one in a search for reasons.

Yet the total irrationality of the Eichmann story must not make us distrust reason or humanity. One is tempted to conclude that reason and conscience themselves have been exploded by the insane cruelties of our bureaucratic age. But that only opens the way to a more complete surrender to a more absolute irrationality, a more total cruelty.

*    *    *

Contrast Fénelon and Eichmann. Fénelon had a conscience and put his insights at the service of statesmen—if they would listen. I like his letters to the young Prince, the Duke of Burgundy, who would have succeeded Louis XIV if he had not died before the old King. Fénelon's warm, discrete, paternal kindness was given generously to all. All were welcome to share his clarity, his reasoned judgment, his human insight. I like his quality. Contact with such minds is indispensable.

*    *    *

What do we mean when we say that such and such an aspect of a war or a persecution is "diabolical?" When it represents a total ruthless contempt and mockery of God's image in man: a special dishonoring of man by associating him intimately in his own worst evil, by degrading him morally while destroying him physically. Example: when the Jews were to be exterminated, "privileged classes" were established. German Jews, Jews who were ex-servicemen, etc., would receive "better treatment." Recall what was said about the "accommodation" offered by the gas chambers! The Jews would all be "accommodated," but some would receive "better treatment." The first indignity of course was that the Jews themselves had to apply for these absurd and insulting privileges, and in applying they automatically seemed to approve the criminal measures taken for the destruction of their race. At the same time, applying for a privilege might mean that one was called upon to earn the privilege by cooperating more actively in the work of extermination by informing on other Jews. In the long run the "distinctions" and "privileges" were meaningless, and served only to add this special burden of moral contempt to that of physical destruction.

✓ ✓ ✓

Morality itself is brought into complete contempt by the Eichmann story, by Eichmann's own appeal to his virtues. This "blind obedience" and his "corpselike obedience." These are not only ethical concepts, they belong to the language of ascetic perfection. Eichmann, however, appealed to philosophy—since philosophy, too, must be contemned! Eichmann claimed that his whole life was lived according to the imperatives of Kant, the Kantian conception of duty. But Kant rules out "blind obedience." Yes, that was true, Eichmann admitted that, when it came to the final solution, this exceptional, limit situation, he had gone beyond Kantian principles. Instead of simply being guided by conscience and duty, he had completely identified himself with the Fuehrer in the most perfect immolation of his own will. His principle was now no longer the categorical imperative, but "Act as if the Fuehrer himself would approve of it if he saw you." Consequently, Eichmann's conscience bothered him not because he had directed the "final solution"—the liquidation of the Jews —but because he had in fact made two exceptions and allowed Jews to escape. Thus he had neglected his duty to the Fuehrer. If the Fuehrer had seen *that* . . .

The awful details of this case can give monks food for thought. Are novices not sometimes trained to "do everything as if the abbot were watching you?" Are monks and priests not sometimes extremely upset over acts that are in fact good, not bad, but which happen to violate some tiny detail of a conventional code of observance? Is it not after all familiar to see that, when there is a choice between real charity and human compassion on one hand, and the violation of a punctilious usage on the other—for instance concerning silence or deportment—they will prefer to violate charity rather than the observance? Violation of the observance would make them feel far more guilty . . .

The Eichmann story shows the breakdown of forensic concepts of morality and demands an existential respect for the human reality of each situation. Without this respect, principles will never regain their meaning in concrete life. Meanwhile, there is no legal machinery to deal with such moral disasters. What judgment could *add anything* to the judgment already implied in the fact that a man who was by certain accepted standards quite honest, respectable, sane, and efficient could do the things he did without feeling that he was wrong? This judgment falls not on Eichmann alone, but on our whole society. What then is the significance of a special judgment pronounced upon Eichmann by our society? This is the real question.

*✓   ✓   ✓*

If the King and Bossuet suspected Fénelon, feared his spirituality, and wanted to find quietism in it—since in those days you could be condemned for quietism as today you might be for Communism, or "imperialism," or "revisionism" —it was because the apparent passivity, the nonaction, the indifference which Fénelon taught were in fact a protest against the active spirituality that could be used in the service of absolutism.

*✓   ✓   ✓*

Spring brush fire. We went out to fight it after our thin Lenten dinner. Smoke was boiling around a hillock on the edge of the monastery land. The flames were just entering a wood, leaping up fiercely through the brambles and into the tops of the small cedars. We went down, skirting the wood, into a hollow, through high brambles, to stop it with a backfire. We came to an old house tucked in the hollow, and built the backfire on the edge of the green grass around it. But the backfire got away and started to circle the house on the other side. We stopped it, however, and meanwhile the backfire stopped the main fire as it came down toward the house, with great flames roaring up in the brambles and dry sage grass. At one point the fire got into some willows that were overgrown with honeysuckle and the flames went twenty feet up in the air, only a hundred feet from the house. The old man sat on his porch and watched us fight the fire, and pretty soon one of his friends came along and they both sat on the porch, talking about the fires in the old days when fires really were *fires*. Meanwhile the main fire had gone off to the south and the monks stopped it out that way too. By midafternoon it was all over.

As we left to go home, I looked back at the lonely old house, tucked primly into the fold of smoking hills, an unforgettable, old, unpainted, ramshackle Kentucky house with a rusty tin roof and a rickety front porch, under an elm tree that was ready to get green. A wasted, washed-out, barren clay road led up to the porch. The archetypal Kentucky house, almost a log cabin but not quite.

ᛣ   ᛣ   ᛣ

Adolf Eichmann, in his last words, at the foot of the gallows, declared himself a believer, a *Gottesgläubiger*, which means, apparently, one who believes in a God who is not personal.

Having made this declaration he addressed those present: *"After a short while, gentlemen, we shall all meet again. Such is the fate of all men. Long live Germany. Long live Argentina. Long live Austria. I shall not forget them."*

What shall one say to this incredible absurdity? Could Beckett or Ionesco do better?

Hannah Arendt's comment: "In the face of death he had found the cliche used in funeral oratory, but his memory had played him one last trick: he had forgotten that he was no Christian and that it was his own funeral. It was as though in his last minutes he was summing up the lesson that his long course in human wickedness had taught him—the lesson of the fearsome, word and thought defying banality of evil."

This is excellent, but it does not begin to silence the awful resonances of this stupid and prophetic piece of perfectly appropriate nonsense. It is so crazy that it is exactly right, and the rightness scares you when you realize that we have not done with Eichmann, and that in a short time we will indeed meet him again. Once again history will repeat, more clearly, what he was trying to say, what he would have said explicitly if he had known a human language of some sort. What Eichmann meant was that these "gentlemen" were really not in a different boat from him at all. "Such is the fate of all men." Do all men have to hang for murdering a few million other human beings? He singled out Germany, Argentina, and Austria as being characteristic of his world, and saluted them buoyantly. Thus in dying *he refused to be dismissed from our world.* "You have not done with me": he said in effect (or the peculiar devil that was doublespeaking in him said it!): "Your world is full of me, I am all over the place, I am legion; and you, whether you like it or not, are going to take the same long course in wickedness and study all its details. When you have finally, with great labor, learned it all, you will be even more banal and more appalling than I."

This, I think, has not come clear. The general impression seems to be that hanging was enough, and that the world is rid of him.

✓ ✓ ✓

Hannah Arendt's very sobering conclusion is that Eichmann represents a new kind of criminal, the *hostis generis humani* who "commits his crimes under circumstances that make it well nigh impossible for him to know that he is doing wrong."

Curious phrase, *hostis generis humani,* "enemy of the human race"—where have we heard that before? Is the "enemy of the human race" a *new* enemy all of a sudden? I was under the impression that he was the oldest enemy we had!

✓ ✓ ✓

Palm Sunday.

Quiet sunset. A cool, still day. Another fire in the woods over toward Rohan's Knob. We did not go after it, since it was far away. Peace and silence, at sunset, behind the woodshed. Nobody there, only a wren playing quietly on a heap of logs. P. Bonnard, the Post impressionist painter, had died after instructing someone where to put the last blob of yellow on a last great painting already bought by the owner of Gimbels.

Pope John has written an Encyclical on Peace, which will be promulgated on Holy Thursday.

✓ ✓ ✓

"The monk is the true philosopher."

This is a commonplace of tradition—monastic tradition of course. Monks have shown no less zeal than others in pointing out the special advantages of their own state!

Originally this statement, which belongs to Christian antiquity, implied a comparison with the stoic, cynic, epicurean, and other non-Christian philosophers. The comparison was suggested not only by the philosophic quest of ultimate wisdom, but also by the discipline and ascesis proper to all "philosophical life." At the same time, the monk was also more than a philosopher, because he did not seek merely an intuition of ultimate principles, but he sought "the Face of the Living God."

Without going into the anti-intellectualism which this phrase sometimes suggests, one can say that for both monks and philosophers the "highest wisdom" was to be sought beyond mere reasoning and clear understanding, beyond intellection as such. The highest wisdom is grasped by man in his totality, and "grasped" is the wrong word, for he who is truly wise is seized by wisdom. He does not gain possession of wisdom by his own power—or by any other. To be wise is, in a sense, to abandon every attempt at gaining wisdom, and to enter into a whole new dimension of existence, where the division of subject and object, ends and means, time and eternity, body and soul either appears in a totally new perspective or vanishes altogether.

Hence, Dilthey said: "The demands upon the person engaged in philosophizing cannot be met. A physicist is a pleasant reality, useful to himself and to others; the philosopher, like the saint, exists only as an ideal."

This would also imply that a monk is a person who sets

himself to meet demands that cannot be met, and exists only as an ideal. True. Nevertheless, he who is called to be a monk is precisely the one who, when he finally realizes that he is engaged in the pure folly of meeting an impossible demand, instead of renouncing the whole thing proceeds to devote himself even more completely to the task. Aware that, precisely because he cannot meet it, it will be met for him. And at this point he goes beyond philosophy.

Here he admits finally that the problem of being a monk cannot be resolved merely by fidelity to a religious ideal. There is much more than that involved. It is a matter of fidelity to the inscrutable demand of God's love, a demand for which there is or can be no purely rational justification. Certainly no ideology will suffice to account for monastic solitude, the flight from the world to prayer and loneliness. All attempts to reduce this to an ideology can only undermine the monastic vocation in the end. A seeming ideology is perhaps necessary for beginners. But one becomes a monk precisely when he renounces the attempt to explain his vocation in terms of ideology. Monastic anti-intellectualism has something to be said for it if it is a renunciation of ideology. Unfortunately anti-intellectualism is itself too often just another very unsatisfactory ideology—the self-justification of the stubborn and the stupid.

In the same way, the true philosopher and the true poet become what they are when they "go beyond" philosophy and poetry, and cease to "be philosophers" or to "be poets." It is at that point that their whole lives become philosophy and poetry—in other words, there is no longer any philosophy or any poetry separable from the unity of their existence. Philosophy and poetry have disappeared. The ordinary acts of everyday life—eating, sleeping, walking, etc., become philosophical acts which grasp the ultimate principles of life in life itself and not in abstraction.

From such unified existence come the aphorisms of great Asian contemplatives or Christian saints—and the poems of Zen masters.

One may add that this unification of life and worship sometimes appears to lack a specifically *religious* quality. In reality

THE MADMAN RUNS TO THE EAST

it is a perfection of the religious life, and not indifference or doubt. It is those who doubt who need the constant expression of religious sentiments and the reiteration of formulas and rites. (Since we all doubt, we all need religion.)

Yet if in resisting doubt we convince ourselves that we truly "know God" we have lost touch with reality, for as St. Thomas said: "The extreme of human knowledge of God is to know that we do not know God."

✓  ✓  ✓

Working on the Russian mystics, I have finally come to Theophane the Recluse, the nineteenth-century bishop and monk who resigned his see at the age of fifty-one to live in solitude. At first he came out of his cell to attend offices in the Abbey Church. Then in six years, after the office of Vespers of Easter 1872, he became a complete recluse, receiving no one except the abbot, his confessor, and a brother who saw to his needs. He lived like this for twenty-two years, doing quite a lot of translating and literary work, and carrying on an immense spiritual correspondence with people he was directing.

This bare outline gives no idea of his true spiritual stature. He is in fact a very impressive figure, standing out above all the Startzi of Optino and the other great Russian monasteries that flourished in the nineteenth century. One feels here that one is in the presence of real greatness, nobility, wholeness, a perfectly integrated and traditionally monastic sanctity. Here is a life which, in spite of its apparent oddity, is seen by its fruits to have been truly balanced. Though it goes against "reasonable" norms, it really makes sense. Theophane was a man who was quite above the vicissitudes of life, who lived in a rare atmosphere and yet remained fully human. He stands out like Isaiah among the prophets.

Here is a man I deeply admire because he was able to see what to do and then do it. He could walk straight forward and follow God. Sometimes I am tempted to think that the complexities of our own cenobitic system hem one in with arbitrary fantasies, keep one in an absurd corner for the sake of some obscure principle or other, some point of ideology.

In such a case, to do what is really right one has to go at it backward, as if he were doing something else.

✦ ✦ ✦

A spring morning alone in the woods. Sunrise: the enormous yolk of energy spreading and spreading as if to take over the entire sky. After that: the ceremonies of the birds feeding in the wet grass. The meadowlark, feeding and singing. Then the quiet, totally silent, dry, sun-drenched mid-morning of spring, under the climbing sun. April is not the cruelest month. Not in Kentucky. It was hard to say Psalms. Attention would get carried away in the vast blue arc of the sky, trees, hills, grass, and all things. How absolutely central is the truth that we are first of all *part of nature*, though we are a very special part, that which is conscious of God. In solitude, one is entirely surrounded by beings which perfectly obey God. This leaves only one place open for me, and if I occupy that place then I, too, am fulfilling His will. The place nature "leaves open" belongs to the conscious one, the one who is aware, who sees all this as a unity, who offers it all to God in praise, joy, thanks. To me, these are not "spiritual acts" or special virtues, but rather the simple, normal, obvious functions of man, without which it is hard to see how he can be human. Obviously he has learned to live in another dimension, that which one may call "the world" in the sense of a realm of man and his machines, in which each individual is closed in upon himself and his own ideas—clear or unclear—his own desires, his own concerns, and no one pays any attention to the whole. One has to be alone, under the sky, before everything falls into place and one finds his own place in the midst of it all.

It is not Christianity, far from it, that separates man from the cosmos, the world of sense and of nature. On the contrary, it is man's own technocratic and self-centered "worldliness" which is in reality a falsification and a perversion of natural perspectives, which separates him from the reality of creation, and enables him to act out his fantasies as a little autonomous god, seeing and judging everything in relation to himself.

We have to have the humility first of all to realize ourselves as part of nature. Denial of this results only in madnesses and cruelties. One can be part of nature, surely, without being Lady Chatterly's lover.

It was one good morning. A return in spirit to the first morning of the world.

✓ ✓ ✓

The less said about the Easter morning Pontifical Mass the better. Interminable pontifical maneuverings, with the "Master of Ceremonies" calling every play, and trying to marshal the ministers into formation and keep things moving. Purple zuchetto and cappa magna and of course it had to be our Mexican novice who was appointed to carry the long train (this inwardly made me furious and practically choked any desire I may have had to sing alleluias). The church was stifling with solemn, feudal, and unbreathable fictions. This taste for plush, for ornamentation, for display strikes me as secular, no matter how much it is supposed to be "for the glory of God." The spring outside seemed much more sacred. Easter afternoon I went to the lake and sat in silence looking at the green buds, the wind skimming the utterly silent surface of the water, a muskrat slowly paddling to the other side. Peace and meaning. Sweet spring air. One could breathe. The alleluias came back by themselves.

✓ ✓ ✓

The riches of this day (in Easter Week). First of all the day itself, brilliant and cloudless. The trees are now almost fully in leaf. Jack Ford brought an ikon (a copy, mounted at St. Meinrad's to look real) of St. Elias. I put it up on the east wall. Fabulously beautiful, delicate and strong. A great red globe of fiery light and glory, with angelic horses rearing up in unison inside it, drawing a simple Russian peasant's cart with the prophet standing in it, looking toward the great globe of the divine darkness to which he ascends—the blackness of the divine mystery. Darker curve and shelves of mountains below. On one of the mountains Eliseus reaches into the globe of glory and touches the prophet's robe.

Below Eliseus, a second Elias, the Elias of sorrow, sleeps. That was the Elias who fled for his life into the wilderness. The same is now in the globe of glory and fire because of the sorrow that went before. An angel leans over and mentions the hearth cake to the sleeping prophet.

What a thing to have in the room. It transfigures everything.

✓    ✓    ✓

Notker Balbulus said: "If you love God's creation, read Ambrose's *Hexaemeron*." The *Hexaemeron* is a book of great simplicity and charm, a poem of love, full of primitive and childlike joy in creation. The joy is expressed in myth and in symbol. Yet it is also a work of intelligence and strength. We can well read such books if we are free enough with them to realize that they are not intended as "science." At the same time, the strictly scientific view of the universe needs this dimension of love and play, which it sorely lacks. That is one thing I like about space flights: at last there is something of cosmic play getting into the somber, unimaginative, and superserious world of science. But what is a little play of astronauts against the great, gloomy, dogmatic seriousness of the death game, nuclear war? Can we recover from the titanic humorlessness of our civilization?

✓    ✓    ✓

Trouble in Alabama (Birmingham). News comes through in fits and starts. I have seen pictures of Negroes drenched with firehoses and policemen setting police dogs on the demonstrators. One picture in particular shows three policemen pinioning a Negro woman to the sidewalk. One of them has his knee on her neck. She was "pushing" them, the little bully! They will show her that they will not be intimidated by a woman, no sir!

✓    ✓    ✓

I am told by a higher superior: "It is not your place to write about nuclear war: that is for the bishops."

I am told by a moral theologian: "How can you expect the bishops to commit themselves on the question of peace and war, unless they are advised by theologians?"

Meanwhile the theologians sit around and preserve their reputations.

Pretty soon they will no longer have any reputations to preserve.

✓ ✓ ✓

I told one of the novices that he had no vocation and he was delighted. With immense relief he prepared to leave.

✓ ✓ ✓

A Chicago policeman writes that he is scandalized over the fact that I am showing concern about nuclear war. Rather, he says, it is my duty to start a "spiritual Los Alamos project." For example? What else but Theresa Higginson and the Devotion to the Sacred Head?

✓ ✓ ✓

Heisenberg's *Physics and Philosophy* is a very exciting book. The uncertainty principle is oddly like St. John of the Cross. As God in the highest eludes the grasp of concepts, being pure Act, so the ultimate constitution of matter cannot be reduced to conceptual terms. There is, logically speaking, *nothing there that we can objectively know*. (Unless you want to use the abstract concept of pure potency, but what does it mean?)

This seems to me to be the end of conventional nineteenth-century materialism—which, funnily enough, now appears exactly for what it was: a "faith," and not science at all. To be more precise, let us say a "myth," which was accepted on faith in the "authority of science." But on this authority the Russians still buy it as a faith. Materialism is the opium of the people. It is an article of faith that the mechanical laws of motion, electronic activity, etc., *must* be a confirmation of dialectical materialism. That is that. Believe or perish.

Heisenberg shows that the naïve objectivity of conventional physics is on the same mythical plane as the ancient conviction that the sun revolved around the earth. The Soviets now struggle against reality to maintain this naïvely objective view. *Eppur' si muove.*

Yet with great sophistication the quantum theory also accounts for the "factual" concepts of everyday life, knowing that they are to be taken into account as part of the observer's reality: and this destroys the myth of the completely separate and detached observer, looking at everything with scientific objectivity. The observer is part of the observed. We are part of nature and our knowledge of nature is nothing if not knowledge of nature as known by us, who are parts of it.

✓   ✓   ✓

Heisenberg concludes with some ideas on politics in the nuclear age: the same kind of thinking as in his physics. "It is probably not too pessimistic to say that the great [nuclear] war can be avoided only if the political groups are ready to renounce some of their apparently most obvious rights—in view of the fact that the question of right and wrong may look entirely different from the other side. This is certainly not a new point of view; it is in fact only an application of that attitude which has been taught for centuries by some of the great religions."

It is precisely the attitude taken by Pope John in his magnificent encyclical *Pacem in Terris*. But it is too much for many present-day Christians to swallow.

✓   ✓   ✓

The profound revolution in man's contemporary religious consciousness is related to the revolution in his sense of *space*. This is naïvely but accurately described by J. A. T. Robinson when he says in *Honest to God* that modern man can no longer cope with a notion of God "out there," a notion of transcendence which in fact presupposes that heaven is a dome over the earth and God is enthroned at the top of it.

The concept of "sacred space," which has in reality formed the religious consciousness of the Christian West, is intimately related to sacred architecture. The Egyptian, Greek, or Roman temple was simply a house in which the statue of the god was located—a cave perhaps. One "went in" to the dark, small sanctuary where the god was present.

But Christian sacred architecture took over the domed aula or the vast basilica, and the fantastic exploitation of space and light in the Gothic cathedral made it a symbolic representation of the whole cosmos. The cathedral is a "world" created by walls on which every kind of being is represented, by windows through which the light of heaven pours in on the people of God, by a spiritual and hidden sanctuary in which the sacred Mysteries are represented. Here the conceptions of transcendence and immanence are both present. Remember that Gothic architecture in France developed under the influence of the theology of pseudo-Dionysius—a theology of apophatic darkness (the God who is known by "unknowing") and the hierarchical transmission of light from God through the angels and the Church.

It is an extremely sophisticated and profound theological vision which of course we have lost.

Today it is no longer possible to fit this kind of church into the "space" of our cities and of our world.

The revolution of our religious consciousness demands a frank understanding that we have a totally different concept of space and of the cosmos. In this new concept there is no *containment*. All limits and boundaries are gone, or if they exist they are infinitely flexible. There is no "room" in which an intelligible light can be contained. There is no spatial location in which the infinite and the finite meet. What we are grasping for is a rediscovery of immanence, but the immanentism of Asian religions, static and fixed in enstasis, will not quite do.

Our most important task is to become aware of the fact that our new consciousness of space no longer admits the traditional religious imagery by which we represent to ourselves our encounter with God. At the same time, we must also recognize that this traditional imagery *was never essential to Christianity*. We must recover the New Testament awareness that our God does not need a temple (Acts

7:47–53) or even a cathedral. The New Testament teaches in fact that God has one indestructible temple: which is man himself (I Cor. 3:17). To understand that God is present in the world *in man* is in fact no new or radical idea. It is, on the contrary, one of the most elementary teachings of the New Testament.

✓  ✓  ✓

Nineteenth-century theorists tried to explain art in materialistic and psychological terms—art was a fulfillment of a biological need; the work of art produced a substitute for a desired material object. Cave art was the product of hunger (!).

In this theorizing, the materialists have unconsciously portrayed themselves as beings for whom life is centered on the external material object—and therefore alienated. The highest realities which man can desire are (they believe) *things*, which he can grasp, possess, eat. In my opinion the "savages" of the Stone Age probably had a much more sophisticated and humane sense of human values than that!

Art is the product of drives? Yes. But specifically human drives. Are there values which man desires more than the satisfaction of hunger, sex, and so on? I certainly think so. Chief of these is the *need for meaning*. This is very obvious today in the breakdown of the naïve materialism of these interesting characters who theorized about cave art. Even in countries where most men have plenty to eat and (it is affirmed) more than enough opportunities for sexual gratification (which, I add, he does not necessarily get), much deeper and more fundamental needs are felt. We are not hungry but neither are we happy. We are in search of *meaning* and the search is consistently frustrated, not only by the fact that ancient and traditional symbols seem to have lost their efficacy, but by the fact that artists, poets, and so on have suddenly become hostile and uncommunicative, frustrating the desire for meaning by declaring that there are no meanings left and that one has to get along without them. I think that is a fair enough reaction against the stupidities of materialism. Let the punishment fit the crime. If what people want is food and sex, let them have that, and see if they can get along with that only, and without meaning.

Meanwhile, of course, what is indecipherable by squares remains significant to the artist and his friends: it is either meaningful or a substitute for meaning, a significant enigma.

✶ ✶ ✶

The Black Muslims, with hard, shiny heads, with frowns, with muscles, drilling for self-defense (and not nonviolent either) have ceased to look upon anything at all in the world as funny. They are one of the very few fanatical movements for which I am able to have any respect whatever. One must grant them this: they have taken men who were wrecks, criminals, men in despair, and made something of them. Of course, the same was said of the Fascists and the Nazis.

Martin Luther King, who is no fanatic but a true Christian, writes a damning letter from Birmingham jail, saying that the churches have utterly failed the Negro. In the end, that is what the Black Muslims are saying too. And there is truth in it. Not that there is not a certain amount of liberal and sincere concern for civil rights among Christians, even among ministers, priests, and bishops. But what is this sincerity worth? What does this "good will" amount to? Is it anything more than a spiritual luxury, to calm the conscience of those who cultivate it? What good does it do the Negro? What good does it do the country? Is it a pure evasion of reality?

✶ ✶ ✶

Vigil of Pentecost, 1963.
Pope John is dying, perhaps already dead. Yesterday at this time he was in a coma, in an oxygen tent. Last night, they say, he was conscious for a moment, smiled, and blessed those around him. I have been thinking about him all day and praying for him, especially at the afternoon Mass. He has done so much in four, four and a half years, to remind everyone that Christian charity is not just a pleasant fiction. For many people he has restored hope in the Church as a living

reality, as the true Body of Christ. He has made the reality of the Spirit in the world once more simply and profoundly credible even to people who are not easily disposed to believe in anything. The world owes him much, and recognizes the fact, for he is much loved. The concern about his death is *real*. And it is universal. For once there is news that is not a pseudo-event. The death of Pope John is an event, and no amount of platitudinous chatter can make it pseudo: it concerns everyone deeply and personally. No one has done so much as he to break through the fixation of hatred and suspicion in the world. Has he succeeded? I do not know. Can people once again really believe that one who has spoken to them of love has not betrayed them? Words like love, truth, justice, God, Church, faith have been so often used to trick and betray that people are mortally afraid of them. Has Pope John overcome that fear?

*✓ ✓ ✓*

Pope John died yesterday.

A holy and good man: and he was both because he was first of all a *man*—that is to say, a fully human being. This is the great meaning of his papacy, of the Council, of *Pacem in Terris*. Being a man, he was concerned with other men. (One felt that Pope Pius XII, for example, was more concerned with *principles*.) Pope John was not just a humanist. He was deeply concerned with the humanity which he shared with his fellow man. *Pacem in Terris* is not theology. It simply says that war is a sin because it is *inhuman*.

Certainly everybody recognized this and responded to the Encyclical sincerely. Even the Russians. In fact one feels that some of those who responded least to this deep humaneness of the Pope were men close to him in Rome. It is a shameful but nevertheless understandable fact.

May he rest in peace, this great good Father, whom I certainly loved, who had been personally very kind to me. I do not think he has stopped being a father to us and to me. If we last long enough, we will canonize him. I do not hesitate to ask his intercession now.

✓ ✓ ✓

Curious effect of newspaper stories of Pope John's death read over and over in the refectory. They are all really one story, but from different papers, different sources, different angles. The total effect of hearing the same material over and over, the same details, repeated each time in a slightly new arrangement, is like a story by Robbe-Grillet. One is left with a strange, neutral sense of dreamlike objectivity. The cast-iron bed, the thick red carpet, the four relatives from Sotto il Monte, the bed table with the black telephone and bottles of medicine. The thick red carpet to muffle the sound of feet. The cast-iron bed. Relatives from Sotto il Monte, Xaverio, Giuseppe, (one whose name I forget), and Assunta, who had been a nurse. The Pope was dying in a cast-iron bed. His sister who had been a nurse was by his (cast-iron) deathbed. Since she had been a nurse she knew what to do. Xaverio and Giuseppe and the other one were not nurses, but they also knew what to do. They sat there. The Pope called his relatives to his bedside. It was a cast-iron bed. There was a rosary on the bed table. The Pope called his relatives. They sat there. Assunta was formerly a nurse. There was a thick red carpet so that when the relatives came closer the sound of their footsteps was not heard. They sat there. The Pope said: "Think of Papa and Mama." He said it in Bergamesque dialect. His relatives were from Sotto il Monte, near Bergamo. Assunta dipped a cloth in a silver bowl of water and mopped the Pope's brow, and the newspapermen knew by this that she had truly been a nurse. They all told about her dipping a cloth in the silver bowl and mopping the Pope's brow. "Think of Papa and Mama," said the Pope. They sat there and thought. The four relatives were there. They sat in four red-damask chairs. The black telephone did not ring. A rosary on the table. The silver bowl . . . The Pope died in a cast-iron bed.

Poor Pope John: none of this idiot mishmash can change his greatness, he suffers nothing from it: even this bug-eyed surrealistic view of his death chamber is somehow great and dignified (much more so than the macabre details—the photographer, etc.—at the death of Pope Pius. One of the first things Pope John had done as Pope had been to protest against the vulgarity and indecency of those who permitted these indiscretions at the death of his predecessor.)

Nothing can change the fact that this was a holy death, a deeply Christian death, a death that was not a pseudo-death and a pontifical cliché. The world knows it, and understands.

*    *    *

I stepped out of the north wing of the monastery and looked out at the pasture where the calves usually are. It was empty of calves. Instead there was a small white colt, running beautifully up the hill, and down, and around again, with a long smooth stride and with the ease of flight. Yet in the middle of it he would break into rough, delightful cavorting, hurling himself sideways at the wind and the hill, and instantly sliding back into the smooth canter. How beautiful is life this spring!

*    *    *

Feast of the Sacred Heart, 1963.

A joyful and exciting day with a great confabulation of crows in the east, and a wood thrush quietly singing in the west.

The conclave for the Papal election began yesterday, and this morning while we were chanting vigils here Cardinal Montini was elected on the sixth ballot. The result was announced in the morning Chapter and at dinner they played a tape of the announcement in St. Peter's square, as it had come over the radio. We never hear such things: this was a momentous exception. Noise, and more noise, and then the voice of Cardinal Ottaviani (who, as everyone knows is one of the arch conservatives) began the news of "great joy" *Habemus Papam*. He started to say the name in Latin: Johannem Baptistam . . . and immediately the whole crowd broke into an immense roar. The Cardinal tried to say "Montini" and choked.

Pope Paul's blessing was clear and strong, very slow, very moving. I did not feel like eating.

In his pictures he looks very tired.

✓   ✓   ✓

An infernal concerto of chain saws broke out on the hillside behind the new water works just before Sext, in the blaze of noon. A deep one and a tenor, a roar and yell of hot metal, diabolical intervals of atonal discord in utter fury. Three or four oaks went down in quick succession. I did not get close, but through the foliage I could see the naked torsos of natives, and a white sun helmet. The typhoon of stygian harmony continued, interrupted from moment to moment with the awful unnatural shuddering of boughs. But it did not last long. The trees crashed and were cut up by dinnertime. An electric line is going through to the water works.

✓   ✓   ✓

A new invention appears in the distant pasture, sliding down the hillside like an Ohio Riverboat or a Sol Steinberg drawing, driven by a brother in a white sun helmet. What is it? An atomic-powered gunboat? An agricultural pagoda? It seems to be made of aluminum—it shines brilliantly—it seems to have a paddle wheel in front, wherewith to persecute some aspect of unoffending nature. A great deal must go on inside. In every direction it has chimneys protruding. It can be heard for miles. It apparently chews the grass and spits it out in all directions. Nobody knows what for. Its name: Behemoth.

✓   ✓   ✓

A helicopter comes over, making its own kind of insane racket. The word "chopper" is appropriate. Insect body, thin tail, half dragonfly, half grasshopper: Louis Massignon calls them the "grasshoppers of the apocalypse." It circles the monastery three times, making an infernal noise. Then, having discerned that the monastery remained for five minutes in the same place and seemed permanent, it departs. This classified information will be filed in triplicate in Fort Knox, the Pentagon, the Department of Justice, and the CIA.

✓ ✓ ✓

I am halfway through the *Ratio Verae Theologiae* of Erasmus, loving the clarity and balance of his Latin, his taste, his good sense, his evangelical teaching. If there had been no Luther, Erasmus would now be regarded by everyone as one of the great Doctors of the Catholic Church. I like his directness, his simplicity, and his courage. All the qualities of Erasmus, and other qualities besides, were canonized in Thomas More.

✓ ✓ ✓

How high the corn is this summer! What joy there is in seeing the tall crests nod ten and twelve feet above the ground, and the astounding size of the silk-bearded ears! You come down out of the novitiate, through the door in the enclosure wall, over the little bridge, and down into this paradise of tall stalks and leaves and silence. There is a sacredness about the beauty of tall maize and I understand how the Mayas must have felt about it: in this feeling there is a pre-Eucharistic rightness and wisdom. How can we *not* love such things? That is why I continue to admire the Mayas and Incas as perhaps the most human of peoples and as those who, so far, have done most honor to our hemisphere.

The completely irreligious mind is, it seems to me, the unreal mind, the tense, void, abstracted mind that does not even see the things that grow out of the earth or feel glad about them: it knows the world only through prices and figures and statistics. For when the world is reduced to number and measure you can indeed be irreligious, unless your numbers turn out to be implicated in music or astronomy, and then the fatal drive to adoration begins again!

The numbers that are germane to music and astronomy are implicated in the magic of seasons and harvests. And there, in spite of yourself, you recapture something of the hidden and forgotten atavistic joy of those Neolithic peoples who, for whole millennia, were quiet and human.

✓ ✓ ✓

No art form stirs or moves me more deeply, perhaps, than Paleolithic cave painting—that and Byzantine or Russian ikons. (I admit this may be really inconsistent!)

The cave painters were concerned not with composition, not with "beauty," but with the peculiar immediacy of the most direct vision. The bison they paint is not a mere representation of an animal, it is a sign, a *gestalt*, a presence of the unique and peculiar life force incarnated in this animal— in terms of Bantu philosophy, its *muntu.* This is anything but an "abstract essence." It is dynamic power, vitality, the self-realization of life in act, something that flashes out in a split second, is seen, yet is not accessible to mere reflection, still less to analysis.

Cave art is a sign of pure seeing, nothing else.

(Personally I do not agree with the way in which cave art is given a magical and utilitarian efficacy. It was undoubtedly associated with the hunters' need for food, but I think it represents an expression of direct awareness of a kind we are no longer capable of conceiving. The cave man's art was before all else a celebration of this awareness and of the *wholeness* of his communion with nature and with life.)

That is probably why Victor Hammer keeps insisting that cave art is "not art." He is right in the sense that it probably involved little or no conscious invention or creation and no concern for form. There is "no frame." But that is precisely what I like about it: it is not limited by deliberation. On the other hand it *is* limited and disciplined, but only by the immediacy of the vision itself. The cave artists admit *nothing* irrelevant.

At the same time, in cave art the drawing is "writing" too. The picture is also an ideogram. I think one of the peculiar sources of power and life in Asian art and philosophy is in its greater fidelity to immemorial modes of vision going back into the prehistoric past. I don't know if it can be proved, but Chuang Tzu, for instance, and Lao Tzu, even more, seem to be fighting to preserve an essentially Stone Age view of the world and of society, in which all that man now needs from his inventions was once attained and realized in himself.

For example—today with a myriad of instruments we can explore things we never imagined. But we no longer *see* directly what is right in front of us.

✓   ✓   ✓

The basic inner moral contradiction of our age is that, though we talk and dream about freedom (or say we dream of it, though I sometimes question that!), though we fight wars over it, our civilization is strictly *servile*. I do not use this term contemptuously, but in its original sense of "pragmatic," oriented exclusively to the useful, making use of means for material ends. The progress of technological culture has in fact been a progress in servility, that is in techniques of *using* material resources, mechanical inventions, etc., in order to get things done. This has, however, two grave disadvantages. First, the notion of the *gratuitous* and the *liberal* (the end in itself) has been lost. Hence we have made ourselves incapable of that happiness which transcends servility and simply rejoices in being for its own sake. Such "liberality" is in fact completely foreign to the technological mentality as we have it now (though not necessarily foreign to it in essence). Second, and inseparable from this, we have in practice developed a completely servile concept of man. Our professed ideals may still pay lip service to the dignity of the person, but without a sense of *being* and a respect for being, there can be no real appreciation of the person. We are so obsessed with *doing* that we have no time and no imagination left for *being*.

As a result, men are valued not for what they are but for what they *do* or what they *have*—for their usefulness. When man is reduced to his function he is placed in a servile, alienated condition. He exists *for* someone else or even worse for some *thing* else. Hence he cannot enjoy life. The ethos of our society certainly places an enormous emphasis on "having fun," but our whole concept of joy is mendacious because it is servile. Even the fun that we have is for a purpose.

It is justified not by its gratuity, its simple celebration of the gift of life, but by its utility. It makes us feel better, therefore helps us to function better, work better, get ahead in life. Since our fun usually costs something—one cannot have fun without buying all kinds of toys, commodities, and refreshments—it helps the economy. Also, since we have more uproarious fun than anyone else, our fun proves the superiority of free enterprise over the grim and admittedly sullen pragmatism of the socialists.

Why then aren't we happy? Because of our servility. The whole celebration is empty because it is "useful." We have not yet rediscovered the primary usefulness of the useless. From this loss of all sense of being, all capacity to live for the sake of living and praising God, all thankfulness, all "Eucharistic" spirit, comes the awful frustrated restlessness of our world obsessed with "doing" so that even "having fun" becomes a job of work, an operation, a veritable production, even a systematic campaign. The phony spontaneity which has to be "produced" in our fun-loving world naturally arouses distrust and guilt, and destroys faith in all real joy. Yes, we still try with all our might to believe in joy, since Madison Avenue tells us to. But we know that Madison Avenue itself is not convinced. The fruit of our servility is the despair that no one can admit—unless of course he is a monk or a beatnik.

I am afraid a monk is not likely to be impressed by the joyous preachments of the new "worldly" enthusiasm of Christians for secular existence in its sheer secularity. What do these glad homilies say, but "since secular servility is inescapable, do not try to escape it: make it your joy, take the world on its own terms and let its servility ['emphasis on use'] become an end in itself, a celebration, a kind of liberality." This is nothing more than the Communists preach with their stakhanovite jubilation in working like mad to increase production and become "heroes of labor." And it is nothing more than we have heard in monasteries where overwork has been sometimes justified with the cliché "your work is your prayer" and where every form of servile futility has been blamed on "the will of God."

Let the secular Christians show us they have some notion of freedom, of gratuitousness, of celebration, of joy that is not made on Madison Avenue, of a respect for persons based on respect for *being* instead of doing. Then they will be more convincing.

(I may add that some of the ones I know *do* have this, but it runs the risk of losing itself in general confusion.)

✦   ✦   ✦

A book about Egypt (read in the refectory) spoke convincingly of the serenity and sanity of Egyptian life under the Pharaohs as shown in the tomb paintings of early centuries. Yet this serenity was not enough. The People of God had to be chosen out of it and flung into hunger, homelessness, anguish, and trouble. They had to leave this placid, well-organized, pleasant life and go into the desert. Can we believe that the civilization of Egypt was the epitome of all that was wicked? We do not have to. The People of God were—and are—called out of Egypt not because it was wicked, but because they had a more bitter and more promising destiny willed for them by God. If we could only have the life of Egypt rather than that of the desert, if we could have it with God's blessing, how happy we could be. There are various historic ways of trying. The serene, joyful, productive, expansive life: and then off into the complex mythical world of death. Is this so different from life in America today? The difference is probably that Egypt was peaceful for centuries. The desert Fathers, too, rejected all this peace. Why? Why not just enjoy it and praise God? That was not possible. And Barth (who is certainly not the most temperate authority on this particular subject) said that if you try to steal the gold of Egypt you simply end up with the idols. Whatever may be the explanation, I am struck and troubled by the fact that if the Jews were called out of Egypt, out of peace and into anguish, it was because God did not will that His People should merely live productive, quiet, joyous, and expansive lives.

✔   ✔   ✔

Guardini, speaking of Caussade, praises his clarity and adds that he is sometimes *too* clear—so clear that the whole doctrine comes into question. He is in danger of short-circuiting our religious integrity with too simple a notion of the "will of God." "In effect," says Guardini, "he simply pre-supposes and takes for granted the strict order of convent life, the status quo in religion." But he does not take into consideration that "this order itself might be a disorder, and that this may raise conflicts that obedience alone cannot re-solve." I think that Caussade does take into consideration the possibility that "order" is really sometimes a mask for dis-order, but his perspectives are so limited and restricted to the individual that he thinks obedience is enough. The trou-ble is, then, with these particular perspectives. Yet within these perspectives it may be possible for abandonment (which is much more than obedience) to leap beyond all conflicts and land in the arms of God's pure freedom.

Guardini then looks to the present situation. Here he sees "the solitude of a Christian in a world detached from Chris-tian order. This is a new and decisive fact, which is not often enough taken into account if one simply is content to say that the world is in error and to set up the previous order as an ideal. . . ." Guardini is speaking of the true situation of the Christian in the world today: called by what does not yet exist, called to help it come into existence *through and by a present dislocation of Christian life.*

This is a point of momentous importance. Aware of this dislocation, we seek to adjust the Church to the modern world by an appeal to principles of order that worked in the past. Caussade is free from systems and principles. He pre-sents the Christian not with an ideology, not with an in-terpretation of the Christian situation, but with the naked will of God. In this sense, he opens the way to a true and heroic freedom—for all who are capable of such simplicity.

He frees us from attachment to principles that are not quite applicable in the present, and makes us already obedi-ent to the future we do not yet perceive or understand.

✦ ✦ ✦

Along with the great work of the Council, there has been a concrete and very disturbing fact—that of the hardening division between progressives and conservatives. This division is something more than one naturally expects where there are men who both temperamentally and sociologically tend to line up right and left. The division is deep enough and bitter enough for some very sound and responsible people, bishops included, to mention even the possibility of schism. This seems at first incredible, but I have seen some of the things that have been written on either side and there is no question that there are profound incomprehensions, deep divisions, stubborn refusals, and even hatreds.

All this is nothing new, unfortunately. We have the history of the Church and of Christian civilization to demonstrate its long ancestry. But it cannot be passed off lightly.

However, one of the great problems after this Council is certainly going to be the division between progressives and conservatives, and this may prove to be rather ugly in some cases, though it may also be a fruitful source of sacrifice for those who are determined to seek the will of God and not their own. I do not speak here of bishops, but of ordinary priests, theologians, lay people, and all who voice their opinions one way or another.

For my own part I consider myself neither conservative nor an extreme progressive. I would like to think I am what Pope John was—a progressive with a deep respect and love for tradition—in other words a progressive who wants to preserve a very clear and marked *continuity* with the past and not make silly and idealistic compromises with the present— yet to be *completely open* to the modern world while retaining the clearly defined, traditionally Catholic position.

The extreme progressives seem to me, as far as I can judge with the poverty of my information, to be hasty, irresponsible, in many ways quite frivolous in their exaggerated and confused enthusiasms. They also seem to me at times to be fanatically incoherent, but I do not sense in them the chilling

malice and meanness which comes through in some of the
utterances of extreme conservatives.

The thing that disquiets me most is the fact that the progressives, though perhaps a majority, do not seem to have
the dogged and concerted stamina of the conservatives. The
extreme conservatives seem to me to be people who feel
themselves so menaced that they will go to *any length* in
order to defend their own fanatical concept of the Church.
This concept seems to me to be not only static and inert,
but in complete continuity with what is most questionable
and indeed scandalous in the history of the Church: Inquisition, persecution, intolerance, Papal power, clerical influence,
alliance with worldly power, love of wealth and pomp, etc.
This is a picture of the Church which has become a scandal
and these people are intent on preserving the scandal at the
cost of greater scandal.

To begin with, while they are always the ones who make
the shrillest noises about authority and obedience, they seem
to be shockingly unready to practice the most elementary
obedience or to display the most rudimentary faith that the
Council is guided by the Holy Spirit as soon as something is
decided which they do not approve. They are so convinced
that *they* are the Church that they are almost ready to declare the majority of bishops to be virtual apostates, rather
than obey the Council and the Pope. At the same time, of
course, their hysteria suggests that they are having a little
trouble handling the guilt which this inevitably arouses in
them.

On the other hand, the refusal of the extreme progressives to pay any attention to *any* traditional teaching which
would give them a common basis for rational discussion
with conservatives is surely scandalous also—especially when
it is allied with an arrogant triumphalism of its own, and when
it simply ridicules all opposition. This is not only foolish, but
seems to show a serious lack of that love to which they
frequently appeal in justification of their procedures. Though
they are continually shouting about "openness" one finds
them hermetically closed to their fellow Catholics and to

the Church's own past, and there is some validity to the conservative accusation that these extreme progressives often are more open to Marxism, to positivism, or to existentialism than they are to what is generally recognizable as Catholic truth.

It has been remarked with truth that conservatives and progressives in the Church are so concerned with total victory over each other that they are more and more closed to each other. If this is the case, one seriously wonders about the value and significance of the much touted "openness" to non-Catholics. An ecumenism that does not begin with charity *within* one's own Church remains questionable.

✓ ✓ ✓

Jacques Maritain has rightly protested against a concept of the lay apostolate which looks at the layman ordinarily only as a sinner who needs to be absolved by the clergy, but sees him now elevated to participation in a clerically organized lay group that runs errands for the clergy. Neither view shows any real respect for the laity and both seem to miss something quite essential in the notion of the Church. The whole Church is the People of God.

The obsession with institutionalism and organization is something the Church has doubtless caught, to some extent, by contagion with modern pragmatism. Yet this accounts for only the accidental aspects, the current ways and means of organizing people. Maritain points out with good reason that this spirit of efficiency has many grave disadvantages, and reminds us that "efficiency" and "success" are not necessarily signs of the Holy Spirit. Or rather the "success" that is the work of the Spirit is not identifiable with the quantitative results verifiable in statistics.

The point is not so much that the layman, guided, instructed, and indeed commanded by the clergy, should organize some movement, set it in operation, get it permanently established with statutes and bylaws, and finally bequeath to the Church a thriving outfit with several thousand busy members. Rather, as Maritain says, speaking of his own Thomist "circle" at Meudon: "The Holy Spirit is not at work *only* in durable institutions which last through the centuries, He is at work *also* in ventures that have no future, which have always to be begun again."*

I underline *only* and *also*. Obviously there must be "durable institutions" and there must be organization. But love is more important than organizations and a small, apparently insignificant and disorganized circle of friends united by love and a common venture in Christian witness may be of far greater value to the Church than an apparently thriving organization that is in reality permeated with the frenzies of activistic and ambitious willfulness.

Maritain adds: "One is paid for one's trouble by that which is best in the world, that marvel of those friendships which God awakens and of the pure fidelities which He inspires and which are like a mirror of the gratuity and generosity of His love."

I would add that *especially in the field of Ecumenism* this dimension of friendship, spontaneity, and spiritual liberty is of the greatest importance, and too much emphasis on organization can be stupefying.

✦ ✦ ✦

These lines from one of Bonhoeffer's *Prison Letters* (January 23, 1944) are very much in the spirit of Maritain, and show how much closer Bonhoeffer is to Catholicism than Barth is.

"It almost looks today as though the Church alone offers any prospect for the recovery of the sphere of freedom (art, education, friendship and play, 'aesthetic existence' as Kierkegaard called it). I am convinced of the truth of this and it would help us to a new understanding of the Middle Ages. What man is there among us who can give himself with an easy conscience to the cultivation of music, friendship, games or happiness? *Surely not the ethical man, but only the Christian.*"

* Preface to *Journal de Raissa*.

If this seems at first sight disconcerting, it is perhaps because we think that the Christian is doomed to be what Bonhoeffer calls the "ethical man"—precisely the non-Christian. The ethical man lives not by God's will perceived in the self-evident demands of concrete life, but by an abstract Kantian imperative, an inscrutable duty that has to be deciphered at every instant in "the glaring and fatiguing light of incessant consciousness."                              —*Ethics*

The Christian simply avails himself of God's command and permission to be a man.

"I am sure we honour God more," writes Bonhoeffer in the same letter, "if we gratefully accept the life he gives us with all its blessings, loving it and drinking it to the full, grieving deeply and sincerely when we have belittled or thrown away any of the precious things of life . . . than we do if we are insensitive toward life."

Worldliness? Yes, of course. The right kind, which sees the world redeemed in Christ.

But one must not conclude from this that a materialistic technocratic worldliness is equally blessed. The "good things" offered in such profusion by the affluent society are not self-evidently gifts and blessings of God. What if they corrupt and destroy life, or pervert it by ruining its true sensitivity and capacity for love, peace, fruitfulness, and joy?

✓ ✓ ✓

Although Bonhoeffer, in his view of the relation of the Church to the world, comes much closer to Catholicism than Barth, he nevertheless stops short—as, it seems to me, a good Lutheran must—and refuses to admit that the Church can speak to the world on the basis of a rational and "natural-law knowledge" which it has in common with the world. No, he says, the Church can preach only the message of Christ, and call the world to conversion and reconciliation in Christ. It can speak of God's love for the world in Christ. It can and must let God's love for the world work also through government, culture, labor, marriage, etc. But it is not concerned with these institutions, only with the faith of Christians living and working within them. Yet the Christian has a Christian duty to obey the state, to go to war, to defend his rights, but in all this he is obeying God *directly*.

Here I do not agree. I hold to the Catholic view which makes an Encyclical like *Pacem in Terris* possible and logical. Pope John could very well have called the world to peace purely and simply in terms of the Gospel of Peace. Instead he called it to peace in the name of humanity and reason. But was this a contradiction of the Gospel? No. Since Christ is fully and truly *man*, since the world, society, humanity, human and social life have been taken up and sanctified in the Incarnation, the Church can speak to the world in terms of a humaneness, a reason, a compassion which both the Church and the "world" are capable of understanding, but of which the Church also has a much deeper, theological understanding than the world.

Pope John's approach, traditionally Catholic yet completely open to dialogue with the world in human and reasonable terms, represents at the same time an explicitly religious position in which, however, religion is not forced on anyone. In his very humaneness and reasonableness he is bearing witness to the Gospel. This also was the spirit of the Catholic reasonableness of Thomas Aquinas.

On the other hand, Bonhoeffer's followers now preach a "religionless religion," a worldliness in which, having accepted an unbridgeable gap between Church and world, they have put themselves on the other side of the gap—where "God is dead" and the Gospel has to be preached as if it were not Gospel but only "worldliness."

I think it is certainly true that the Church must not claim to propose ecclesial and official answers to all human problems, and that her respect for reason must not confine itself to scholastical and clerical prescriptions for all our troubles. On the contrary, the possibility of meeting the world on the ground of dialogue and reason is now recognized as a great opportunity for the Church to develop her understanding of contemporary man, and in so doing to deepen her understanding of herself in relation to Christ, by serving Him in godless and worldly man.

It is in this way, I think, that the Church can, by humility and lucidity, awaken in man the sense of his real identity, and restore him to the hope of sanity and peace.

✶ ✶ ✶

The Church and the world: the medieval temptation, which unfortunately became an integral part of "Christendom," was, crudely and oversimply stated, the belief that because Christ is Lord of the world, and the world owes Him absolute submission in everything, and because the Church is the Body of Christ, then the world owes the Church absolute submission in everything.

The world belongs by right to Christ. The Church is the "whole Christ." The world therefore belongs by right to the Church. Pushed to its extreme, this view ended by demanding the temporal sovereignty of the Pope.

This implied first of all a confusion between the "whole Christ," the Mystical Body as such, and the visible, institutional framework of the Church. It implied a further confusion between the Church and "Christian society." Also it implied forgetfulness of the Church's function of *service* to the world, since the Lord made clear that He had come into the world to serve (Matthew 20:28), not to judge or to rule (John 3:17), and while He rules in heaven it is the Church's function to serve, to suffer, to preach, to witness on earth, and not to rule. Certainly she rules herself and makes laws to organize her own life, but only in function of her mission and her service in the world. Nor can she insist that in order to carry out this service she must have a certain power to exercise rule and control over men through the secular arm —to "make them believe." (Such a concept of the world implies that the world is simply insane in its wickedness and has to be subjugated by force, for its own good, before it can be calmed down enough to hear the word of salvation!)

If this concept is taken too seriously, then unconsciously the Church begins to concentrate too much on her own power and prestige rather than on her mission of service, preaching, and love. She takes her institutional power too seriously as an essential means for fulfilling her function in the world, and as the world itself grows more and more arrogant and hostile to religion, the Church tends more and more to entrench herself in her power and to assert her claims *against* the world. Instead of serving the world, she struggles with it in order to preserve her influence in it. And in the struggle, her influence is in fact diminished, since people come less and less to expect from her anything but the truculent assertion of her right to their respect and their obedience, rather than the proclamation of the truth revealed to the world in Christ. For since the Church *is* Christ, what need has she to proclaim anything but herself?

This summary is of course grotesque and unfair, but it does, I think, bring out the nature of the past failures and confusions which the Vatican Council is now honestly and courageously confronting.

✓ ✓ ✓

I quite understand and sympathize with the Christians—Protestant mostly—who are preaching a "religionless religion" and a frank admission of the "secular" and the "profane" in Christianity. But I think they have taken one aspect of Bonhoeffer's teaching and expanded it beyond measure, ending up with a superficial and naïve fad, rather than serious faith. I think they have cheapened grace, and Bonhoeffer said that "cheap grace is the deadly enemy of the Church."

However, I agree with their protest against the impertinences of a "religious" tactic that tries to cajole and pressure modern man, scientific and technological man, into having religious needs which he does not have. This "religiousness" is negative, ambiguous, moralizing: it preaches on one hand that one must run to God and the Church as to a refuge from life, yet once one has given the sacred its due, one can be unashamedly secular as regards making money and enjoying the good things of life, provided one maintains a rigid and negative set of standards in the matter of sex. One need not worry too much about things like war, civil rights, and so on, regarded as moral issues. One leaves such things to the secular authorities, and one prays for those concerned to get the right answers.

"Religiousness," then, preaches a need of and a dependence on God in order to emphasize a need of and dependence on certain specific religious forms, a definite style of life which sets itself up as the only authentic Christianity and which relies heavily on externals.

I think that, like most other converts, I faced the problem of the "religiousness" and came to terms with it. God was not for me a working hypothesis, to fill in gaps left open by a scientific world view. Nor was He a God enthroned somewhere in outer space. Nor did I ever feel any particular "need" for superficial religious routines merely to keep myself happy. I would even say that, like most modern men, I have not been much moved by the concept of "getting into heaven" after muddling through this present life. On the contrary, my conversion to Catholicism began with the realization of the presence of God *in this present life*, in the world and in myself, and that my task as Christian is to live in full and vital awareness of this ground of my being and of the world's being. Acts and forms of worship help one to do this, and the Church, with her liturgy and sacraments, gives us the essential means of grace. Yet God can work without these means if He so wills. When I entered the Church I came seeking God, the living God, and not just "the consolations of religion." And I can say that even in the monastery I have been able to put up with the "religiousness" that is sometimes more an obstacle than a help. Also, of course, I freely admit that I am myself deeply in sympathy with, and I think imbued with, the traditional religious culture of the West. I have said it often enough in this book and in others.

Furthermore, it is in this tradition itself—in St. Thomas, St. John of the Cross, the Greek and Latin Fathers—that I find the strongest warrant for this immediate and direct access to God in everyday Christian life, which is to be regarded not merely as a moral preparation for a heavenly existence but, as St. Thomas said, the very beginning of eternal life *incohatio vitae aeterna.*

Where I differ with the "religionless religion" people is that they seem to me to lack a real sense of God, the living and indwelling God, and to end up in a rather pitiable infatuation with everything that is superficial, mendacious, and cheap in technological culture. And this is not so new either. I can remember that one of the things I found most exasperating in Anglicanism—or in the peculiar sort to which I was subjected—was the facility with which preachers could enthuse over airplanes, radios, and other wonders of that time. It was this fatuous "joy-of-living" view of Anglican religion that made me want to become a Roman Catholic. I am afraid I am not able to find anything very new in the brave new secularity.

*  *  *

Why does the Church insist so much on "turning to the world" with acceptance and positive assent? Setting aside the answers that might point to human and pragmatic motives among some Christians—such as the desire to be accepted in and by the world—I think we must admit a much deeper reason.

The Church, considered now not merely as an institution but as the Body of Christ and the witness to God's merciful love for the world, senses in the crisis of modern man the ultimate danger of *man's refusal of himself.* Whereas conservative Churchmen are still afraid that the modern world presents a moral danger by its incitements to joy and its affirmations of humanism, freedom, and earthly delights, the Church, in her wisdom, realizes that the greatest danger comes from the power of *negation* that is latent in this great and powerful society of ours. Teilhard de Chardin himself realized this—he feared the possibility of "strikes in the noosphere" and the *refusal* of fulfillment on the part of the world itself. "There is danger that the world should refuse itself when perceiving itself through reflection," said Teilhard. Nietzsche was one of the prophets of this refusal, and the fact that man's technological skill and power are diverted more and more into preparing instruments and tactics for absolute destruction make the final refusal all too obviously possible.

The Church realizes that now she has to help the world

to accept itself. She clearly sees that blame, complacency, and recrimination will clarify nothing as long as they are accompanied only by exhortations to antique piety and the primness appropriate to another age.

The gravity of the situation is seen in the fact that Catholic theology has had to plunge into the task of acquiring entirely new perspectives in the space of a generation or two. But the fact that these perspectives are Biblical, concrete, existential, thoroughly based on respect for the world and for man in their actuality, gives definite hope—I do not say of solving all the problems of the modern world, but of bringing to that world the light it needs in an hour of risk and uncertainty. But that light is, as always, the light of the Gospel.

What is new in modern theology is not the essential message, but our rethinking of it, our rediscovery, in it, of insights we had lost. These insights provoke in us neither naïve enthusiasms nor petulant slander of the world, but awaken us to the deep truth of man's sinfulness and hardness of heart, overcome by the love of God and by His restoration of the world in Christ.

Without the awareness of God's wrath and of His mercy, the modern world makes no more sense (religiously) than a drunken hallucination. If we remember what the Bible means by the wrath of God, we can see how terribly the world needs mercy, pity, and peace—none of which things can come to man merely by his own wishing. Yet they are all within his reach, since he is loved by God, and more so than ever when he feels himself on the verge of utter despair. To speak of that despair is therefore no crime if it reminds man that his very despair is a good reason for not despairing.

✓ ✓ ✓

The most challenging thing the "religionless Christianity" people have to say, as I see it, is their demand that the Christian should be a man who, like Christ, lives and gives himself entirely for others and "to live for others means to accept life on their terms, to serve within the structures in which they live."                    —J. A. T. Robinson

But the great question is: Precisely what is meant by "accepting life on their terms?" What are "their terms?"

Bishop Robinson, in this context, is speaking of letting the Church's institutional structures entirely dissolve, so that the Christian lives in and accepts only purely secular institutions. The priest will work in the factory, etc. This is the current *diaspora* context which is not just a matter of imagination: it is lived, and with fervor, by Christians in Eastern Europe under Communism.

However, it does *not* mean simply accepting the Communist world view "on its own terms"; and let us always remember that Bonhoeffer was far from accepting Nazism "on its own terms." He died resisting it.

The question I ask, then, is: To what extent are we to accept the affluent society of the West on *its* own terms? It is here that I do not get too clear a picture from the *Honest to God* set. Robinson protests against an expensive Church "machinery" for "fighting the world." In so far as the fight itself is ambiguous, I agree with him. And I am not especially interested in his own special problem of how to keep a Church going where there are no more Churches.

The real point he wants to make seems to be this: that since modern man has lost the capacity to believe in "a gracious God" we should not speak to him about God at all. Thus in taking modern man "on his own terms" we accept his agnosticism or his atheism and start from there. There is nothing new about that, unless it means that for all practical purposes one becomes oneself an atheist or agnostic in order to be "all things to all men!" And in spite of protestations to the contrary, I sometimes feel that this is where "religionless Christianity" finally ends up. It is in the same predicament as everybody else, and has only added the final triumphant discovery that *it is really not a predicament*. It is here that the new faith begins! Everything is all right after all!

✓ ✓ ✓

Robinson is right, I think, when he says that Christianity has tended more and more to preach the "disincarnate word," to reduce Christ to formal abstract concepts which ordinary people are no longer able to cope with. There has to be theology, and theology has to be abstract, at least to a degree. What matters is that the theologian himself should not be dealing with a cold "disincarnation," a mental Christ that is no longer visible to him when he meets his fellow man. The sin of bad theology has been precisely this—to set Christ up *against* man, and to regard all flesh and blood men as "not-Christ." Indeed to assume that many men, whole classes of men, nations, races, are in fact "anti-Christ." To divide men arbitrarily according to their conformity to our own limited disincarnate mental Christ, and to decide on this basis that most men are "anti-Christ"—this shows up our theology. At such a moment, we have to question not mankind, but our theology. A theology that ends in lovelessness cannot be Christian.

On the other hand, together with flesh and blood man, "the world" is constituted by the illusions, the myths, the prejudices, and all the mental fictions with which man torments himself and from which Christ came to deliver him. If our mental image of Christ does nothing to deliver the world from its confusion, this does not mean that we can find a truer light by plunging into the same confusion. What we need is a deeper understanding of Christ and of the mystery of His presence in the world, in man. From this we will gain a much truer, less arrogant, more humble and more merciful awareness of the true meaning of the Church and of her mission to man.

To begin with, "the world" has no need of Christian apologetics. In saying this I speak as one who lived quite happily without apologetic arguments for the faith before I became a Christian, and when I became a Christian my conversion had absolutely nothing to do with apologetic arguments. The world has no need of Christian explanations of the world. It explains itself to its own satisfaction. That is why I think it is absurd to approach the world with what seems to me to be merely a new tactic and a new plea of sincerity—a "religionless religion" which cheerfully agrees that "God is dead."

Obvious answer from "the world": "So what?" The world does not need a "religionless religion" any more than it needs the traditional kind. It fabricates its own religion as it goes along, and its products are far more exciting. Nazism for instance!

In a word, "the world" feels no need of God either to explain itself or to be at peace with itself, or to regulate its activity. *The struggle of Churchmen to maintain their place in the world by convincing the world that it needs them* is, to my mind, a confusion and an indignity which "the world" rightly regards as ridiculous. What does it imply? That "having a place in the world" is a major concern of these Churchmen. They want to be needed, and God is the justification of their desire.

Therefore, it seems to me, personally, that the basis of the Christian mission to the world is precisely that the Christian is "not of this world." He is first of all freed from its particular myths, idolatries, and confusions by his Christian faith. His first mission is to *live that freedom* in whatever way God gives him to live it—whether in the world or out of it does not matter.

The Christ he "preaches" (whether by word or by silence) is the Christ of Christian freedom, Christian autonomy, Christian independence of the arrogant demands and claims of the world as illusion. Obviously the Christian is not "free" from the world as nature, as creation, nor is he free from human society. But he is free, or should be, from the psychic determinisms and obsessions and myths of a mendacious, greedy, lustful, and murderous "worldly" society—the society that is governed precisely by the love of money, and the unjust, arbitrary use of power. Does such a world "need God?" Obviously not!

The point then is not to convince "the world," in this sense, that it needs a Christian God because at one time it did justify itself by an appeal to Christianity. What is important is to show those who *want to be free* where their freedom really lies!

✶ ✶ ✶

The most valid intuition of the "religionless religion" people is, I think, their awareness that, though the vast majority of men today cannot adjust themselves to the idea that life acquires meaning only when one "joins the Church," these men who "cannot believe" are nevertheless, somehow mysteriously, encountering Christ. It is not the Christ of theology, or of Christian devotion and art. It is not the Christ of "Christian civilization," literature, ethics, philosophy. It is an anonymous and unknown Christ who comes in merciful hiddenness to the distraught pilgrim, as He did to the travelers to Emmaus. In this I agree, not so much on the basis of theological principles as on the basis of intuition and experience. I honestly think that there *is* a presence of Christ to the unbeliever, especially in our day, and that this presence, which is not formally "religious" and which escapes definition (hence the inadequacy of terms like "invisible Church" or "latent Church"), *is perhaps the deepest most cogent mystery of our time.* The Lord who speaks of freedom in the ground of our being still continues to speak to every man.

The thing that Christians must understand about this is that there is no use whatever trying to "get these people into the Church" or to make "believers" out of them. There is perhaps no way of bringing them a specifically Christian comfort which would in any case only disturb or confuse them. What is needed is to love them with a love completely divested of all formally religious presuppositions, simply as our fellow men, men who seek truth and freedom as we do.

This love is not simply an act of benevolent, condescending, and tolerant charity on our part. It can also be for us a means of knowing Christ better, by entering into the mystery of the hidden encounter which marks the lives of these others in a way that neither they nor we can understand. We cannot understand it, but by means of love we can experience its reality nevertheless.

✓   ✓   ✓

Though the liberty of St. Anselm and the liberty of Sartre may seem at first sight to be poles apart, yet I think they have much in common.

Both reject a concept of liberty that is confined to choosing between objects which pretend to confer happiness upon us from outside ourselves: both reject a pragmatic liberty which claims to orient the will to the possession of an object that will fulfill it. One might say immediately that Anselm, as a Christian, directs the will to the possession of God as the beatitude of the will. But wait a moment. Is God merely an "object" that the will can possess?

For St. Anselm, the union of the will with God takes place in the *justitia*, by which the will clings to freedom for its own sake. "Freedom for its own sake" may not seem like a good rendering of *rectitudo propter se servata*, and really it is not, since I am deliberately biasing the translation in the direction of Sartre. Yet for St. Anselm *rectitudo* is not merely the "uprightness" of a will that takes a self-complacent pleasure in its own moral exercise knowing that it is "right" and is "doing its duty." *Rectitudo* is in fact the right and authentic use of freedom: and this means spontaneous love of God for His own sake.

(This notion of loving God "for His own sake" is very ambiguous today. It might almost seem to mean loving Him because He has the power to make us love Him—being the "infinite good." For Anselm that would really be a distortion of its meaning. Anselm does not start from a *notion* of God, though in the *Proslogion* he seems to. He starts from the direct awareness of God as the ground of being that cannot-not-be. To love God "for His own sake" is therefore not just to love the notion of an omnipotent and all-good Father. It is, on the contrary, to love Him who is *without knowing really who or what He is* simply because He *is* and because His Being is existentially present to us as the ground of all existence, all knowledge, all freedom, and all love.)

In all the medieval Augustinian tradition the concept of *amor amicitiae*, or the love of God for love's sake and for

God's sake (God is love), is contrasted with the *amor commodi* or *concupiscentiae,* which is the love of an external object that confers happiness upon our own selves. The *amor amicitiae* is, then, love for love's sake, or freedom for freedom's sake, freedom always being understood in the light of the perfect self-giving which is the divine *caritas.* (In this context the "freedom" simply to grasp objects and appropriate them to oneself, the freedom to dominate and possess "things" or people as if they were things—is seen really as unfreedom.) Hence Anselm's *rectitudo* is not just the prize that is given the virtuous Christian in reward for making the right choice of a truly happy-making object: it is that which confers the final perfection of freedom on man's own free will, removing all obstacles to its perfect and authentic exercise.

Thus, for both Anselm and Sartre, the exercise of true freedom is required for a man to become truly what he is. Man is truly himself when he makes an authentic choice of freedom and abides by his choice. He who uses his freedom only for convenience, for "happiness," or even for "inner peace" and self-satisfaction, is in Sartre's term a *salaud,* which, in the most idiomatic translation I can think of, is a "bastard," not in the juridical but in the familiar and colloquial sense of the word. The concept of the *salaud* is not absent from St. Anselm, though he has a milder term: he simply calls him the *insipiens.* The *insipiens* is not so much a fool as what in American slang would be a "square," that is to say a self-satisfied and self-complacent positivistic type who is incurably pleased with his own mental clichés. The *insipiens* of Anselm happens also to be an agnostic, and he is addicted to frivolous and inconsequential verbalizing. Hence, there is a resemblance between Anselm and Sartre, and Anselm is not without a certain affinity for existentialism. At the same time, Sartre's freedom is the freedom of Anselm with a short circuit. In Anselm the perfect exercise of freedom is measured (or unmeasured, liberated from measure) by the boundless freedom of God. In Sartre it is measured by the act itself: thus, claiming to be limitless, it limits itself to itself. Sartre's ideas of commitment do not re-establish the circuit. Meanwhile, for Anselm, it is clear that God's will is not a force that presses down on man from the outside. It works on man from within himself and from within the ontological core of his own freedom. Made free, in the image of God, man's freedom contains in itself a demand for infinite freedom which can be met only by perfect union with the freedom of God, not only as an external norm, but *as the source of our own love.* Here philosophical notions of freedom necessarily break down and the perfect freedom of the Christian can be accounted for only by the indwelling Holy Spirit.

✓ ✓ ✓

One of the things St. Anselm has to say to modern man is that the power to sin (*potestas peccandi*) is first of all not a "power." Nor is it an expression of freedom, and finally it does not even enter into the definition of freedom. Freedom is not measured by our power and capacity to sin.

One might say that modern man has no interest whatever in the notion of sin. That is partly because he thinks that "sin" is a use of natural power forbidden by ethical authority, and this implies precisely that freedom equals the power to sin. From this one concludes, and I am afraid that religious and irreligious vie with one another in coming to the same idiot conclusion, that in order to prove one's freedom and "experience" it, one has to "sin": while, in order to grow in freedom one has to sin more and more. In so doing, one liberates himself from the tyranny of guilt. Finally, the acme of freedom is reached when one becomes like Lucifer and refuses to serve God or anyone else. This completely ludicrous concept, which is one of the characteristic myths of the modern world in so far as that world is "post-Christian,"*

---

* "Post-Christian" here refers to a type of thinking which, while rejecting Christian conclusions, still starts from presuppositions that are, or sound like, vaguely Christian views. Though our "post-Christian" society claims to have no interest in matters of good-and-evil, it still continues in fact to accept the division between the two and then, and in order to justify itself proceeds to confuse them in order to make clear that its conclusions are "not-Christian." The

actually destroys all possibility of genuine and mature freedom wherever it is taken seriously.

Here is where Sartre falls short of true freedom. In groping for the kind of freedom of which Anselm speaks, and in excluding *a priori* the Anselmian *rectitudo*, which is really a much more existentialist concept than one would imagine (it corresponds to "authenticity"), Sartre condemns himself to a puritanism in reverse, a doctrine of justification by sin (since absolute liberty in sinning is the ultimate canonization of freedom). That is one of the disadvantages of being French: Sartre is so logical that he will follow his absurdity to its ultimate limit. But it is also one of the disadvantages of being a "post-Christian"—and of being unconsciously determined by the myths and illusions of semi-Christians in the past. Really, one cannot blame Sartre for taking seriously the totally inadequate notion of sin which was, and still is, popular among Christians who have not really understood their religion. (The old idea that virtue is grim and unpleasant but one must practice it to be happy in the next life, even though one could really be happy and fully human by sinning in this! Thus Christianity is nothing but the renunciation of humanity, liberty, joy, etc.)

*✓ ✓ ✓*

A curious fact that calls for study: the part played by the *myth of momentous choice* in our current moral crisis. Our image of ourselves (constructed of cultural and subcultural elements) is that of firm, enlightened, decisive men who, when we are faced with the momentous choice, quickly calculate the pros and cons, decide, and then advance resolutely to carry out our decision. At the same time we assume that these momentous decisions are to be faced at every turn. We are always making momentous decisions—says the myth; we stand at the crossroads two or three times a week, and decide on our new course. The traffic problem resulting from this

---

"post-Christian" mind, then, is a mind which is no longer Christian but is still self-conscious about it, and still concerned with vestiges of Christian thinking.

would defy imagination. Fortunately there is no such problem: *it just does not happen.*

We do not make momentous decisions. They are made for us, and we either accept or not, with good grace or not. The myth of the man of decision, enlightened, determined, calculating the pros and cons, jutting out his jaw and ready to go —this is our consolation for being passive, petulant, confused, ineffectual, dominated by routines.

All right then. But at least we *try* to be decisive, determined. . . . Maybe that is the source of the trouble.

The time has perhaps come to ask ourselves if this myth has not finally become so unreal, so unproductive, so paralyzing that it ought to be altogether discarded for some more honest and more workable image, as a center of a more realistic scheme of meaning.

Why do I ask?

Because this myth has reached its ultimate absurdity in our image of ourselves as men of decision, determination, etc., etc., with our fingers on the button which can let loose nuclear destruction on our civilization. The demonic ironies of this pitiable image of ourselves ought to alert us to the fact that there are unsolvable contradictions in our present scheme of meanings. These ironies ought to alert us to the fact that while we have been talking our heads off about freedom we have in fact surrendered to un-freedom.

Our myth of ourselves as men of momentous choice is then simply a disguise for the more basic falsehoods that corrupt our real motives. What are they? Who knows?

My guess is that instead of being men of *decision* we are in reality men of *velleity.* And our pitiable confusion is due to our total submission to desire: not desire in its strong and passionate form (as we would like to imagine), but desire in a weak, erratic, querulous, resentful, subhuman caricature. This desire *seems* strong because it can express itself in a symbolic use of powerful machines (the high-powered car), but in reality it is flabby and dependent on things, on commodities, on money, on artificial stimulation.

The myth of the momentous decision cloaks our pitiable lack of identity and of autonomy.

But we cannot free ourselves from this illusion simply by making another momentous decision. For then the vicious circle begins all over again.

Where do we begin? Perhaps by learning to admit *values which we fear,* from which we are trying to escape. Values like solitude, inner silence, reflective communion with natural realities, simple and genuine affection for other people, admission of our need for these things, admission of our need for contemplation. But at every step we confront the same vicious myth, because we have forgotten how to "let things alone," and live first of all by simple trust. Naturally there is much more involved than this: but this might be a conceivable point of departure, a preparation for the recovery of freedom. Then "decision" would once more have a meaning.

(Note: we live in a society in which for many people the values I have just mentioned are for the most part completely inaccessible.)

✓ ✓ ✓

Magnificent lines from Barth:

"Everyone who has to contend with unbelief should be advised that he ought not to take his own unbelief too seriously. Only faith is to be taken seriously; and if we have faith as a grain of mustard seed, that suffices, for the devil has lost his game."          *—Dogmatics in Outline*

This is one of the great intuitions of Protestantism. And, of course, from a critically Catholic viewpoint, one can find fault with it: but why? To say "only faith is to be taken seriously" can be understood in the light of that Christian—and Catholic—humility which puts all its trust in God. Our "good works" are necessary, but they are not to be *"taken seriously."* The Catholic dogma of justification never told anyone that he had to take his good works *seriously* in the sense of trusting completely in his own righteousness, for to take one's good works seriously is to be a pharisee. Only faith is to be taken seriously because only the mercy of God is serious. And if we put too much emphasis on the seriousness of what we do, we not only make the judgment of God the most serious reality in our life, but we are in fact judged: we are judged as men who have taken seriously something other than His infinite mercy. He who takes mercy seriously will hardly sin seriously. He who takes his own works seriously will not be kept, by that seriousness, from sin. It is pseudo-seriousness. It is not good enough.

What about unbelief, then: if faith is to be taken seriously, it follows that unbelief is also serious. No, because in taking faith seriously it is God whom we take seriously, not ourselves, not our faith. I do not take faith seriously as something which I definitely possess, but I take seriously God Who gives me faith and renews that gift, by His mercy, at every moment, in spite of my unbelief. This I think is one of the central intuitions of evangelical Christianity, and it is something which we must all learn. It is something, too, which many Protestants have themselves forgotten, becoming instead obsessed with faith as it is *in themselves*, constantly watching themselves to see if faith is still there, which means turning faith into a good work and being justified, consequently by works. "To believe is to *be free to trust in Him quite alone*" and to be free from every other form of dependence and reliance. This is true freedom, and from it springs the capacity for every good work, for it removes all obstacles to love in our hearts.

*     *     *

Barth stresses the fact that God must not be regarded as "pure power" in the sense of unbridled and arbitrary *potentia*. His power, *potestas*, is the power of love and truth. It is not the infinite, arbitrary will that flies into action unchecked by any responsibility to anything but its own whim: He is responsible to His own Love and His Truth. His power is the power of love.

"Absolute power," power responsible only to itself is the program of the devil—it becomes the ideal of man who thinks that the "power" to sin is essential freedom.

Barth's concept of evil: that which has been denied existence by God, and which we affirm by our own choice, thus attempting to give it existence in spite of God.

The world is the theater of God's glory—says Calvin, following Augustine. Man is the witness of the great acts of God, and "has to express what he has seen." It is a great conception, but it is inadequate. I like better St. Irenaeus, who brings it even closer: *man himself* is the glory of God, but this glory in himself is not a spectacle which man contemplates. It is something that he *lives*. *Gloria Dei vivens homo*. I think it is most important today to get away from the idea of God, God's glory, God's attributes merely as "objects" which man contemplates, and then praises. Even though man may see nothing whatever of God, his life may still be filled with God's glory. To say that he will "know" this in another world is all right, as long as we remember that we do not know precisely what we are talking about.

*ɪ   ɪ   ɪ*

Zoë Oldenbourg, who writes passionately well about the Cathars, has cast her choice upon a cold, burning religious beauty, a kind of quintessential Protestantism, and she celebrates it in books of great fervor. But again, this is "post-Christian." How much of this beauty is surreptitiously taken over from Catholicism itself? (The Fathers writing about Exodus said it was right for the Church to take along the gold of Egypt when leaving the world, and now in "post-Christian" clichés they are taking along our gold, too, as the "gold of Egypt.")

One can hardly help being rocked by the fantastic religious eros of *Destiny of Fire* (about the Cathars who were burned at Montségur). But is it the eros of Catharism, or rather the genius and eros of the author herself, the beauty and fascination of religious aspirations so much like those of Simone Weil? How can one stand by without compassion and love for such people? I cannot comprehend the Catholics who revile them, tear them down. One can have compassion surely without being "bewitched"—it is supreme uncharity to treat them as witches, yet that is in fact what we do. It shows our fear of them.

Here is the haunting beauty of religious passion, something quite other than just ordinary, dull faith. But in the end it gives me a feeling of absence and emptiness. The whole Albigensian crusade (in which the Cistercians by the way were so involved) seems to me to be one of the first great prophetic signs of the modern void, the "absence of God," as if in the crusade both sides, clashing with different styles of passion, conspired to destroy the true memory of God while attempting to substitute for it the madness of a peculiar religious style, a spirituality, a brand of fervor.

*   *   *

In the climate of the Second Vatican Council, of ecumenism, of openness, the word "heretic" has become not only unpopular but unspeakable—except, of course, among integralists, who often construct their own identity on accusations of heresy directed at others.

But has the concept of heresy become completely irrelevant? Has our awareness of the duty of tolerance and charity toward the sincere conscience of others absolved us from danger of error ourselves? Or is error something we no longer consider dangerous?

I think a Catholic is bound to remember that his faith is directed to the grasp of truths revealed by God, which are not simply accessible by reason alone. That these truths are not mere opinions or "manners of speaking," mere viewpoints which can be adopted or rejected at will—for otherwise the commitment of faith would lack not only totality but even seriousness. The Catholic is one who stakes his life on certain truths revealed by God. If these truths cease to apply, his life ceases to have meaning.

So then: what is a heretic?

A heretic is first of all a *believer*. Today the ideas of "heretic" and "unbeliever" are generally confused. In point of fact the mass of "post-Christian" men in Western society can no longer be considered heretics and heresy is, for them, no problem. It is, however, a problem for the believer who is too eager to identify himself with their unbelief in order to "win them for Christ."

Where the real danger of heresy exists for the Catholic today is precisely in that "believing" zeal which, eager to open up new aspects and new dimensions of faith, thoughtlessly or carelessly sacrifices something essential to Christian truth, on the grounds that this is no longer comprehensible to modern man. Heresy is precisely a "choice" which, for human motives (rationalized perhaps as "grace"), selects and prefers an opinion contrary to revealed truth as held and understood by the Church. It then proceeds to teach this opinion contumaciously even against the sincere protest of the faithful (not merely the carping of a few bigots).

I think, then, that in our eagerness to go out to modern man and meet him on his own ground, accepting him as he is, we must also be truly what *we* are. If we come to him as Christians we can certainly understand and have compassion for his unbelief—his apparent incapacity to believe. But it would seem a bit absurd for us, precisely as Christians, to pat him on the arm and say: "As a matter of fact I don't find the Incarnation credible myself. Let's just consider that Christ was a nice man who devoted his life to helping others!"

This would, of course, be heresy in a Catholic whose faith is a radical and total commitment to the truth of the Incarnation and Redemption as revealed by God and taught by the Church. Without this commitment there is no serious basis for his "Christian humanism," or indeed for his mission to the world and to his fellow man.

What is the use of coming to modern man with the claim that you have a Christian mission—that you are sent in the name of Christ—if in the same breath you deny Him by whom you claim to be sent?

✓ ✓ ✓

There are some very strong and moving quotations on the religious life in the history of Anglican religious orders by A. M. Allchin, the *Silent Rebellion*. I have an especial admiration for Father R. M. Benson, whose theology is perfectly traditional and sound, it seems to me. There is a special monastic quality in Anglican ideas of the religious life, and a genuine touch of protest, of "witness against" the torpor of the nineteenth-century Anglican establishment. The book is interesting and disturbing, and one cannot get away from a certain ambiguity in Anglican religious orders. I am glad I came all the way to Rome.

✗ ✗ ✗

Father Paul Evdokimov, the Orthodox theologian, writes a splendid and challenging article on the Desert Fathers and on the radical tradition of monasticism, both Eastern and Western. He frankly regards monastic chastity as a refusal to procreate and to continue the existence of a society that has reached its term (a view which in modern Catholicism would shock even the most convinced of monks). This refusal is creative, not negative: those who claim to be so positive about the value of "the world" and of our society are precisely the ones who are so busy building the bombs that are capable of destroying it. Which is better: an optimism of hope which takes the world with only relative seriousness and looks to a supernatural end, or an optimism which is based on mere power, arrogance, and affluence, and leads to nothing but the proliferation of instruments for destruction? Which shows the more real respect for life?

Evdokimov demands a virile ascesis, not simply gentlemanly retirement into leisure. The monk does not build his monastic city "on the margin" of the world, but *instead of it*. This is important. The monastic consciousness of today in America is simply a marginal worldly consciousness. It won't do. On the other hand, I do not think the crumbling lavras and sketes of Athos will do much better.

For Father Evdokimov, the monastic life is there to proclaim the abolition of history. How many Western monks could swallow that? Few, I imagine. Yet I see what he means. He aims this statement shrewdly against the activistic, care-worn, busy-busy preoccupation of monks with ephemeral projects that have no deep significance. He has nothing to do whatever with the facile optimism of beatified agitation. His view of the Church and the world: since the world presents a *lying* vision, the unworldliness of the monk must be not only noncomformist, but provocatively so. The monk is *in revolt* against the false claims of the world. This has to be properly understood. There are enough emotionally disturbed people around who ask nothing better than to be dendrites and column sitters, to prove they are right and everyone else is wrong. Yet the principle is true.

I profoundly agree that in fact the monastic turning away from the world leads the monk, naturally, into a kind of prehistoric condition. Hence we are foolish to be too excited about playing an imaginary part, as monks, in "history." But nevertheless, we are in history, not prehistory. (One might ask the question whether we will shortly be in posthistory.)

The literature of the Desert Fathers is iconography, rather than character study. It shows us the spiritual radiation of men who are outside history: men who have taken history to themselves and transcended it, who render it transparent, thus showing its inner and secret dimensions. The monastic life, then, is not a mere refusal of history. But for this fruit to mature, there must be true sanctity, and truly *monastic* sanctity. As long as the solitary life is systematically played down, discouraged, and even forbidden, I do not think that even the cenobitic life will bear its proper fruits.

This is an extreme and radical view, implying the rejection of culture, (in order to elevate it also to the "transparent" level), the frank adoption of a life lacking in rational measure, as against the "moderation" and "good sense" of merely ethical norms. But once again, when we consider our monks in the concrete, who of them is able to do this without breaking down?

One of his most impressive phrases: *one goes into the desert to vomit up the interior phantom, the doubter, the double.* It is the monk's office to do this for himself and for others, since others are not in a position to do it. The ascesis of solitude is, then, a deep therapy which has uncovered the ascetic archetype in man. But again, the risk is enormous. When one considers monks in the concrete, one finds them dangerously bound to their double, incapable of "vomiting him out." It is precisely this phantom, this impostor, that dictates the pseudoasceticism and the contemplative posturing of the misfits.

In the end, Father Evdokimov himself admits that the radical, desert phase of the monastic development cannot be renewed today in its original form. We are in history, for better or for worse. We are not ikons, and we are not transparent. If we were dendrites, we would not for all that be living in "arks of air above the level of the flood." We are men of prayer and love, and being men of love we can move in the world though unseen by it. The world is no longer bewitched. But we must recognize clearly that we have ancient roots to which we must be faithful.

Meanwhile the Red Cross came again for the yearly visit with the blood wagon. I went out at a crowded time, and discovered that I was in better health than last year, weighing a hundred and eighty-five pounds, which is certainly too much. As an ikon, I am not doing too well. Maybe I ought to try living in a tree.

✓ ✓ ✓

A priest speaking at the funeral of Bernanos said of him: "That demand to exist authentically, that anguish at the thought that perhaps he might have only pretended to live: these marked with a devouring dissatisfaction his own estimate of himself, his view of us, his judgment of the world."

The whole thing is in this.

The real trouble with "the world," in the bad sense which the Gospel condemns, is that it is a complete and systematic sham, and he who follows it ends not by living but by pretending he is alive, and justifying his pretense by an appeal to the general conspiracy of all the others to do the same.

It is this pretense that must be vomited out in the desert. But when the monastery is only a way station to the desert, when it remains permanently that and nothing else, then one is neither in the world nor out of it. One lives marginally, with one foot in the general sham. Too often the other foot is in a sham desert, and that is the worst of all.

✓ ✓ ✓

Dead, dry, fall weather: the dry leaves tinkle like flakes of copper when the breeze passes over them. Hot haze. I wrote a short article on the Shakers, something I had been intending for a long time. Why were they first hated so much, then loved so much? Perhaps they were hated because of their mixture of celibacy and common life—both sexes living together in chastity in the same houses, each house divided with one side for the men, the other for the women. In any case this disturbed their attackers, and the Shakers were much slandered for it. Because of this and public confession, as well as their strict discipline and obedience, they were reviled as "Catholics" in New England. Why loved? For their work? In the markets they did not scruple to drive a hard bargain. Probably they were loved for an angelic gentleness, which after all was related to their celibacy. Thus they were loved for the very thing for which they were hated.

*✓ ✓ ✓*

Barth's visual imagination sometimes reminds me of that of the medieval German cathedral builders. He does not hesitate to introduce a droll image in his theology. And it always comes at the right moment. "We Christians," he says, "must not sit among them [unbelievers] like melancholy owls."

One could compile a whole lively and charming medieval bestiary out of Barth. *The snail* (which the Church is not): "The Church runs like a herald to deliver the message. It is not a snail with a little house on its back and so well off in it that only now and then it sticks out its feelers and thinks that 'the claim of publicity' has been satisfied."

*The dog.* Pilate is the dog: "How does Pilate come into the creed . . . ? Like a dog into a nice room!" However, Barth is insulting politics rather than Pilate himself. It is politics in the Church that is "the dog in the nice room." The point is that Barth does not even describe his dog, and yet you see him instantly, a dog from the street who does not belong in a nice room, but comes ambling in with a mixture of assurance and guilt.

Sometimes, Barth admits, the Christian in the Church is like a bird beating its wings against the bars of a cage because everyone will not adopt *his* ideas, his new ritual, his projects. "If you do not know this oppression you have certainly not seen the real dynamic of this matter." But this is to be accepted too, and we all wait patiently for the Kingdom, "recognizing each other in longing and humility in the light of the divine humor."

—all quotes are from *Dogmatics in Outline*

✦ ✦ ✦

In St. Anselm's book on the Redemption (*Cur Deus Homo*), as well as in his *Proslogion,* one cannot really follow his argument unless one shares something of the inner light and experience of his faith. Dialectics are not enough, even though Anselm thought himself chiefly a dialectician in his writings. What is the "light" in which he sees and discusses the Redemption? Again it is the intuition of *rectitudo* as authentic freedom, and not simply the accomplishment of duty. The *rectitudo* of Christ in the Redemption does not consist for Anselm primarily in the acceptance of a condemnation to death imposed by the Father. Many interpreters of Anselm see it that way. Christ was not condemned to death by the divine justice. He came into the world, was made man in order to live perfectly as man, in the freedom and truth of man, to do what was fitting for man, and thus to save other men. In accomplishing "all justice" He is condemned *unjustly*. He could justly have used his power to save man in some other way, but He preferred explicitly *to save man by a renunciation of power*. Therefore he willingly and freely underwent death. The Father willed the salvation of man but left Christ entirely free to choose His own means. What is pleasing to the Father is not precisely the suffering and death of Christ, but the fact that the Son uses His freedom to choose that which He thinks best and most perfect in saving man— that which is in fact the purest exercise of freedom without any afterthought of self-interest. Hence, strictly speaking, the Father's will did not arbitrarily impose suffering and death on Christ, but *sent Him into the world to use His freedom to save man*. It is out of love for the Father that Jesus chooses this particular way, the way of humiliation and of the total renunciation of power, in order to save man by love, mercy, and self-sacrifice.

Note that the will of the Son and the will of the Father are One in God. It is the *human* will of Christ that makes this choice of the renunciation of a divine power that He could justly use. God's will was that the human will of Christ should freely specify by what means man should be saved. Christ as man chose the way of total poverty, humiliation, self-emptying, since in this way He was most completely identified with man, and also most freely witnessed to the nature of love as supreme freedom—a freedom that is not limited or stayed even by death.

The death of Christ was, then, for Anselm, anything but a passive, blind, desperate subjection to an absolute decree that He must die. At the same time, Calvin's intuition of Christ at all times "bearing the wrath" of God is true too, in a more somber aspect of the same thing. Anselm, however, makes clear that freedom in Christ accomplishes all justice; that perfect freedom alone is strong enough to bear the full weight of God's wrath. But in us that freedom can only be a gift of the Spirit and of grace. Our nature cannot provide it. Such freedom is not accessible to us outside the love of Christ, which means also love of the *humanity* of Christ, that is to say of man.

*✝ ✝ ✝*

Liturgies, new and old.

For the junior brothers, new liturgy, parts of the Mass sung in English, homily, offertory procession (sung), etc.

In the infirmary: old liturgy, in fact very old and very unique—and very moving in its own way. Father S——, for example, leans on the altar, hangs on to it, grapples with it, veering sideways he gangs up on the book with a rush, then holds on for dear life, reading from it in a quaking whisper. His server, Brother L——, who is deaf, kneels in strange places so that he can see to lip-read, and gives out the responses in a high-pitched Latin that he has not heard for a long time and has consequently become a liturgical language all its own. Then the *plebs sancta:* Brother J——, in his wheel chair, with a red blanket over his shoulders and glasses perched on the end of his nose; Brother D——, the oldest, sixty years in the monastery, bowed far over, very low. . . . Then in the midst of all this the aquiline nose and powerful frame of the cellarer, who is there to get early communion and take off on a trip. Early Mass in the infirmary (2:30 A.M.) is an altogether unforgettable liturgy. There is nothing like it on earth.

At the brothers' Mass the altar now faces the people. One of the more conservative Fathers says Mass angrily at it, and at the *nobis quoque peccatoribus* digs his fist violently into his stomach. Liturgical *hara kiri?*

✦ ✦ ✦

Eadmer's life of Anselm has a wonderful "healing" air about it—simply because in the rather violent monasticism of that time Anselm himself was a saint with a tender and almost motherly concern for his monks. One of the monks, who hates Anselm (no bones are made about this), is dying. Suddenly he finds himself attacked by two wolves. He is "in their arms" (one immediately sees the half-human wolves of a romanesque sculptured capital) and their teeth are at his throat. It is siesta time and nobody is around except Anselm, who is in the nearby cloister correcting manuscripts. He comes in and the wolves vanish.

✦ ✦ ✦

When I came down to the monastery from the woods this afternoon (November 22, 1963) one of the novices met me in the door of the novitiate and told me that President Kennedy had been shot and had died, in Dallas, Texas, an hour and a half before. At first I could not believe it. I told him it must be an irresponsible rumor. No, it was quite true. There was a notice on the board about it, and when I went to see Father Abbot he said the latest news was that a rifle had been found in a building that overlooked the street where the President was shot through the head.

The whole thing leaves one sick. Sick at the madness, the useless ferocity, the aimless violence that marks so much of the life of this country. No matter who killed the President or what his motives were, this act was simply one more in a whole long series of senseless, brutal, stupid, pathological killings. We have had one after another, especially in the South. The Negro leader, Medgar Evers; the little children in the Birmingham Sunday school; the Baltimore postman—and now this. Was it something to do with the race question, or was it just some vague fantacism, some free-floating need to destroy?

As for Kennedy, he was one of the few good Presidents we have had in my lifetime. Not that he did not have his limitations, but he was far above people like Truman, Eisenhower (whom I nevertheless respect as a person), not to mention the Hoovers, Coolidges, and Hardings. Kennedy was on a level with Wilson and FDR, and probably better than both, if only he had had his chance to go on and do something. Why should people want to kill him?

Later: I am told they have captured "a Communist," someone who was pro-Castro, and that this man shot the President. News comes into the monastery by phone to Father Abbot and gets around fast, sometimes very twisted.

Later: outside, people are simply shattered. The country is undergoing a real emotional crisis . . . all the more so as Oswald, suspected of shooting Kennedy, has now been shot himself by a superpatriot, a curious, impulsive type; a nightclub owner. The whole thing is so odd it is barely credible.

✓ ✓ ✓

The whole question of the Kennedy assassination is extremely complex and obscure. It is probably much graver than people seem to believe: but now everybody wants it to be "settled" and "settled" it is. All have agreed on the answer, and the question is no longer seriously asked, except by a few. The general justice is "satisfied." One feels that all have wanted a solution at any price and have taken the first one that was at hand. Is it good enough? (November 30, 1963)

✓ ✓ ✓

The seventeenth chapter of St. Anselm's *De Casu Diaboli* (*The Fall of the Devil*) raises a rather modern question: our creativity, that is to say the creative power of our liberty in the world, is resolved perhaps into the choice to be nondestructive and to freely cooperate in creation. Creation itself is beyond our power. If we accept creation, if we are open to the mysterious creative power of God's will (even when it appears to us to pose a threat) we concur in creation. We do not have the power to create, but we have the seeming power to destroy, by reason of our capacity for the refusal of creative and positive power from God. Actually the power to destroy, like the apparent power to sin, is no power at all. It is a metaphysical illusion, though destruction itself can be very objective and real. More truly creative is the free consent by which we really participate in the dynamism of the world created by the love of God.

But our power to destroy, like our power to sin, seems to us more of a power because it seems to be more unique, more personal, more autonomous. It seems to be uniquely *ours*. Especially when we cannot really believe in our consent and our freedom, we fall back on this illusory power. We destroy in order to affirm our freedom and our "reality." The more we doubt our freedom and our identity, the more we are impelled to destroy.

St. Anselm, accepting this negativity in man, even says that to refrain from destruction is to participate in creation. We "make" something when we are capable of unmaking it and do not do so. This, of course, is not our only way of making things, but it is important to remember this rather humble estimate of our power in this age of destructive passion and violence.

Problem: the difficulty of *realizing* that our power of consent is real and creative, when it vanishes into the creative background of God's will and does not affirm us clearly in our own eyes as having singular autonomy. God's will and love are the only true power, and we are truly powerful when our autonomy is lost in Him. But we prefer the appearance of power that we have when we stand apart, refuse, and destroy. In the modern world it is this which counts more and more as power, and not the creative love that simply nurtures, consents, and helps to live.

⚹ ⚹ ⚹

Cold stars. Steam coming up out of the kitchens into the freezing night (4:00 A.M.). Frost on the side of the coal pile outside the furnace room. Dirty bread lying in the gravel, frozen, for birds. Creak of the frosty wooden steps down to the infirmary kitchen. Flamingos on the Standard Oil calendar in the kitchen. Hot tea.

⚹ ⚹ ⚹

An ex-postulant sent a few pages torn out of a magazine, concerning the Kennedy assassination. Once again, though it is barely a month since his death, the same conclusions are all dogmatically reaffirmed. Everyone is content with the answers. The curious thing about this magazine was that it showed with what anxiety everybody wants Oswald to be really and truly the guilty one so that no one will have to worry about the affair any more. He is an acceptable murderer, and that is that. How acceptable? Listen to this: "Oswald was a lone wolf whose background showed that he was *inclined to nonviolence up to a point where his mind apparently snapped . . ."* With this perfect equivocation, how could the case be anything but settled? Oswald has with the greatest of ease become the incarnation of everything that the American mass media ridicule or distrust: and now, this concentration of evil qualities in this one man becomes so intense that opposites stand together without the slightest discomfort. Nonviolence equals violence. And it is scientific. (His background showed it. And when your background shows it, baby, it is *proved.*) Of course (just a matter of unimportant detail) Oswald's background was Communist and Communism is violent, not nonviolent. No matter. His mind snapped, and that was what everybody wants to know. If it turns out that his mind snapped because of a violent predisposition to nonviolence, so much the better. That makes him a beatnik as well as a Communist and thus by implication the President's murder is pinned on the beatniks and not by any means on Dallas, which (in spite of having the highest homicide rate of any city in the country) has officially declared itself "without sin."

✶ ✶ ✶

"To be a man," says Barth, "means to be situated in God's presence as Jesus is, that is to be a bearer of the wrath of God."

I do not want an "optimism" that shrinks from this truth. But it must be understood. Jesus bears the wrath, and He lives. Because He bears it and lives, we bear it also, not by our own strength but by His. And by His bearing it on the Cross, the wrath becomes love to us, saves us, purifies us. Here perhaps I am adding my own Catholic ideas to Barth: ideas so well and so terribly expressed in St. John of the Cross.

Compare this, from the Calvinist catechism, with the *Dark Night*.

"What understandest thou by the little word 'suffered'?"

*"That He all the time of His life, but especially at the end thereof had born in body and soul the wrath of God against the whole human race."*

There is nothing in this of the "dolorism" of certain types of piety. Its perfect seriousness is of a kind to overthrow one's whole life in an instant. Other perspectives speak of Christ's sufferings in exquisite physical detail, but miss the essential, the theological wrath. His pains are enumerated as the pains of one who has not truly been struck. They are quantitative, detailed, wrung out to the last essential drop of agony, but the seriousness of the wrath is not there because, as one gradually realizes, in the mind of the preacher, God is pleased with this pain. But when the word "wrath" is spoken, this whole pious elaboration becomes sickeningly frivolous. Wrath means that God is not pleased, is not "gratified" by the pains of the Redeemer, whose love bears the wrath and

redeems us from it. We have lost our sense of the wrath
of God. It is only thunder, power. True wrath is ontological.
It reaches into the very depths of being.

I think I will have to become a Christian.

✓  ✓  ✓

Persistent rumors are going around that Jacques Maritain
has been made a cardinal. This is not in itself impossible,
since laymen have been made cardinals before. But it is difficult to see how Pope Paul, even with his well-known affection for Jacques, would make him a cardinal. Still, I know
someone who even claims to have seen it in print. Meanwhile, I am writing a preface to Julie Kernan's translation of
Raissa's beautiful little book on the *Pater*.

✓  ✓  ✓

Priests and ministers suddenly believe it urgent to assure
everyone that "the world" is telling us the truth—not always
making clear what world they mean. And often those who
insist that "the world" is deceiving us mean only the world
which refuses them and their message, not their own world,
their own tight system of fragments of the past held together by money and armies.

I think only the poets are still sure in their prophetic sense
that the world lies, and George Oppen has said it well:

> They await
> War, and the news
> Is war
> As always
>
> That the juices may flow in them
> And the juices lie.

This psychic and chemical dialogue of news, glands, juices,
opinions, combat, self-affirmation, despair: this is "the world"
and no poet need be doctrinaire about it. It is there for anyone to see, and they see it. They see how the people act
in it.

> They develop
> Argument in order to speak, they become
> unreal, unreal, life loses
> solidity, loses extent, baseball's their game
> because baseball is not a game
> but an argument and difference of opinion
> makes the horse races. They are ghosts that endanger
> One's soul.

News, argument, and the juices flow. We do not want the news, but the flow of juices. Stimulation is the lie, and we cannot get along without it.

> Wolves may hunt
> With wolves but we will lose
> Humanity in the cities, stores
> And offices
> In simple
> Enterprise.

✓   ✓   ✓

Yet the poet, Oppen again, knows another and more real world, the world not of lies and stale air in the subway, but of life. The world of life is itself manifest in words, but is not a world of words. What matters is not the words but the life. If we listen particularly to the world's speech about itself we will be lied to and deceived, but not if we listen to life itself in its humility, frailty, silence, tenacity. This poem of Oppen's is about a Jewish baby.

> Sara, little seed,
> Little, violent, diligent seed. Come let us look at the world
> Glittering: this seed will speak,
> Max, words! There will be no other words in the world
> But those our children speak. What will she make of a world
> Do you suppose, Max, of which she is made?

Will the words of the children be lies also, like those of our generation—or worse lies still? When one takes this deeper view he does not have to ask. There is the hope, there is the world that remakes itself at God's command without consulting us. So the poet, here, does not ask about lies or worry about them. He sees only the world remaking itself in the live seed, and Max can confidently take the baby to the window to see the false, glittering buildings, about which some speech will probably come later.

The glitter is false? Well, the *light* is true. The glitter has ceased to matter. It is even beautiful.

# INDEX

Abraham, 14, 90, 127, 137
Acts, bible quotation, 299–300
Adjust, trying to, 264–68
  yes and no, 265–68
Affluence, 73
Affluent society, 98, 316, 323
Africa, 31
Alabama, 39, 296
Albert the Great, St., commentary on Aristotle, 203
Albigensian Crusade, 335
Allchin, A. M., *Silent Rebellion*, 336
Alphonsus Rodriguez, St., 100
Ambrose, *Hexaemeron*, 296
America, 34–37, 39, 71, 74, 76, 163, 249, 336
American monasticism and John Wu, 231
American myth, 33, 39, 76
American society, white, 111
Andrade, Carrera, Ecuador poet, 13
Anglican religious orders, history of, 336–37
Anselm, St., 135, 327–30
  *De Casu Diaboli*, 344–45
  *Cur Deus Homo*, 341–42
  life of, by Eadmer, 343
  *Proslogion*, 341
Anti-Americanism, anti-Semitism, 281
Anti-Semitism, 19, 133, 134, 170, 171, 281
Antoninus, Brother, 278
Antiphon, poem, 176
Ape into space, 60–61
Approval, need of, 97–98
Aquinas, St. Thomas. *See* St. Thomas
Arabi, Ibn al', 208, 210
Arendt, Hannah, 285, 289–90
  *Totalitarianism*, 104, 108
Aristotle, 203–6, 208
Arnold of Morimond, Abbot, 151

Art
  and artists, 149–50, 283–84
  Byzantine, 307
  cave, 300, 307–8
  Egyptian tomb paintings, 310
  future of, 282–83
  pop, 283–84
  Russian ikons, 307
Asia, 31, 37
Atheist, 323
  existentialist, 17
Auden, W. H., poem, 129, 275
Augustine, St., 53, 334
Aunt Kit, 200–1
Auschwitz, 59
  poem, 57–58
Automobile, meditation on the, 76
Autonomy of individual, 114–17
Averroes, 208

Babylon, 35
Bandeira, Manual, 13
Bantu philosophy, 55, 307
Baron, Dom, 136
Barth, Karl, 6, 11, 19, 160, 170, 194, 201, 310, 315, 316, 333, 347
  Christmas sermon, 17–18
  concept of evil, 333
  *Dogmatics in Outline*, 332, 341
  dream of, 11–12
Basket weaving, 26–28
Baudelaire, Charles Pierre, 182
Beatnik, 80, 347
Bede, the Venerable, 229
Behan, Brendan, 45
Being, 220–23, 266
  respect of, 310
  sense of, 308
Belgium, 141
Belinsky, Russian intellectual, 104

Benedict, St., 285
  principle of, 96
Benedictines of St. Denis, 181
Benson, Father R. M., 336
Berdyaev, Nikolai, 86
Berea, L., 103
Bergson, Henri, 182
Bernanos, George, 165
  funeral of, 339
Bernard, St., 136, 151, 268
Berrigan, Father Dan, 251
Bhave, Vinoba, *Talks on the Gita*, 153
Binyon, Laurence, 252
Black Muslims, 301
Black widow spider, 24
Blake, William, 176, 188, 285
Bloy, Leon, 99, 182, 183, 188
Bogota, 149
Bonhoeffer, 6, 63, 65, 71, 73, 125, 167, 170, 195, 202, 253–54, 316, 317, 323
  *Ethics*, 66, 76, 194, 201, 315
  *Prison Letters*, 315–16
  teaching of, 319
  and total war, 73–74
Bonnard, P., 291
Boone, Daniel, 36
Boredom, 254, 256
  and rioting, 254
Bossuet, Jacques, 282, 288
Bouyer, 269
Braque, Georges, 182
Brecht, Bertolt, 63
  poems of, 133
Bubonic plague, 251–52
Buddhism, 45, 144, 230, 267
Burckhardt, J., 11

Calvin, John, 227, 334, 342
Cambridge, 182, 186, 244–45
Camus, Albert, 63, 182
Cape Hatteras, 12
Cape Horn, 12
Cardenal, Ernesto, 13
Cassiodorus, *De Anima*, 229
Castro, Fidel, 44, 84
Catherine the Great, 104

Caussade, 311
Celtic Church, 133–34
Ceylon, 137
Chagall, Marc, 182, 188
Chandler, Albert, Governor of Kentucky, 16
Change, fear of, 208–9
de Chardin. *See* Teilhard de Chardin
Charlemagne, 53, 133, 179
Chartres, 181, 183, 260
  bomb at, 183
  school of, 135, 260–61
Chenu, M. D., 134
  *Guide to Understanding St. Thomas*, 203
Chicago, 194
China, 37, 75, 185, 277
Choice, momentous, 331–32
Chou kings, 243
Christian culture, 205
  Father Tavard on, 217
  renewal of, 195
Christian Socratism, 218
Christian theology and creation, 220–21
Chrysostom, John, 44, 165
Chuang Tzu, 42, 173, 307–8
Churchill, Winston, 192
Church and the world, 45–47, 49, 50–51
Civil rights, 47, 125, 163, 172, 247
  concern for, 301, 319
Civil War, 36, 220
Clement of Alexandria, 187, 188, 190
  *Protreptikos*, 188
  *Stromateis I*, 93
*Cloud of Unknowing*, 198
Cocteau, Jean, 182
Cold war, 32, 200, 263
Colombia, 149, 160
Columbia, 183
Communism, 22, 23, 31, 32, 44, 74, 126, 146, 163, 288, 323, 346

Communists, 33, 156, 174, 175, 236, 308, 344
mentality, understanding of, 102–3
and propaganda, 239
Comparison, monastery and G. E., 232
Confession, signing of, 108
Confucius, Confucianism, 185, 198
Congo, 31
Conrad, Cistercian hermit, 150–51
*Contemptus mundi*, 45–47, 50–51, 53
Coomaraswamy, A. K., 25, 188
Copernicus, Nicolaus, 34
I Corinthians, 110, 300
Council. *See* Second Vatican Council
Counterreformation, era of, 270
Cramp, spiritual, 224–25
Creation, doctrine of, 220–21
Crusades, 135
*Crusoe*, Defoe, St. John Perse, 12
Cuba, 37, 84
Bay of Pigs, 84
crisis, 272–73, 277
Russian missile sites, 272
Cyprian, St., tracts on patience, 226

Dalai Lama, 42
in India, 49
Daniélou, Father, 270
Dante, 188
Dawson, Christopher, 217
*Historic Reality of Christian Culture*, 55
*Understanding Europe*, 194
Death
and bubonic plague, 251–52
of Christ, 126
permanence of, 138
wish, 73, 235, 263
and zero, 107
Declaration of Independence

and automobile accidents, 39
Defoe, Daniel, *Crusoe*, 12
Democracy, 79, 100–1
on trial, 80–81
in United States, 101
Descartes, René, 181, 265, 285
Despair through servility, 309
Destiny of man, 95
Diadochos of Photike, 143
Dilthey, Wilhelm, 291
Dionysius, 181
Dolci, Danilo, 259
Dreams, 29–30, 188–89, 230
Duns Scotus, John, 29

Eadmer, life of Anselm, 343
Easter Liturgy, 136
Eberhart, Richard, 215
Ecclesiastes, 202
Eckhart, Meister, 53–54, 187, 188
Avignon, 54
sermon of, 187
Ecumenical movement, 40
view, 6–7
Ecumenism, 270, 314, 315, 335
for monks, 143
Ego-identity, 265
Egypt, 35, 310
book on, 310
tomb paintings, 310
Eichmann, Adolf, 289, 290
case, 285–86, 287, 288
Eichrodt, 135
Einstein, Albert, 99
Eisenhower, Dwight D., 192, 344
Elias, St., 296
Eliot, T. S., 162, 186
*Murder in the Cathedral*, 154
Ellul, Jacques, 236, 237
Emerson, Ralph Waldo, on Thoreau, 249
Encyclical and Russians, 302
Engels, Friedrich, 21, 105
England, 71, 132, 186, 193, 200, 251–52

Ephesians, bible quotation, 219
Erasmus, 249
  *Ratio Verae Theologiae*, 306
Eschatology, 52, 55, 74, 102, 133, 211
Essence, man's, 145–46
Eucher, St., *De Contemptu Mundi*, 247, 248
Eulogius, 143
Europe, 34, 35, 37, 47, 52, 69–71, 74–75, 102, 240, 281
Evdokimov, Father Paul, on Desert Fathers, 337–39
Existence, 262–63
Existentialism, 167, 168, 170, 196, 328
Ezechiel, lament of, 247

Faber, 24
Fallout shelters, 191, 194
  *See also* Shelters
Fast for Peace, 219
Fénelon, 24, 187, 282, 285, 288
  and Eichmann, 286
  letters to Duke of Burgundy, 286
Festival of a martyr, 144–45
"Firewatch," *Sign of Jonas*, 212
Ford, Henry, 102
Forester, E. M., on Eliot, 162
France, 48, 132, 141, 180–81, 185–86, 259, 271, 299
Freedom, principle of, 88–92, 100, 168, 180, 310–11, 325–30
French Revolution, 179

Galileo, 34
Game, 232
  and suspension of conscience, 228
Gandhi, 44, 58, 59, 85, 117, 118, 119, 120
  *My Non-violence*, 117
  Nonviolence, doctrine of, 84
  by Romain Rolland, quote, 54
  on Western democracy, 80

Garrigou-Lagrange, Thomist revival, 271
Gaulle, Charles de, 192
Genesis, 137
Germany, 17, 48
Gilson, Etienne, 29, 268
Giono, Jean, *Le Poids du Ciel*, 42
Glossolalia, 125
Goliards, beat monks, 136
Good and evil, 166, 167, 168, 329
  *See also* Right and wrong
Gospel, 82, 93, 126, 127, 128, 159, 170, 180, 218, 317, 322, 339
  of Peace, 317
Great Way, 199–200
Greece, 180
Greeks, 98, Tantalus in Hell, 98
Green, Julien, 143, 153–55, 188
  *Journals*, 183
Gregorian chants, 136, 175, 229–30
Gregory the Great, St., 183, 229–30
  dream of St. Odo of Cluny, 230
  and medieval Benedictinism, 230
  *Moralia*, 229
Guardini, 311
Guerric of Igny, 135, 136
  Christmas sermon, 135

Hammer, Victor, 307
Harlem grapevine, 239
Harrington, *Life in the Crystal Palace*, 232
H-bombs, 47, 126, 218, 252, 281
Heidegger, Martin, 232–33
Heisenberg, *Physics and Philosophy*, 297
Henry IV, 181
Heresy, heretics, 335–36
Hilary of Arles, St., *Life of St. Honoratus*, 248

Hildemar, 14
Himmler, Heinrich, 242
  speech of, 241–42
Hindus, 144
Hispaniola, description of discovery of America, 34
Hitler, Adolf, 138, 175, 192, 240
Holland, 183, 197
Hugo, Victor, 13
Hujwiri, Al', 210
Hulst, Monsignor, 153

Ignatius of Loyola, St., 181
Incas, 306
India, 49
Indians, American, 35, 37, 112
Industrial Revolution, 52
Inquisition, 104
Irenaeus, St., 195, 334
Islam, 90, 181, 194, 205
Ivan the Terrible, 34

Jackson, Mahalia, 113
Jacob, Max, 181
Jehovah's Witnesses, 46
Jerusalem, 66
Jews, 14, 90, 112, 127, 134, 135, 144, 171, 174, 240, 281, 286, 287, 310
Joachim of Flora, 52, 207
  Joachimism, 52
Joan of Arc, 162
Job, 153, 164, 285
  and his friends, 164
John XXIII, Pope, 38, 217–18, 250, 269, 291, 298, 301, 312, 317
  death of, 302–4
  story about, 269–70
John, bible quotation, 170, 234, 318
John of the Cross, St., 137, 271, 297, 320, 347
John of Salisbury, 135, 181, 259, 260
Johnson, Lyndon B., 193

Johnson's Great Society, 35
Julian of Norwich, Lady, 211–12
Jung, Spiritual Disciplines, 251

Kabir, 9
Kacmarcik, Frank, 172
Kennedy, John F., 58, 192, 199, 270, 272, 343
  assassination of, 344, 346
  inauguration speech, 57
  new frontier of, 35
Kentucky
  and brushfire, 288–89
  governor of, 16
Kenya, 254
Khrushchev, Nikita, 34, 44, 192, 272
Kierkegaard, Sören, 170, 315
King, Martin Luther, 301
Kingdom, Thy . . . , 123–24, 159, 202, 340–41
Kirov, Sergei, 104
Knowles, David, quotations from
  Monastic Order in England, 135
  Religious Orders in England, 187
Koan, Zen, 269, 282
Komachi, Japanese poetess, 252–53
Koran, French translation, 18

La Bruyère, Jean de, 181
Lamartine, A. M. L. de, 139
Language, 161
  learned, 99
  misuse of, 92–93
Lanza del Vasto, 228
Lao Tzu, 177, 307
Lax, 14
Lee, Robert E., 36
Lenin, Nikolai, 103, 105
Lieh Tzu, 215
Life and death, 224–26
Lima, Jorge de, 14

Liturgical Easter Trope, 134
London, 182, 201, 244
Lord's Prayer, 124
Louisville, 155, 156, 173, 182, 232, 257
Love, law of, 120–22
Luther, Martin, 170, 268
Lwanga, Charles, 144

McCarthy era, 172
MacCauley, Rose, *Personal Pleasures*, 244
Madison Avenue, 94, 309–10
Malraux, André, 142
  *Royal Way*, 143
Manet, Edouard, 182
Mao Tse-tung, 44
Marcel, Gabriel, 150
Maritain, Jacques, 6, 182, 183, 188, 270, 314–15, 348
  Preface to *Journal de Raissa*, 314–15
  *The Range of Reason*, 244
  Thomist circle at Meudon, 314–15
Maritain, Raissa, 183, 188
  *Journal*, 270
  translation by Kernan, 348
Mark, bible quotation, 126
Mars, 61, 280
Marshall Plan, 37
Martinique, 197
Marx, Karl, 19, 21–23, 60, 105, 145
Marxian humanism, 145–46, 202
Marxism, 314
Mass before sunrise, 270
Massignon, Louis, 144, 147, 305
  and African boys, 144
  dialogue with Islam, 147
  *Mardis de Dar-es Salam*, 151
  mass for, 144
Mass for Louis Massignon, 144
Mass media, 77, 226, 346
Mass society, 238
Matisse, Henri, 172

Matthew, bible quotation, 318
Mayas, 306
Meditation on the automobile, 76
Mencius, parable, Ox Mountain, 137
Merton, Thomas, "Song for the Death of Averroes" in *Emblems of a Season of Fury*, 208
Mexico, 38, 273
Michelangelo, 269
Middle Ages, 124, 135, 136, 180, 181, 229, 315
  writers of the, 248
Mila Repa, 49
Milosz, Czeslaw, 138
Mind, heart and body, 278–79
Mirgeler, A., *Mutations of Western Christianity*, 53, 124
Molière, 181
Monasticism, 179–80
Monet, Claude, 182
Montauban, 183
Montini, Cardinal, 304
Moon, 61, 99, 223, 280
Moral reasoning and technology, 65
More, Thomas, 249, 306
Mounier, Emmanuel, 43
Mozart, Barth's dream, 11–12
Mumford, Lewis, *City in History*, 137, 138, 222
Music in cow barn, 166
Muslims, 18, 135, 144, 147, 151
Mussolini, Benito, 138

Nanayakkara of Kandy, Bishop, 137
Napoleon, 181
Nashe, T., 63
Natural Law, 124–25
Nazi: 19, 202
  Germany, 73, 281
    and Communist Russia, 243

Nazi (*cont'd*)
  persecution of Christianity,
    194–95
  terrorism, 104
Nazism, 325
  and Bonhoeffer, 323
Near East, 147
Negroes, 31, 32–33, 39, 109,
    111, 112, 113, 152, 174,
    239, 243, 301
  and Alabama, 296
  leader of, 112
Neruda, Jan, 13
Nessus shirt, 70
Newman, Cardinal, 24–25,
    187–88
New Orleans incident, 109–10
New Testament, 14, 52, 118,
    133, 134, 180, 218, 300
New York, 149, 182
New Zealand, 200
Nicholas of Cusa, 285
Nicholas of Flue, 162
Niebuhr, Reinhold, 56, 243
Nietzsche, Friedrich, 127, 227,
    321
Nonviolence, 58–59, 102, 144,
    346
  doctrine of Gandhi, 84, 85,
    86
  and Rome, 101
North Africa, 147
Nothingness, 17, 266
  idea of, 263
  is being, 266
Notker Balbulus, 296
Novices' scriptorium, 213–14
Nuclear tests, 251, 273
  war, 272, 277, 296, 298

Oakham, 186, 187, 259
Odo of Cluny, St., 136
  dream of, 230
Oldenbourg, Zoë, *Destiny of
    Fire*, 334
Old Testament, 14, 133–36, 180

Oppen, George, poems, 348–50
Order, possibility of, 254–55
Oriental religions, 90
Orthodoxy, 194
Orwell, George, 142
  on immortality, 143
Ottaviani, Cardinal, 304
Ox Mountain, parable, Men-
    cius, 137

Parables, 137, 142
Paris, 144, 180–82
Parousia, 123–24, 211
Pascal, Blaise, 181
Paschasius Radbertus, 136
Patience, 227, 264
Paul VI, Pope, 304–5, 348
Paul, St., 134, 154, 219
Pauline, Sister, 231
Péguy, 40, 182
Pelagius, 180
Perse, St. John, 18
  *Crusoe*, 12
  poems, 140
Peru, 39
Peter of Celles, 248
Peter the Venerable, 136
Pharisaism, pharisaical argu-
    ments, 92, 103
Pharisees, 77, 171, 332
Picasso, Pablo, 182
Pieper, quotations from
  *Guide to Thomas Aquinas*,
    203, 204–5
  *The Silence of St. Thomas*,
    206–7
Pius XII, Pope, 302, 304
Placide Tempels, Father, 55
Plato, *Phaedo*, 58
*Point vierge*, 131, 151, 158
Poland, 240
Post-Christian, 329, 334, 335
Prayer, 177–78
Propaganda, 235–40, 241–42,
    243
  mentality of, 240
Proust, Marcel, 182

Proverbs, 8th chapter, 14
Psalms, 135–36, 271, 294
Pugachev, Cossack leader, 104
Pyramids, 88
    and extermination camps, 88

Quasimodo, poem on Auschwitz, 57

Racine, 181
Read, Sir Herbert, 283
Red Cross, 245, 339
Redemption, St. Anselm, 341–42
Reginald, 264
Rejection of others, 174–75
*Relax and Live*, 173
Religion, religionless, 283–84, 318–26
Renoir, Pierre A., 182
Repentance, 127
Reyes, Alfonso, 13
Right and wrong, 166, 167, 168, 191, 227
    *See also* Good and evil
*Right to be Merry, A*, 20
Rimbaud, Arthur, 141–42
Robinson, J. A. T., 6, 323
    *Honest to God*, 298, 322
Rolland, Romain
    on Gandhi, 54–55
    India, 54
Romans, bible quotation, 225
Rome, 101, 180, 182, 261, 302
Roosevelt, Franklin D., 172, 192, 344
Rufinus, 165
Rumi, Sufi poet, 234–35
Rupert of Deutz, 136
Russia, 34, 47, 48, 71, 75, 105
    and China, 277
    and conversion, 259
    prayer for, 87
Ruysbroeck, Jan van, 188

Sartre, Jean Paul, 168, 182, 327–30

*La Nausée*, 140
    meditation on root, 139–40
Satie, Eric, 182, 188
Schweitzer, Albert, 31
Science, resistance to, 50–51
Scotus Erigena, 181
Second Vatican Council, 7, 261, 270, 312, 313, 314, 319, 335
Sermons, mention of
    Father John, 159–60
    Guerric of Igny, 135
    Isaac of Stella, 18
    Meister Eckhart, 188
    in New Orleans, 109–10
Servility, 308–10
Shakers, 132–33, 220, 339–40
    builders, 220
Shelters, 258–59. *See also* Fall-out shelters
Shirer, W. L., *The Rise and Fall of the Third Reich*, 241
Smaragdus, 14
Social action, Christian, 81–83, 94–95
    transformation by, 82–83, 94
Socratic principle, 218
Soldier and martyr, heroism of, 101
Solipsism, 210
Solitude, 96–97
Song, refrain of, 20
Sophrony, Archimandrite, *The Undistorted Image*, 164
South Africa, 73
Space, concept of, 298–99
Speaking in tongues, 125
Stalin, Joseph, 34, 102, 103, 138, 192, 202
Steere, Douglas, 86
Steinmann, *St. Jerome*, 165
Stone Age, 138, 300, 308
Story
    of tiger cub, 198
    Zen, 199
Sufism, 208, 210–11
Suicidal age, 223, 226

Sunrise, 280, 294
Suvarov, Tsarist general, 104
Suzuki on "New Knowledge in Human Values," 246
Sword and cross, 102
Sylvan, Staretz, 164

Tao, 149
Taoists, 185
Tauler, Johannes, 188
Tavard, Father, 217
Technological culture, 308
    skill and destruction, 321
Technology, 25, 65, 72, 76–77, 157, 222–23, 225, 253, 284
    and death, 241–42
    and moral reasoning, 65
    and science, 75
    and unbalance, 72
Teilhard de Chardin, 17, 51, 52, 321
Tertullian, 252
    tracts on patience, 226–27
Theologia Germanica, 182
Theologie monastique, 230
Theophane the Recluse, 293–94
    and Isaiah, 293
Theresa, St., 211
Thomas Aquinas, St., 129, 135, 201, 203–8, 220, 264, 293, 317, 320
    commentaries on Aristotle, 203
    theology of, 206–7
    and University of Paris, 203
Tibetan monks, 48, 49
Total war, 75
    Bonhoeffer, 73
    Russian view, 74
Toulouse-Lautrec, Henri de, 182
Traherne, Thomas, 9
Transformation, 225–26

Uganda, martyrs of, 30
United States, 47, 48, 73, 83, 98, 101, 125, 137, 252, 269, 273
    Catholicism in, 87
    See also America
Unity among Christians, 21, 143
    foundation for spiritual, 95
Ur, 35
Urban culture, 138

Valéry, Paul, 182
Van der Meersch, Maxence, 231
Van der Meer de Walcheren, Pierre, 188
    Rencontres, 183
    The White Paradise, 183
Van Doren, Mark, 12
Venezuela, 39
Venus, 269, 280
Vergil, Georgics, 259, 260
Victor, St., School of, 135
Viet Nam, 39
Violence, reason of, 85–86
Vivarium, library of, 229
Von Hügel, Friedrich, letter of, 20
Von Rad, 135–36

Ward, W. G., 20
Warnefrid, 14
Washington, D.C., 138
Weil, Simone, 40, 138, 142, 334
Western culture, 71
Whale, dead of ulcers, 231
White society, 32–33
William of St. Amour, 207
Wilson, Edmund, on Marx, 21–22
Wilson, Woodrow, 37, 344
Winandy, Dom Jacques, 197
Wind, 29
Wisdom, book of, 18, 59
Wise heart, 211–12
Worldliness, 284, 294
    technocratic, 316
World War I, 37, 271
World War II, 73, 74
Wu, John, 231

Yang and Yin, 149
Yes and no, 265–68, 270
Yin kings, 243
Yvo, conversation with, 155–56

Zen, 152, 185, 285

koan, 269, 282
poems, 292
proverb, 275
story, 199
Suzuki, quote, 246
Zero, 107, 238